SNOOKER

THE PLAYERS • THE SHOTS • THE MATCHES

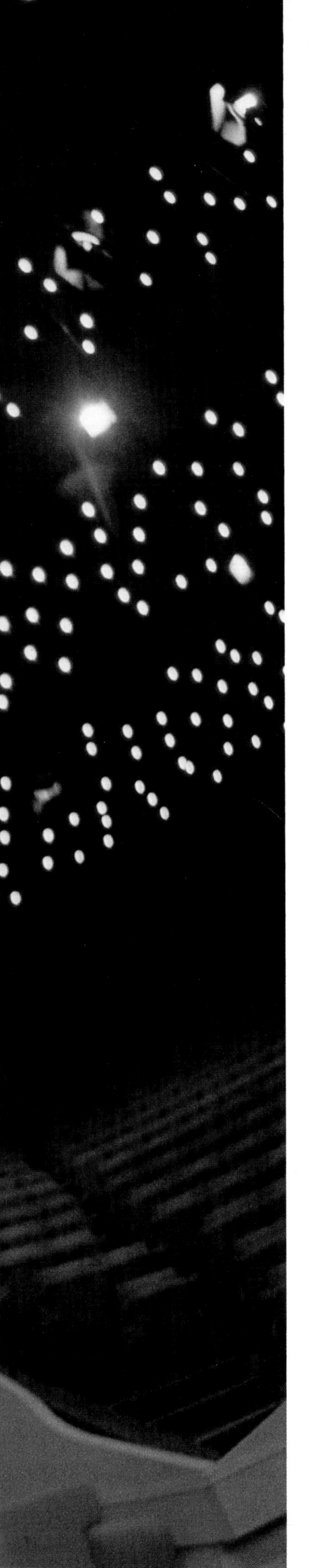

SNOOKER

THE PLAYERS • THE SHOTS • THE MATCHES

TERRY SMITH
INTRODUCTION BY STEVE DAVIS

Macdonald
Queen Anne Press

This edition first published
for Marks and Spencer plc in 1989 by
Macdonald & Co (Publishers) Ltd
London & Sydney
A member of Maxwell Pergamon Publishing
Corporation plc
66–73 Shoe Lane, London EC4P 4AB

Typeset by Brian Smith Partnership, Bristol.
Printed and bound in Great Britain by
BPCC Paulton Books Ltd.

Editor: Roger Tritton
Text Editor: John Wainwright
Art Director: Linda Cole
Designed by The Image
Picture Researcher: Amanda Baker
Production Controller: Guerwyn Thomas

Front cover: Steve Davis, perhaps the greatest snooker player of all time.
Back cover: (left) Jimmy White, 'The Whirlwind', still with the desire to be world number 1; (right) Stephen Hendry, has shown a maturity way beyond his years.
Page 1: Steve Davis during his 18–3 destruction of John Parrott in the 1989 World Final.
Page 2: Steve Davis shows off the 1989 Embassy World Championship trophy, his sixth.
This page: John Parrott contemplates impending defeat at the Crucible.
Page 6: Steve Davis is one of the Britain's wealthiest sportsmen, earning more than £1 million a year.

This edition published 1990 by Queen Anne Press
a division of Macdonald & Co (Publishers) Ltd
1 New Fetter Lane, London EC4A 1AR

British Library Cataloguing in Publication Data
Smith, Terry
Snooker: the players, the shots, the matches.
1. Snooker
I. Title
794.735

ISBN 0-356-19507-4

CONTENTS

THE
147S

INTRODUCTION BY STEVE DAVIS

AS WE APPROACH THE 1990s IT IS CLEAR THAT SNOOKER HAS NEVER FACED A MORE CHALLENGING FUTURE. WITH THE GAME GROWING ALL THE TIME, ESPECIALLY OVERSEAS, THERE IS MORE PRESSURE THAN EVER ON THE PROFESSIONAL PLAYERS. AS THE REWARDS FOR SUCCESS HAVE RISEN DRAMATICALLY THROUGHOUT THE '80s, AS MEDIA COVERAGE HAS MUSHROOMED, AND AS INTERNATIONAL TRAVEL HAS TAKEN OFF, A MORE EXCITING AND HECTIC LIFESTYLE HAS BECOME INEVITABLE FOR THOSE OF US PLAYING THE CIRCUIT.

BUT DESPITE THE FACT THAT I HAVE BEEN LUCKY ENOUGH TO TRAVEL ALL OVER THE GLOBE IN MY CAREER, I WOULD HAVE TO SAY THAT I STILL FEEL MOST AT HOME DOWN AT THE MATCHROOM CLUB IN ROMFORD, WORKING ON MY GAME WITH MY FATHER, BILL. AND EVEN THOUGH I HAVE WON THE WORLD CHAMPIONSHIP SIX TIMES, I NEVER TIRE OF PRACTISING AND PLAYING. THE REASON IS QUITE SIMPLE. FOR ME, SNOOKER IS THE GREATEST SPORT IN THE WORLD.

I DO HOPE THAT YOU WILL FIND THIS BOOK, COMPILED BY MY GOOD FRIEND, TERRY SMITH, BOTH INFORMATIVE AND ENTERTAINING, AND I WOULD LIKE TO THINK THAT IT WILL INSPIRE YOU WITH ALL THE ENTHUSIASM THAT I HAVE FOR THIS GREAT GAME.

THE HISTORY OF THE GAME

THE HISTORY OF SNOOKER AND BILLIARDS IS CLOUDED IN MYSTERY. THERE ARE SOME FACTS WE CAN BE CERTAIN OF, AND OTHERS THAT HAVE UNDOUBTEDLY BEEN ELABORATED ON OVER THE CENTURIES. BUT THE STORIES OF HOW IT ALL BEGAN MAKE FASCINATING READING, AND IN THE FOLLOWING CHAPTER WE TAKE YOU FROM THE EARLIEST DAYS RIGHT UP TO THE MONEY-SPINNING BOOM OF THE 1980S.

The game of billiards (left) had without doubt much to do with the origins of snooker. Precisely how the latter game developed into what it is today is the subject of fierce debate.

THE ORIGINS OF THE GAME

For the last fifty years it has been generally accepted that snooker was invented by Col. Sir Neville Chamberlain, while he was serving in the Devonshire Regiment of the British Army, stationed in Jubbulpore, India, in 1875. But did he? Indeed, was snooker invented by any one individual, or did it just gradually develop from an eclectic combination of similar games?

Colonel Chamberlain's story states that while playing Pyramids on the billiards table (a betting game that employed 15 red balls), he introduced a set of different coloured balls (which were used in another fashionable game at the time – Life Pool), and thus snooker was born. The name certainly has military origins, as a 'snooker' was slang for a first year cadet who had little military knowledge and consequently was of low standing. Chamberlain claimed all his fellow players of this new game were of low standing!

This may all be true, but the question must be asked: why did the colonel wait until 1939 to release this story – a gap of some 65 years since the game's alleged inception? Chamberlain's name had never been mentioned before in billiards and snooker literature, prior to his 1939 statement, but his story was fully accepted at that time by Compton Mackenzie, the well-known and respected writer from the first half of this century. Perhaps the long silence was mere modesty on the part of the colonel, an admirable quality that was finally swept aside by anger when a rival claim to the origins of the game 'forced' him to supply the facts as he saw them.

'THE SHOP' IN WOOLWICH

That rival claim came from 'The Shop' at the Royal Military Academy, in Woolwich, where a Lt. Col. G. H. Howell maintained that in 1894 he had played snooker with senior officers, who informed him that the game was a hybrid of Pyramids and Pool, and that they had played it when they were cadets in 1865. First term cadets had been known as 'snookers' at 'The Shop' as far back as 1840, and the rules that they played to in the 1880s were those printed by Burroughes and Watts, with the table set up as shown in the illustration *below*.

As can be seen, the yellow ball was placed on the centre spot of the D, the green ball at the apex of

A game of pyramids in 1884: a rare illustration of this 19th century game.

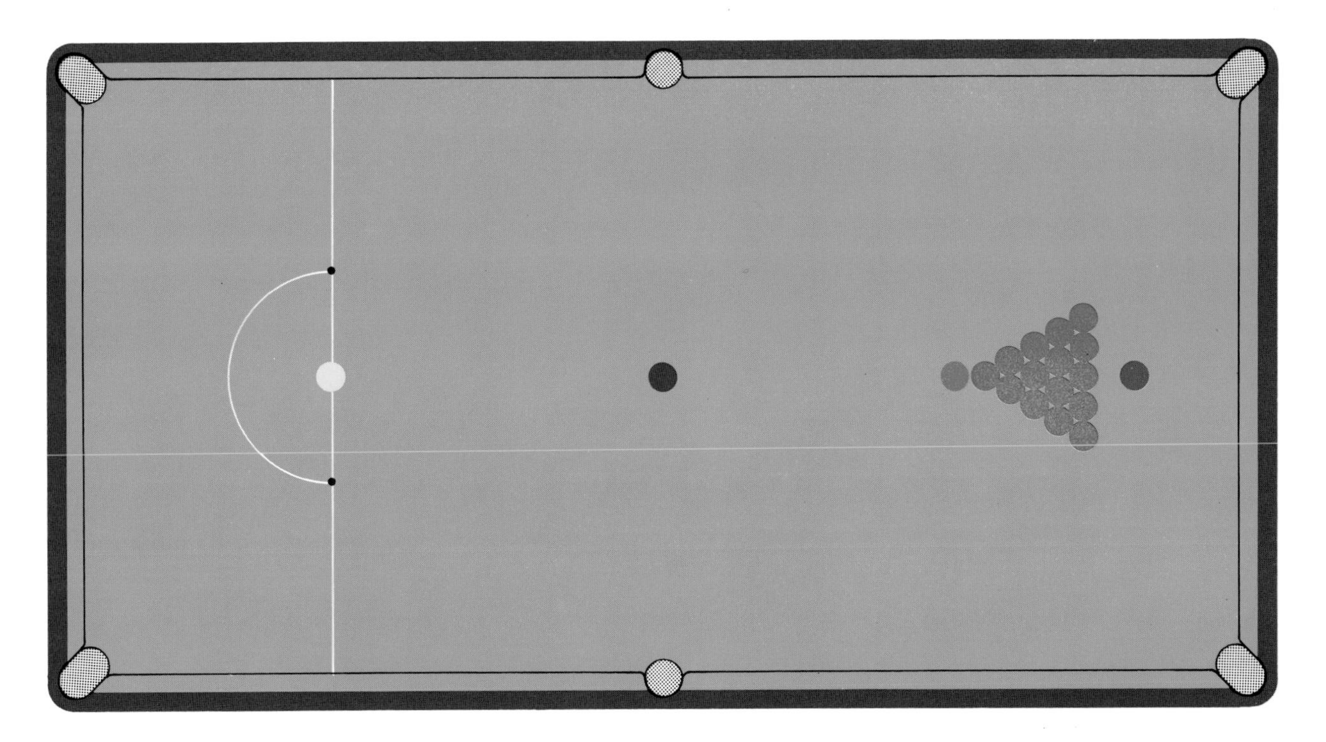

A table set up for the earliest game of snooker; played in the 1880s.

the pyramids, the brown ball on the centre spot, and the blue ball on the billiard spot (our black spot). The red balls were valued at 1 point each – except the last red, which was worth 2 – while the yellow was worth 3, the green 4, the brown 5 and the blue 6. Another big difference to the modern game was that after all the reds were taken, the striker was allowed to pocket 'any colour' after pocketing a colour in correct rotation. For example, after taking yellow he could take blue (or any other colour), but then had to take green with the following stroke, and so on . . .

In fact, two or more quite distinct versions of snooker were being played by the end of the 19th century, and there were no well-defined and generally accepted rules until they were formulated by the Billiards Association in 1900. Even up to 1926, very few snooker rooms were run with the same set of rules.

A 'snooker' was slang for a young cadet who had little military knowledge and consequently was of low standing.

So, as far as the origins of the game are concerned, it would seem as if a germ of an idea, which combined two 19th century table games, was sown some time during the 1860s or '70s. Whether the idea was first conceived by Col. Sir Neville Chamberlain and his officers in India, or by gentlemen at 'The Shop' at Woolwich, we can never be sure. Maybe, like 'Topsy', it simply 'grow'd – and possibly from different locations at the same time.

FANCIFUL ORIGINS

However, some explanations of the origin of the game are more dubious than others – though nonetheless entertaining for that. For example, in a letter to the 'New World of Billiards', in December 1907, the correspondent stated: *'Unlike most billiard games, Snookers' Pool is a comparatively modern invention and it would appear a fairly easy matter to trace its source. Yet this is not the case, and those who well remember the introduction of the game into this country seem to have no certain knowledge of where it came from. Some credit our American cousins with the honour of devising this fine game and others say it originated in India. In connection with the latter theory, the writer well remembers playing at Snookers' Pool with a distinguished army officer who had seen much service in India'.*

The letter goes on to say that a dispute arose during the game and, after consulting the rules, the military gentleman had to admit they were against him. *'But he thought the rules must have been wrong and claimed he knew the inventor of the game very well indeed. He was a Captain Snooker in the*

Bengal Artillery and he played many games with him in The Shiny East (India)'!

ORIGINS OF BILLIARDS

Whilst there is a degree of confusion surrounding the birth of snooker, it is impossible to place a date, even an approximate one, on the appearance of its mother game – English billiards. However, it has a fascinating history – a look at which will help us to appreciate the high standard of equipment and play that snooker enjoys nowadays.

Imagination has done much to place the origins of billiards in the realms of fancy. For example, Shakespeare makes but one mention of the word 'billiards' in the whole of his works, when in Anthony and Cleopatra (act II scene V) Cleopatra says to Charmian 'let us to billiards'. Undoubtedly Shakespeare knew the game in some form, but for Cuthbert Bede, in his 'Book of Beauty', to show his

Charles Cotton, in his book 'The Complete Gamester', in 1674, seems to have been the first writer to have considered billiards worthy of serious attention. He describes it as a 'most gentile, cleanly and ingenious game'.

idea of Cleopatra playing billiards is a complete falsification of history. In a literal sense, Shakespeare errs when he places a cue in the hands of Cleopatra. He might as well have given Anthony command of a company of machine gunners! Billiards, or any game remotely resembling it, was unknown to the ancient civilizations.

Another early reference to billiards is Ben Jonson's simile: 'Smooth as a Billiard Ball', in 1637. But it is Charles Cotton, in his book 'The Complete Gamester', of 1674, who seems to be the first writer who thought billiards worthy of serious attention. He refers to it as the 'most gentile, cleanly, and ingenious game', and makes it clear that in his opinion the game was imported from a foreign land.

Billiards *by Arthur Roger Dighton in 1790. One player is using a cue, the other a mace. The scoreboard is marked up to 12.*

However, against this latter point, we have the indisputable fact that billiards was played in England for many years before Cotton's day. The only sensible conclusion to be drawn is that the balance of probabilities favours the assertion that English billiards, on a table fitted with pockets, is as national in its origin as cricket, and that a similar game, on a pocketless table, evolved at about the same time on the European mainland.

We do know that Mozart's favourite pastime was billiards and that apparently he played it with great skill. He had a billiard table in his room upon which he frequently practised. Hummel, who was his pupil, related that Mozart would often interrupt the lesson and propose a turn with the cue and balls. When the fervour of musical inspiration was upon him, he would have a game of billiards. He could then let his imagination run free, composing the elaborate phrases within his brain, tapping the billiard table to the ever-flowing rhythms in his mind.

THE PAWNBROKER

Like snooker, billiards also has its own (fanciful?) 'birth of the game' story, which is as follows: 'Billiards was first invented by a pawnbroker', says an old authority. 'About the middle of the 16th century there was one William Kew, a pawnbroker who, during wet weather, was in the habit of taking down the three balls from his sign and, with yard-stick, pushing them around from his counter into his stalls, which became a great amusement for the young clergymen from St. Pauls (hence the term: canon). The game is now known by the name Billyard, because William, or 'Bill', did first play with 'yard' measure. Cue coming from William Kew's surname.'

Above: Mozart at the billiards table where he spent many fruitful hours.
Right: John Thurston, father of the billiards trade.

So, working on this theory, perhaps snooker was invented by a Mr. Snook – which is not an uncommon name today, as a look at the telephone directory will reveal! But what is certain is that billiards, for more than 200 years after the earliest references to it, was played with a mace on tables of various shapes and sizes, and was a very crude and different game to the one that is played today.

THE FIRST MATCHROOM

The father of the modern billiard and snooker table was undoubtedly John Thurston (1777 – 1850). He

introduced slate beds (1826) and rubber cushions (1835), which were formerly made of wood and stuffed felt respectively, and thus provided the game with two essential components of a modern snooker table. A cabinet-maker by trade, Thurston became the first specialised producer of billiard tables, when he opened his headquarters at 14 Catherine Street, London, in 1814. This property housed the first Match Room, from where he arranged exhibition games for visiting professionals – an idea which was to be repeated some 150 years later in Romford, by Mr. Barry Hearn!

Thurston also originated the idea of a Licensed Victuallers Championship, as well as handicap competitions within the trade. Any profits went to the Licensed Victuallers Schools or Asylum – an institution with which billiard players seem to have been associated over the years. Indeed, one story goes that a well-known professional once played a game of billiards in an asylum against one of the patients, gave his opponent a 25 start and was hopelessly beaten. The patient took him quietly to one side and said: 'Look here, if you go on giving away points so recklessly as that, you'll be inside the asylum instead of me'.

BILLIARDS IN THE ASYLUM

Both the size and facilities of these asylums are well-illustrated in the following tale: Mr. George Nelson, who was a well-known professional player and table manufacturer during the early part of this century, was playing an exhibition match in an asylum in Yorkshire, which had 2,000 patients and 12 billiards tables. When it was not his turn to play he dropped into the nearest available chair. In doing so he sat next to a fat, amiable-looking patient. After repeating this several times, he then sat next to one of the head warders, who said to him: 'You see my ear' (out of which a good-sized piece had been clearly bitten), 'well that fat chap you keep sitting next to bit that out'. Nelson thanked him, and proceeded to concentrate more on where he was to sit-out next time, rather than on the game in hand!

DEVELOPMENT OF THE CUE

The earliest games of billiards were played with a mace, which wasn't replaced by the cue until the latter half of the 18th century. During the transition

Billiard Playing *by Guiseppe Piattoli (1787 – 1807). The players are using a mace while the table has holes and not pockets.*

period, games were arranged between players using mace against cue. But it didn't take very long for the experts to realise the advantages of the cue, and it became the predominant implement for the enthusiast of the 1780s.

It is often wrongly assumed that the two-piece cue is a modern innovation. In fact, a patent was given to Mr. W. Buttery on July 22 1885, which relates to an improvement in the making of cues in two or more parts (and describes a joint made with a screw, firmly fixed by a shank in one part, and screwed into the socket of the other part). The modern two-piece cue came into fashion among snooker players after John Spencer's victory in the World Professional Championship in 1977.

Another development that had to take place before any real progress in cuemanship could come about was the fitting of a leather tip to the end of the cue. This was accomplished by a Captain Mingaud in 1807, who was at the time a political prisoner in Paris – his incarceration having been caused by a too-free expression of opinion! In his place of confinement was a billiard table to which he had daily access. Playing the game served to while away the long, tedious hours, and in time Mingaud became quite skilful, but suffered frequent disappointments through his cue sliding off the ball.

Captain Mingaud, who invented the leather tip for the cue in 1807.

It is incorrect to assume that the two-piece cue is a modern innovation. In fact a patent was given to a Mr. W. Buttery on July 22, 1885, and relates to the making of cues in two or three parts.

By devising a leather tip he was able to substantially reduce the problem.

THE MAGICAL PROPERTIES OF CHALK

Around this time, the search for greater control when striking the ball led to the practice of chalking the tip of the cue. As to who actually came up with the idea is unclear. Although one 'hoary old yarn' concerns Jack Carr from Bath who, in 1825, claimed to be the 'father of the side stroke', with the help of his 'twisting' chalk. Well, he may have made a fortune from the 'magical' properties of the ordinary chalk he sold in small boxes to a gullible public, but the use of side is documented in a book some 20 years earlier. An amateur writing in 1806 states: 'A lateral twist or rotation may be given by striking the ball sideways, with the point of the cue chalked', and thus disproves Carr's claim.

Regardless of its origins, the use of chalk became so widespread that in the billiard rooms of the late 1800s it was not uncommon for notices to state: 'Players are requested not to chalk their cues on the ceiling'. It appears that this was quite a serious problem, as the chalk was usually missing from the room and players used to rub the tips of their cues against the white-washed ceiling. Other notices, which today seem humorous, included: 'Players are requested not to poke the fire with the club's cues' and 'Players are requested not to strike matches on the cloth'. They make the modern snooker club sign of 'No smoking over the table' look quite tame!

DEVELOPMENT OF THE BALL

Like the table and cue, the development of the snooker ball has an interesting, if bloodthirsty, history. Before 1820 the balls were wooden, but for the next century ivory balls were in favour – bad news for the elephants of Africa and India! From

Africa alone, 130,000 tusks were exported annually, solely to satisfy the worldwide billiard ball trade, and many natives lost their lives assisting in the very dangerous business of capturing and killing the elephants.

At one time it was estimated that the manufacture of billiard balls, in Britain alone, involved an annual slaughter of 12,000 elephants. The number of balls cut from a tusk averaged five, and the best ivory came from the elephants of Equatorial Africa. Their tusks weighed on average between 12 to 18 pounds (approx 5½kg to 8kg) each, and were cut into blocks, turned on a lathe and then stored for several months to dry and season – after which they were turned again into perfectly circular balls. As to the value of this trade in ivory: in 1904 a hundredweight (approx 50kg) of best ivory would fetch £120 at the London auctions!

Eventually, dwindling supplies of ivory, combined with a rapid growth in the popularity of the game, especially in Britain, together with the unsuitability of the material under certain climatic conditions overseas, meant that a substitute had to be found. The result was the composition ball. The first to be marketed in Britain, in 1901, were the crystalate balls, which finally came to the public's attention in 1909, after a series of large breaks (including one of 2,196) were made with them by the Australian, George Gray. Although a 'composition versus ivory' war raged until the end of the 1920s, from 1930 onwards the composition ball was used almost

Above: Twenty thousand billiard balls, made by Burroughes and Watts from the ivory of 2,000 elephants.
Below: An advertisement from the front cover of The New World of Billiards*, 1908.*

exclusively under one name or another. But by 1972 it was felt that something more modern was required, and so the brightly coloured super crystalate used today was introduced.

ADVANTAGES OF THE MODERN BALL

The modern ball is about a 'two bob bit' (a 10p piece) lighter than the old crystalate and is much 'livelier' for screw and side. However, the one

The Australian George Gray who, using the new crystalate balls, amassed exceptional breaks.

advantage the older balls did have was with follow-through shots, which were more consistent and less likely to 'kick'. But to think that 'kicks' are a modern problem would be wrong as, back in 1900, balls made of the 'inferior' Indian ivory often did just that, bringing many a promising break to an undeserved end. Just imagine, for example, that occurring on Dennis Taylor's final black ball against Steve Davis in the 1985 Embassy World Championship final! It would have been heart-breaking and would have certainly led to a far less lucrative career for Dennis than the one he has since secured.

Having stated that the old ivory balls were less reactive than the modern crystalates, the following shot seems almost unbelievable. Riso Levi, who was undoubtedly one of the game's great writers, could screw in-off the black on its spot from the D, without the black rebounding into baulk! It was witnessed by many notable cue-men, and was performed on an average-paced table. It was a slow screw shot which, at the time, the great Willie Smith thought was impossible.

As to the size of the balls, Riso Levi also recalls an astonishing feat of a totally different kind. How many snooker balls can be picked up with only one hand and without any assistance from the cushion? The average man can only pick up five, and, with practice, six. Apparently George Hunt, a Barnsley professional, could pick up nine, and did so in the presence of Joe Davis, who had to count them to believe what he had just seen. George Hunt obviously had very strong fingers, as his hands were only of average size!

The modern super crystalate ball is approximately the weight of a 10p piece lighter than the old crystalate balls, is more suitable for the application of 'screw' and 'side', but is also more likely to 'kick' than the heavier, top-quality ivory balls used in the past.

THE LIGHTING

The all-important lighting of the table also has an interesting history. Contrast, for example, the modern television lighting over our major snooker tournament tables with that of candlelight, as illustrated in the print of Louis XIV playing billiards, in 1694. The dripping wax was always a problem so the candles were later replaced by oil lamps. However, these were also not without their drawbacks, as the story of a diminutive boy who was given the job of looking after a table reveals. Apparently he brushed and ironed the cloth alright, but when lighting-up time came he clambered on the table and walked around it in hobnailed boots to light the lamps!

By the end of the 19th century, gas lamps had become the standard form of lighting, but they were in turn eclipsed by electric lighting during the first decade of this century – an innovation that no doubt reduced the risk of damage to the playing surface!

THE GREEN BAIZE

As standards of play improved, the condition of the playing surface became increasingly important – as the following anecdote highlights. Apparently,

By the end of the 19th century gas lamps had replaced oil and candle, to become the standard form of lighting. But they in turn, were eclipsed by electric lighting during the first decade of the century.

two professionals were playing a match at a club near Leeds. After a while they both noticed how strangely the balls were running and, despite a close inspection, were uncertain of the all-important factor of which way the nap of the cloth was lying. So, at half-time they asked who had ironed the table, and the steward's wife said that she had. On further inquiry as to which way it had been ironed the good lady replied: 'Ah! I forgot which way it had to be ironed, so I ironed it both ways to be sure'!

Of course, confusion surrounding the state of the cloth has not always been confined to the direction of the nap, nor indeed to the wives of stewards. The chairman of a little club in Lancashire had been on his holidays and, during his absence, the committee had had the cloth of the snooker table shifted round and a new baulk line and D marked out at the other end. On his return the chairman went into the snooker room and looked with admiration at the table, expressing pleasure at the improvement and concluding with the remark: 'but I cannot understand how you managed to turn such a big, heavy table around in such a small room as this'!

An engraving by Antoine Trouvain showing Louis XIV playing billiards by candlelight.

EARLY EXPONENTS OF BILLIARDS

The high standards of play that we see today have been made possible not only by innovations in and improvements to equipment, but also by the achievements of the leading exponents of the game over the years.

JONATHAN KENTFIELD

The first recognised champion of English billiards was Edwin Kentfield, whose treatise on 'The Game of Billiards', in 1839, is one of the most treasured books of any billiard collector's library. Edwin, or as he was generally known, Jonathan, was strictly speaking never entitled to call himself the champion inasmuch as he never played for the title, but from 1825 until 1849 he was regarded as the best player in England. A contemporary of John Thurston, they together introduced most of the improvements that led to the modern table. Moreover, Kentfield may fairly be described as 'the grandfather of modern billiards', for it is clear that he was the first player to approach the game with the precision of a science – much in the same way as Joe Davis played snooker in the 1930s. Kentfield died in 1873 and, sadly, for some years before his death he lived in poor circumstances.

John Roberts Senior.

Jonathan Kentfield.

JOHN ROBERTS SENIOR

His successor, John Roberts Senior, was born on June 15, 1823, in Liverpool, and assumed the premiership of the game in 1849, after Kentfield, who had passed his peak, sensibly declined to play him. For twenty years Roberts' position was unchallenged. A powerful man, he had the reputation of being something of a rough diamond, as this letter to the World of Billiards, in 1901, clearly shows:

'Dear Sir, I once saw in an exhibition match in the provinces, between the late John Roberts Sen and William Cook, a curious incident. The local marker, who had probably never marked more than a 'hundred up' at a time in his life, got bewildered and called the game incorrectly. Roberts noticed this and mentioned it, saying at the same time: "Marker, I must hit you for that". And sure enough he did hit him. He had his ball in hand with the red on its spot. Roberts knocked the red ball clean off the table, striking the marker full on the chest, to the amusement of everybody. Which unbelievably was not a foul in those days.'

Roberts remained at the top of the tree until 1870, when he lost to William Cook by 117 points in 1,200

By taking on all-comers, John Roberts Senior was the first to exploit the competitive aspects of billiards and thus attract the interest of the public.

up, the match lasting five hours. After this he played infrequently in public, and died on March 17, 1893. His influence on the game was enormous. By taking on all-comers he had been the first to exploit the competitive aspects of billiards and thus capture the attention of the general public. A 19th century version of Alex Higgins, in style if not in stature, Roberts was also the first pioneer of overseas billiards – visiting Australia in 1864, and later also going to America.

John Roberts Junior.

William Cook.

WILLIAM COOK

William Cook, who beat John Roberts Sen, had a great delicacy of touch. He was at his best from May 1871 to February 1874, when he won four Championships, beating John Roberts Junior three times and Joseph Bennett once. His last appearance in the championship was in 1885 and he died of consumption in 1893 in his 44th year.

JOHN ROBERTS JUNIOR

John Roberts Junior, who quickly avenged his father's defeat by beating Willie Cooke for the title in 1870, was from 1875 to the early 1900s the 'King of English billiards'. He stands out as one of the great Victorians in the world of sport. He was to billiards what W. G. Grace was to cricket and was easily the most commanding figure the game has ever known, both on and off the table. For years he was able to give a third of a game start to any opponent, and he invented the top-of-the-table game – that delightful combination of pots and cannon play at the spot end which remains the *pièce de résistance* of billiards to the present day.

Mitchell
Sala
Taylor
Bennett
"A HO

erts
Cook
Peall
North
POOL."

Previous page: A photograph from 1882 probably taken at the first Match Room at Thurston's, Catherine Street, London (left to right) W. Mitchell (1854 – 1931), J.G. Sala (1857 – 1901), T. Taylor (1857 – 1927), J. Bennett (1841 – 1905), J. Roberts Jun (1847 – 1919), W. Cook (1849 – 1893), W.J. Peall (1854 – 1952), J. North (1857 – 1902).

Tall in stature, with a commanding physique and an arresting personality, Roberts was a showman, for in his dress and deportment he never forgot that people had paid to come and see his play, and therefore were entitled to see him at his best in every respect. Fortunately, that tradition has remained, as witnessed by today's smartly-dressed professionals.

However, the other side of the coin was his constant tendency to behave as if he was a law unto himself in everything connected with billiards. The governing body and other professionals were waved aside by a sweep of his dictatorial hand. This is well illustrated by the story of a tournament that was held under his management. The rumour got out that due to the success of the event the fees to the players were to be increased, and it was left to Cecil Harveson, a well-respected professional, to approach their paymaster on this matter. As he entered the office, Roberts was writing and did not look up. 'Mr. Roberts', said Harveson, 'there is an impression amongst the players that our fee for winning a heat is to be increased from two to three guineas'. 'Harveson, that impression will soon wear off', was the reply. Cecil quietly left!

JOSEPH BENNETT AND W. J. PEALL

Contemporaries of John Roberts Junior included Joseph Bennett (1841 – 1905), who advertised himself for years as 'The only man who ever defeated John Roberts Junior for the Championship'. He achieved that feat in November 1870. W. J. Peall (1854 – 1952) was another peer, whose speciality was the 'spot stroke' – that is potting the red off its spot without interruption – from which he made a break of 3,304. This is where Peall left his mark on the game, by being the first to reveal the invincible scoring power of a series of strokes all directed towards the same objective. As a result, rules had to be brought in to limit the number of successive reds that could be potted, and these were a forerunner to similar restrictions placed on incessantly repetitive methods of scoring. Of course, this has never been a problem in snooker for, unlike billiards, it is quite impossible to stereotype the scoring sequence. No two opening strokes at the triangle of reds ever gives the same result and thus each game is inevitably unique.

DUELS

At the turn of the century, top players seem to have come in pairs, with great duels between Charles Dawson and Harry Stevenson, followed by Tom Reece and Melbourne Inman. There was rivalry between them, and in one match Inman was fluking in a manner which made Reece's hair stand on end. At last he jumped up and asked with solemnity and disbelief: 'how did you get that shot, Mr. Inman?' After a momentary pause Inman replied: 'I believe you know my terms for tuition, Mr. Reece'.

But no matter how much Inman and Reece supposedly hated each other, they would never have considered a 'billiard ball duel', which actually took place in France, in the 1840s. The quarrel was between two men, named Lenfant and Mellant, over a game of billiards. Challenges were exchanged, the red ball was selected as the weapon and lots were drawn to see who should throw it first. This Mellant did, and struck Lenfant on the forehead, killing him instantly. And nowadays we think deducting ranking points is tough!

A 'SNOOKERS' POOL CHAMPIONSHIP'

It was during 1907 that a 'Snookers' Pool Championship' was first played for. Admittedly the match was tagged onto the end of a billiards tournament which was promoted by the table manufacturers, Burroughes and Watts, at their room in Soho Square. However, it was the first time that the paying public began to show an interest in the 22-ball game. The ultimate winner was Charles Dawson but, curiously, the scoring was still recorded in billiard terms, as it was the total aggregate points scored, and not the frame scores, which decided the winner of this round robin competition.

One of the earliest authenticated breaks at snooker was recorded in the following year – a 73, by James Harris against Albert Raynor in a Bonzoline tournament in Manchester. This was equalled a few months later by John Roberts Junior in a rare snooker match against Tom Reece – a game noted for its exciting, though unusual, climax.

All the coloured balls had been taken, except the pink and black. The pink was left in the jaws of the right middle pocket, while the black and cue ball were near the top cushion. To take the pink, it was necessary to play off the baulk end cushion first, and this Roberts elected to do. Roberts and Reece both

1. Dawson watching Stevenson's play. 2. Preliminaries. Testing weight of balls. 3. Old stagers in the audience. 4. The Champion watching the Challenger. 5. Stevenson defending his title on Messrs. Riley's specially-made standard table. 6. Stevenson contracted. 7. Dawson extended.

had three attempts to hit it, and it was not touched till the veteran's fourth go, when he managed to hit it and, catching the bump of the pocket, it came out into the middle of the table. However, the game didn't end there, for Roberts snookered Reece behind the black a couple of shots later. Reece then tried to get past the black with a *masse* (severe swerve) but hit it and also holed the pink. Roberts now had the black to go at, brought off a brilliant double, but unfortunately the white just managed to find the top right pocket. So, with the last two balls on the table, the players had given away no less than 50 points between them. Moreover, the pink was not re-spotted after the foul shot, which was probably a good thing, otherwise the number of penalty points might have been even higher!

ANNO DOMINI

Around this year of 1908 John Roberts Junior was still a force to be reckoned with, although time was beginning to take its effect. The story goes that Charles Dawson was playing him after receiving a considerable start, when one of Roberts' supporters asked the referee who he thought would win. The referee replied that he thought Dawson would. 'Well he can't', replied the supporter, 'nobody will ever beat Roberts'. The referee then suggested that Roberts was not so young as he used to be and that Anno Domini might beat him. 'Oh', said Roberts' backer, 'I didn't mean any of your foreign players, I meant an Englishman'! Needless to say, Anno Domini did finally beat Roberts and the 'King of English Billiards' died on December 23, 1919.

THE GROWTH OF THE BILLIARD HALLS

At the beginning of this century, billiard halls were few and far between, but from 1909 to 1914 a steady boom occurred. Like today's snooker clubs, billiard halls sprang up like mushrooms in every town and city in the country. Billiard hall proprietors read their balance sheets with smiling faces and billiard table manufacturers enlarged their works to cope with the increasing demand for tables. In those days, £1 per week per table revenue and a ten-table room gave a proprietor a very comfortable existence.

During the First World War (1914–18) the business steadied up, except of course in the munition and military centres. But 1919–1925 saw an unprecedented upsurge in halls, with money no object. From 1925–30 things began to tail off, and by 1934 supply had certainly exceeded demand. Some of the halls still kept a fairly good trade through the 1940s and '50s, some no more than held their own, and by 1960 a lot had closed down.

The present upsurge in up-market snooker clubs and centres (which took off in the 1970s) has coincided with the growing popularity of snooker on television. The boom has also been fuelled by the change in the law which allowed jackpot gaming machines in working mens' and social clubs. The increased revenue that ensued allowed the clubs' entertainment and sporting budgets to be increased – hence, better snooker room facilities and increased exhibition work for the professionals.

WILLIE SMITH AND TOM NEWMAN

The 1920s was the decade which saw billiards reach its peak and snooker start to become the test of strategy and skill it is now acknowledged to be.

At the start of the decade, the next duo of great players had come along in the form of Willie Smith and Tom Newman. Smith (1885–1982) only entered the Billiard Championship twice, and he won it both times. The first time was in 1920, against that wonderful touch player, Claude Falkiner, and then in 1923 he regained the title from Newman. Willie was possibly the best non-specialist all-round billiard player of all time. His reasons for not entering the Championship more often were due to his constant wrangles with the game's governing body – a problem which seems to have bedeviled both games since 1885, when the first committee was formed.

Newman (1894–1943), on the other hand, was a far more easy-going person and a great sportsman. After a match it would be impossible to tell if he had won or lost, such was his amiable character. He won the championship six times between 1921–1927, the last two against a rising star who would dominate the sport for the next 20 years . . . Joe Davis.

There has been much speculation over who would have been the likely winner in a match between Steve Davis and Joe Davis. This is a question Newman used to reply to rather well when the same comparison was made between John Roberts Junior and Joe Davis. 'He began where Roberts left off', was Tom's reply. As a showman, however, Roberts was first and the rest nowhere.

THE STANCE

Before we go on to look at the career of Joe Davis in detail, a mention must be made of how the

Tom Newman, World Professional Champion 1921–27, watches Clark McConachy.

players' stance has changed over the last century. Both John Roberts Senior and John Roberts Junior were very upright in their stance, having both legs virtually straight, with the right behind the left and with both feet facing forward. Willie Smith in contrast seems to have been the first professional to have got his chin down to anywhere near the cue, a style which was taken further by Joe Davis. Their stance was very much like that of a boxer, with the weight mainly on their left leg, and their right foot still behind their left foot, but nearly at right angles to it. The modern stance, on the other hand, has brought the right foot virtually level with the left, so that the whole body is standing square to the table, which gives almost a 'knock-kneed' effect, as in the case of John Parrott. This position, in the opinion of John Pulman, is incorrect. But one certainly cannot 'knock' the results that the stance produces.

AN AMBIDEXTROUS ADVANTAGE

But whatever style has been used, to be able to play with either hand has always proved to be a most useful attribute over the years, as it all but eliminates the need to use the dreaded rest. Many's the player who would have given his right arm to be ambidextrous! Of course, given the right opponent, one hand will often do, as the following anecdote reveals.

At the opening of a billiard tournament in New York, that great novelist Mark Twain was called upon for the inevitable speech. He chose billiards as his topic, and began by stating that the game had destroyed his naturally sweet disposition. 'Once when I was an underpaid reporter in Virginia City, a stranger came and opened a billiard parlour. I went to seem him and he proposed a game to which I agreed.' ''Before we begin'', he said, ''knock the balls around a little so that I can assess your capabilities''. 'I did so for a while and then he said: ''I will be perfectly fair with you, I will play you left-handed.'' I felt hurt for he was cross-eyed, freckled and had red hair, so I was determined to teach him a lesson for his audacity. He won the toss, got in first, and continued to play the game out, after which he took my half-dollar and all I got was the opportunity to chalk my cue. ''If you play like that with your left hand'', I said, ''I'd like to see you play with your right''. ''I can't'', was the prompt reply, ''I'm left-handed'''!

JOE DAVIS - AND THE GROWTH OF SNOOKER

Joe Davis was born on April 15, 1901, in the coal-mining village of Whitwell, Derbyshire. He grew up to become the man who made snooker a real test of tactics, turned it into an exciting spectator sport, and dominated the game for 20 years. His apprenticeship was, of course, served in billiards, and early reports (in 1923) of his professional career gave a clear indication of his potential and the success that was to follow.

There were new, quite distinctive features in Joe's cueing action – which were to hold him in good stead when he later turned his attention to snooker. For example, his method of sighting right down over the cue, and his ultra-rigid stance, were both considered worthy of note in the billiard press at the time. Tom Newman remarked some years later, when Joe was getting the better of him in the billiards championships, that it was Joe's potting which made the difference, resulting in as much as 3,000 points advantage over a fortnight's play.

Joe's record certainly bears this out. After early reverses in 1926 and 1927, he proceeded to win the World Championship of Billiards against Tom Newman in the finals of 1928, 1929 and 1930. There was no championship in 1931, due to contractual wrangles among the top professionals, but Joe won the title again in 1932, this time against the New Zealander, Clark McConachy.

THURSTON'S

During this period, most of the important tournaments and exhibitions were played at Thurston's club, in Leicester Square. Playing there against Joe, in 1927, Tom Newman made a world record break of 97 at snooker – which beat the previous highest, made by Joe in 1925, by one point. Indeed, many records, and much of the game's history, were made at Thurston's, and the venue attracted many celebrities from all walks of life.

For example, in 1929, J. B. Priestley, the great author, visited Thurston's and watched a match between Tom Newman and Joe Davis, and of the one and a half hours he spent there he later wrote, quite simply: 'I was happy'. But perhaps the greatest compliment was that, after watching for a few minutes in that 'small, snug and companionable room of Thurston's', Priestley said he was in absolute awe of those great players, and much more so than he could have been towards any contemporary writer. 'It would have to be

Joe Davis demonstrates the 'masse' shot while Walter Lindrum looks on in 1930.

Shakespeare to compare, and when you are in this remote little world of billiard and snooker, players like Messrs Davis and Newman are Shakespeare: they are as good as that.'

Interestingly enough, another author of that period, Sir Arthur Conan Doyle (the creator of Sherlock Holmes), was a very keen billiard player – so much so that he entered the English Amateur Championships during the 1920s.

WALTER LINDRUM

Looking at the statistics, it would appear that Joe Davis reigned supreme at English billiards from 1928 to 1932, but in fact this was not the case. In 1929, a man arrived on our shores from Australia – a player who would in the next five years completely dominate the game. His name . . . the legendary Walter Lindrum.

Quite simply, Walter was a genius who conquered his chosen sport perhaps more thoroughly than any other sportsman has ever done, and his record break of 4,137 remains unchallenged to this day. (Incredibly, immediately after Walter's record break, Joe Davis replied with a 1,247, which in many ways he considered his finest, bearing in mind what he had to follow!) Such achievements made Lindrum a national celebrity, and he was invited to Downing Street to meet the Prime Minister, Ramsay McDonald. Not long after, in February 1931, he was summoned to give an exhibition of potting to King George V and Queen Mary at Buckingham Palace.

So superior was Walter, in every department of the game, that by 1930 he was giving Joe Davis, Tom Newman and Clark McConachy 7,000 starts in a fortnight's play! And by the end of his first tour

Walter Lindrum was a genius who conquered his chosen sport perhaps more thoroughly than any other sportsman has ever done. His record break of 4,137 points hasn't been bettered to this day.

he had scored 346,362 in public matches, made 67 thousand-plus breaks, and exceeded the 500 mark on no fewer than 211 occasions! Indeed, his fellow countryman and friend, Don Bradman – who many consider to be the world's greatest ever batsman – modestly, but probably very accurately, claimed that in terms of their abilities at their respective sports, Walter was by far a long way ahead of him.

Walter's domination of the game was such that, during his long breaks, he would occupy the table for two or three sessions at a time. On one such occasion a stranger wandered into Thurston's match room, and after watching Lindrum for some considerable time turned to the doorman and asked: 'What is the game he is playing?' 'Billiards, sir', came the reply. 'Oh', said the stranger, 'they play billiards with two players where I come from, but I suppose it's different in London'.

But, despite all this recognition and record breaking, Walter had still not become world champion – the obstacle being that he was contracted to one table manufacturer, Burroughes & Watts, while the Championship was played on a Thurston's table. However, this was all put behind him in 1933, when at the Dorland Hall, London, Walter beat Joe Davis by the fairly close margin of 21,815–21,121 points, and thus finally captured the world crown.

Lindrum successfully defended his title in 1934, in Australia, again against Joe Davis. But sadly this was the last time he entered a tournament. The rest of his career was spent for the most part in giving

Walter Lindrum receives the World Professional Billiards trophy after beating Joe Davis (2nd left) at the Dorland Hall, London in 1933.

exhibitions, helping the war effort and playing for charities. He was awarded the OBE in 1958 and died two years later, in 1960.

THE BIRTH OF THE WORLD SNOOKER CHAMPIONSHIP

All through the Lindrum era of the late '20s and early '30s, Joe Davis really had two careers. We have seen how he developed into a world class billiard player, second only to Walter Lindrum, but at the same time he was beavering away at instigating the first World Snooker Championship, in 1927 – although it had been way back in 1924 that Joe, together with two billiard traders, had first put forward the idea of such a championship to the committee of the ruling Billiard Association and Control Council.

Curiously, the amateur game had its first snooker championships approved way back in 1916. But the idea of an equivalent professional tournament was met with a marked lack of enthusiasm, and it was not until 1927 that the first World Championship was held at the Camkin's Rooms in Birmingham. There were ten contenders for this first title, most of whom were far better known for their prowess at billiards – Tom Newman and Melbourne Inman being the most notable. Perhaps the relatively low entry was something to do with the conditions which were placed on it.

Joe Davis after winning the inaugural World Professional Championship in 1927.

At a meeting on September 1, 1926, an entrance fee of five guineas (£5.25) was enforced, along with stake money of five guineas for each round. The competition was open only to professional billiard players, and the trophy was to be paid for out of the pay fund. This was to represent 50% of the total entrance fees – the other 50% going to the finalists, with 60% of that going to the winner and 40% to the runner-up. The gate receipts, after payment of expenses, were equally divided between the winner and loser of each match so that: 'every competitor may be assured of receiving a certain modicum of remuneration for the time that he devotes to the competition'. It can be safely stated that no-one made a fortune.

Once Joe had beaten Tom Dennis 20–11 in the final, a more financially rewarding challenge went out from the new champion, in the form of a press statement. It read that Joe would play for £100 a side, in a match of 15, 31 or 61 games, against any player in the world. Or, play for £25 or more in a match of 9, 15 or 31 games against any player in Great Britain, except Willie Smith, and concede his opponent a start of 12 points per frame. (Willie Smith was considered to be the best snooker player prior to 1927.)

It is interesting to note that Joe's highest break up to that time was a 96 he made against Tom Newman on February 4, 1925, at Burrough's Hall, St. James Street, London. Whereas his highest in the first World Championship was 57, which was only bettered by Albert Cope in his semi-final against Joe, when the former produced a break of 60.

A DOUBLE WORLD CHAMPION

In 1928 the Championship was played on a challenge basis, with one player coming through to compete against Joe, the defending champion. That player was Fred Lawrence, who had beaten Tom Newman in the qualifier, only to lose to Joe 16–13 in the final. This was a great year for Davis, for at the age of 27 he had become champion at both billiards and snooker.

The Championship of 1929 proved to be a repetition of the first tournament, although there were only five entrants. Davis beat Dennis again, this time by a margin of 19–14, and increased the top Championship break to 61. The same pair went on to meet in the 1930 final, this time with Joe winning 25–12 and producing a top break of 79 – a Championship record. After making one of those record breaks, Joe had hardly taken his seat

Joe Davis shown in action, this time on his way to beating Tom Newman in the 1928 World Professional Billiards Championship.

when a friend of his sat down next to him and exclaimed 'When I watch you play, I wonder how you ever break down'. 'Don't you sometimes wonder', retorted Joe, 'how I manage to keep on scoring as long as I do.'

THE BIG FOUR

In the early 1930s, the 'Big Four', as they were known, consisting of Davis, Lindrum, Newman and McConachy, would tour the country playing billiard tournaments. On one such tour, in 1930, a snooker tournament was played on a round-robin basis, with each playing their opponents twice. Although Lindrum had made century breaks at the 22-ball game, he never really took to it. What he might have achieved had he done so is anyone's guess. Looking at old archive film of him today, his style, touch and speed was very similar to that of Jimmy White.

In fact it was Davis who won all his matches, and while playing Walter made a break of 105. He secured all the red balls, together with nine blacks, two pinks and three blues, and after the last red had a fairly easy pink on. Unfortunately, in trying to get to the yellow, he wobbled the pink, and the break went no further.

Each match was awarded on the best aggregate score, with only Newman given a 200 start. And as the final placings show (see table below), it was Davis who was considered superior to all the others when it came to snooker.

Player	Played	Won	Lost	Aggregate
J. Davis	6	6	0	10,332
T. Newman	6	3	3	8,897
W. Lindrum	6	2	4	7,591
C. McConachy	6	1	5	8,058

Two years later, in the spring of 1932, Lindrum and Newman set off on a three month tour of Canada and the USA, and while in New York they actually played snooker matches against the American player, A. St-Jean. Lindrum beat St-Jean, whilst Newman lost to him, in a game again played on an aggregate points basis.

THE WORLD CHAMPIONSHIP IN THE BACKROOM OF A PUB

It must have seemed strange to Joe Davis that, despite public interest (both national and international) in these snooker tournaments, there were so few entrants for the World Championship.

In 1931 there were just two entrants: Joe Davis and Tom Dennis. The match was staged in the back room of a Nottingham pub owned by Dennis, and played over 49 frames. However, home advantage did not help Tom, who lost 25–21, giving Davis his fifth consecutive victory.

THE LIONS' DEN AND ON HORSEBACK!

Playing a World Championship final in the back room of a pub may seem strange today, but that's nothing compared to some of the odd places in which billiards has been played. A match of 25 up took place in a lions' den at Stoke, in 1906, and during its progress the lions sat around the cage on pedestals. Apparently disappointed at a shot made during the game, one of the animals gave vent to a loud roar. This startled the player into dropping his cue, and in a few moments the lions became so dissatisfied with the display that they commenced to 'cannon' round the cage – which inspired the 2,000 spectators with anything but confidence. The lady trainer had great trouble in making them stop, which proved too much for some of the spectators who yelled at the top of their voices, while a number of women fainted!

Billiards has also been played on horseback, in New York. Needless to say, both players were experts at the game and fine equestrians. They played for £200 a side and although progress was slow, one of the cueists contrived to make a break of 15, which was the best of the match!

THE CHAMPIONSHIP GETS BIGGER

In 1932, the World Professional Snooker Championship had three entrants, with Clark McConachy joining the previous year's finalists. In the preliminary heat at Skegness, McConachy beat Dennis 13–11 and made a top break of 72. Then in the final at Thurston's, he lost to Davis by the convincing margin of 30–19 – Joe making a Championship record break of 99.

WILLIE SMITH

In 1933, Willie Smith at last decided to try his luck and entered the Championship. Had he done so in 1927 the history books might have been re-written, but by now Davis had developed his skill and strategy way beyond the chasing pack. This was clearly demonstrated when Joe, in an exhibition match against J. Harris, made a break of 132 on February 9, 1932. After Harris had taken a red and a pink, Davis cleared the table – taking 14 reds, one blue, one brown, two pinks, ten blacks, and all the colours.

WALTER DONALDSON

1933 was also the first year in which Walter Donaldson from Scotland entered the World

Willie Smith and Joe Davis 'stringing' for break during an exhibition match in 1933.

Championships. In later years, Donaldson was to have his name engraved twice on that now world-famous trophy. Previously, he had won the Boys Billiards Championship in 1922, and was later the Professional champion of Scotland. His first opponent in the 1933 Championship was Willie Lee from Nottingham, whom he defeated 13–11, making a 71 break in the final frame. He was then unfortunate enough to meet Joe Davis in the semi–final. In the other semi-final, Willie Smith defeated Tom Dennis by 13 frames to 4. And in the final, Willie lost 25–18 to Joe.

In 1934, as an experiment, Joe Davis and the challenger, Tom Newman, were contesting the championship in the provinces. Two places were selected for the final; The Lounge at Nottingham was to stage the first 30 frames and The Central Hall, Kettering, the last 19 frames. The crowds came out and Davis won by 25 frames to 22 – a frame score which belied Davis' superiority.

CONRAD STANDBURY

Willie Smith was back in contention in the 1935 finals. And other contenders, apart from Joe, were Tom Newman, Alf Mann from Birmingham, and Conrad Standbury, champion of Canada. Standbury first came to the public's attention when he made a record break of 117, in 1923. He played very well in this Championship, and should have beaten Willie Smith by the odd frame, but missed a very ordinary pink into the middle bag in the last game. Had he made the shot, he would have been odds-on favourite to beat Mann in the semi-final, and thereby go on to meet Davis in the final. As has often been seen in modern snooker, careers can be made or lost on the pot of one ball!

But perhaps the most significant feature of the 1935 Championship was that for the first time in its history it attracted large and continuous crowds to Thurston's, where in the final Joe Davis beat Willie Smith by 25 frames to 20. In his semi-final against Tom Newman, Joe had made a Championship record break of 110.

CHANGE IN FORMAT AND A RECORD BREAK

In 1936 the whole basis of the Championship changed when it took on the regular knock-out format that we know today. This new structure attracted 12 entrants, one of whom was Horace Lindrum, nephew of the great Walter. And it was in Australia, at the famous City Tattersalls Club, Sydney, on February 5, 1936, that Norman

Horace Lindrum was Joe Davis' biggest challenger during the 1946 world final. Davis won 78–67.

Squires, a visitor from New Zealand, compiled a magnificent break of 139, clearing the table from the break-off by J. Morton. This break bettered the 137 that Horace Lindrum had made in a friendly match at Melbourne, on May 3, 1932.

SNOOKER COMES OF AGE

In the 1936 Championship, Sydney Lee, who much later on was well known as The Pot Black television referee, first entered the professional game, and lost by the odd frame to Clare O'Donnell, the hard-hitting Canadian. But it was in Horace Lindrum that Joe Davis probably saw his biggest threat to date.

Against Tom Newman, Joe won all ten frames on the first day, and the next five on the second day, before poor Tom could put one on the board – Joe eventually winning 29–2. Willie Smith fared a little better, losing 'only' 22–9, and in the semi-finals Joe beat Alec Brown 21–10. Meanwhile, Horace was also in devastating form, beating O'Donnell 19–6 – this after the Canadian failed to turn up for the final session. He then played Stanley Newman, a less gifted brother of Tom's, and won convincingly by 29–2. And so the stage was set for the grand final between 'The Emperor of Pot', which Joe was nicknamed (no drugs tests in those days!), and the young pretender from Australia.

Before we look at that epic final in some detail, it is important to understand the significance of this

Championship. This was the first time when snooker could at last be said to have overtaken billiards in popularity as a spectator sport. Thurston's were turning money away, session after session, and every seat was sold for the last day's play before a ball was struck. This was all brought about by Joe Davis, the first player to treat snooker as something more than a mere sideline, or just a 'fill up' to give the people something to look at when the old style 'sessional points' in billiards were achieved rather too quickly. It can be said without fear of contradiction that Joe made a study of the game, perfected its technique and positional possibilities and gave it every atom of his outstanding ability – and justly reaped the rewards.

THE 1936 WORLD CHAMPIONSHIP FINAL

The five-frame opening session of the final produced a highest break of only 26, and showed that both men were feeling the pressure and strain of the occasion. At the end of the first day Lindrum led 6–4. The second day saw both men in better break-building form, and Lindrum still led by two frames at the close. However, Davis struck a patch of his best form during the afternoon of the third day, and by winning four games out of five took the lead for the first time, making breaks of 75 and 78. Lindrum then hit back during the evening to make the score 15–15 at the end of play.

The next day brought a great deal of strategy and safety play, but Lindrum had the better of things, finishing ahead at 26–24. When the decisive Saturday came Lindrum won the first frame of the day and his lead of three frames seemed to make him a strong favourite for the title. And then, as we have seen so many times in modern matches, when the winning post was in sight Lindrum faltered and Davis took command. Playing the best snooker of his life, as a true champion does when he needs to, Joe won the next ten frames straight off, and thereby took the World Championship for the tenth year in succession, by 34 games to 27.

FRED DAVIS AND 'SWIVEL LENSES'

The 1937 Championship was a repeat of the previous year, with the same venue, the same finalists and the same result. This time it produced a 32–29 win for Joe, with a top break of 103. In a qualifying round, Fred Davis, Joe's younger brother, made his début and surprisingly lost to Bill Withers, 17–14. However, it made sense after Fred discovered that he was beginning to suffer with myopia. Up to that time no leading professional player had ever worn glasses, and Fred thought his career was over. But a solution to his short-sightedness was eventually found with a pair of 'sportsman's glasses', with special swivel lenses – now made famous by Dennis Taylor. In the meantime, Joe avenged his younger brother's defeat by hammering Bill Withers 30–1 in the next round!

Fred was again present in the 1938 Championship, and this time he fared a little better, beating Herbert Holt 23–8, and Alec Brown 14–6. Fred then lost in the next round to Sidney Smith, who went on to the final and lost to brother Joe by 37–24 – which was repeated in 1939 when Joe won 43–30.

In 1937, Sidney Smith took his place in the record books by completing the world's first 'official' total clearance – scoring a 133 break in tournament play.

FIRST OFFICIAL TOTAL CLEARANCE

However, Smith could take comfort from the fact that he had already won a place in the record books by cueing the world's first 'official' total clearance – scoring 133 in a separate event in 1937. Other total clearances had been reported earlier than this, but as they were not ratified by the BA & CC (for various reasons) they didn't count.

Similarly, Kingsley Kennerley became the first amateur ever to score an 'officially recognised' three-figure snooker break, after making exactly 100 in January 1939. Yet several other amateurs had made century breaks prior to this. They included Pat Matthews, Sydney Lee when he was an amateur, W. D. Hargest and the Welshman, Bryn Gravenor. In fact Kennerley, too, had made an earlier century break, but like the others it had been made on tables not up to the specifications required by the BA & CC. What's more, over the years a number of players had made large breaks abroad, but in the absence of measuring templates official ratification wasn't forthcoming.

Fred Davis, at 18, when he became the Junior Professional Billiards Champion in 1931.

Walter Donaldson pictured in training before competing in the World Professional Snooker Championship in 1947. There he beat Fred Davis in the final.

JOE VERSUS FRED

Although Joe won the 1939 Championship he had a tough semi-final against his brother Fred, eventually winning 17–14. Fred also raised the Championship best break to 113. Encouraged by this, Fred's progress was startling. So much so that by 1940, after beating Sidney Smith 17–14 in one semi-final while Joe was beating Walter Donaldson 22–9 in the other, he felt he had his first real chance of beating his legendary brother. Joe just made it by 37 frames to 35, making a century in the last frame, but sadly, because of circumstances beyond everyone's control – the 1939–45 World War – and Joe's decision after it, the two brothers never met again in the World Championship.

The War was, of course, a great disruption to everyone's lives, and many a career took a different course because of it. However, the billiards and snooker trade can be proud of its war effort, with the game's leading players raising large sums of money both for it and related charities – an effort that was sustained throughout the Commonwealth.

FIRST CHAMPIONSHIP AFTER THE WAR

After the war, in 1946, Joe Davis had lost none of his competitive edge, and was back to take the title for the 15th consecutive time. In the semi-finals, he beat Stanley Newman 21–10, while in the other semi Horace Lindrum beat Fred Davis 16 – 12. The final was played at the Royal Agricultural Hall in London and proved to be the longest match to date – being the best of 145 frames played over a two week period.

During the final, Joe made his 200th century break with a Championship record of 133, the game being broadcast live on radio to Australia. A few days later he improved the record to 136 and in all, during the fortnight's play he made six century breaks, finishing on the right side of a 78 – 67 frame score-line.

This was the measure of the man, that after six years of non-tournament play he could raise his game for the big occasion. Maybe the effort required was partly the reason that soon after he announced his retirement from the World Professional Championship. He wanted to retire undefeated, and with the likes of his younger brother Fred making a strong challenge, Joe obviously thought that this was the right time. He stated that he felt it was not good for the game that one man should dominate it. But simply retiring from the Championship proved to be not enough, as he was to remain a dominant force in snooker for another 15 years. And of course, Joe's decision also took a little of the glory away from his successors, because although they were acclaimed world champions, in the public's eye, for the next decade at least, Joe was still No. 1.

In 1874 the French billiard professional, Mons Izar, introduced his 'Fingers Spin' act to this country. His display of twisting and spinning the balls around the table using fingers and thumb was so clever that it became 'all the rage' for many years.

AMAZING FINGER SPINS

Before we turn to the new era of snooker ushered in by Joe Davis' 'retirement', a mention should be made of an art-form which seems to have died in recent years. Namely: 'Hand Stroke Billiards', later billed as 'Amazing Finger Spins', and once often demonstrated by leading professionals during exhibition play.

In approximately 1874 a French billiard professional called Mons Izar paid a visit to this country and introduced the then unknown 'Fingers Spin' act to our professionals. His display of twisting the balls into pockets, and making cannons with side and other strokes with his fingers and thumb, was so clever that it soon became the rage everywhere. Herbert Roberts, brother of the great John, took up the task of learning the skills, which was slow work at first, but as his fingers became more supple he began to steadily improve, and before long began a series of public exhibitions.

Meanwhile, John Roberts himself, never slow to spot a good business proposition, arranged a tour of the colonies which proved to be a great success. When giving a show before a club room filled with locals, John would perform one particular trick to perfection. He would stand behind the baulk cushion and whizz a ball up the table. From the pace at which the ball started it looked as if it was sure to rebound up and down the table several times. But just as it reached the vicinity of the black spot, John would shout: 'Stop!' and the ball would indeed stop dead as the powerful under-spin he had imparted took effect. On one occasion the sight was altogether too much for those watching who, one by one, began to file out and before long there was a rush to the door. 'We do not mind what Mr. Roberts does with his cue to the balls, but when he talks to them, and they obey him, there is black magic in it', was the fearful explanation!

Other great exponents of the art around the turn of the century were R. De Kuyper followed by Eugene Carter. They would stand at the baulk-end and send a ball up the table with spin on it to curl around a top hat placed on the black spot! It is quite likely that the inventor of cricket's 'Googly', a Mr. B. J. T. Bosanquet (1878 – 1936), worked out his theory after watching such a finger-spinning expert. Indeed, Bosanquet was a keen billiards player too, representing the University of Oxford in 1898 and 1900. In more recent years, during the 1940s and '50s, Horace Lindrum and Herbert Holt also used their 'finger-spinning skills' to great effect.

There has never been a hand stroke championhip, although on the continent there is an 'Artistic Billiards Championship' where similar strokes are attempted, but with the use of a cue. It should be mentioned that if one takes the trouble to practise screwing a ball with finger and thumb for a few minutes, it will be readily apparent that a considerable amount of skill is required to achieve the desired effect. Certainly it was and is a pretty and attractive art, would prove a great addition to the modern day professional's exhibition play, and should be greatly appreciated by the viewing public.

SNOOKER AFTER THE WAR

With Joe Davis retired from World Championship play, the next great duo of snooker champions to hold centre stage were Fred Davis and Walter Donaldson – who met for the first time in the finals of the 1947 Championship, a confrontation which was to be repeated for the following seven years. This first encounter was at Thurston's, which had now been renamed the Leicester Square Hall after re-opening following bomb damage during the War. This was also the first year that the inimitable John Pulman appeared in the Championship.

Even when Donaldson beat Horace Lindrum in the semi-final, it was still thought by most observers, including Joe, that the name Davis would be engraved on the trophy for the 16th time. But they hadn't reckoned on the wily Scot, who was dour but effective – qualities accentuated by his having been one of Monty's 'Desert Rats'.

Walter's orthodox style of play was of the highest standard, and he never used side if there was the chance it would compromise his potting. Before the final, he locked himself away with a table in a friend's loft to perfect his long potting – which Fred later acknowledged as some of the best he had ever seen. The result was that Walter beat Fred in their first encounter 82–63.

Unfortunately, Walter was not at his best whenever he lost a match. For example, when a consoling friend said to him: 'Walter, I don't know what to say', after he had lost six frames in a row to Fred, Walter's pointed reply was: 'Well, don't bloody well say anything'!

They met again in the final of the 1948 Championship, which was played at the same venue, the Leicester Square Hall, over 145 frames, and this time Fred matched Walter with safety play, taking no risks and giving few chances. This is well illustrated by the fact that there were no century breaks. Fred won 84–61 and both players were honoured by the attendance of the Marquess and Marchioness of Queensbury, plus Joe – there to watch his brother in his hour of victory.

PHYSICAL ENDURANCE

John Pulman did rather well in the Championship of 1949, again played at Leicester Square, making it

Four World Snooker Champions cueing up in 1954. From left to right: Walter Donaldson, Joe Davis, Fred Davis and John Pulman.

to the semi-final before losing to Donaldson 49–22. In this match Donaldson made his 100th century break, with 100 and 115 in successive frames. In the final, Walter was leading Fred by six frames as

Fred Davis beat Walter Donaldson 73–58 in the 1949 World Championship final. Playing competitive snooker six hours a day for fourteen days made the game more of a test of physical endurance than it is today.

late as the 84th frame, but he failed to last the course and Fred came back to take the title in the 131st frame, and went on to win 80–65. It should be pointed out that having to play competitive snooker for six hours a day for fourteen days made the game much more a matter of a physical endurance than it usually is today. In this final Donaldson seemed to crack after frame 117, when Davis who was leading 60–57, then won 13 out of the next 14 frames. Fred's play around this time was nothing short of magnificent, and in other tournaments he

Fred Davis after winning the World Snooker Championship in 1948 at the Albany Club, London.

was managing to beat his brother off a level start – the only man ever to achieve this feat.

The quarter-final matches of the 1950 Championship, which was sponsored by the Empire News, were scattered all over the country. In the semi-final held at Oldham Town Hall, Fred Davis beat the Canadian champion, George Chenier, 43–28. Shortly afterwards Chenier gained some compensation by making a world record break of 144, only for that man Joe Davis to beat his score by one point just five weeks later. In the other semi-final at Newcastle, Walter Donaldson beat Albert Brown 37–34, after a somewhat dour struggle. When the final came round, Fred played far below his best form, which allowed Walter's safety game to come out on top. The game was held at the Tower Circus in Blackpool, and Donaldson won 51–46.

DISPUTE WITH THE BA & CC

It was soon after this Championship that the professional players 'fell out' with the game's governing body, the BA & CC. Initially, it was over a rule which today we take so much for granted, but at the time was the catalyst for the parting of the ways. The rule in question was: 'When a foul has been committed, a player can elect the offender to

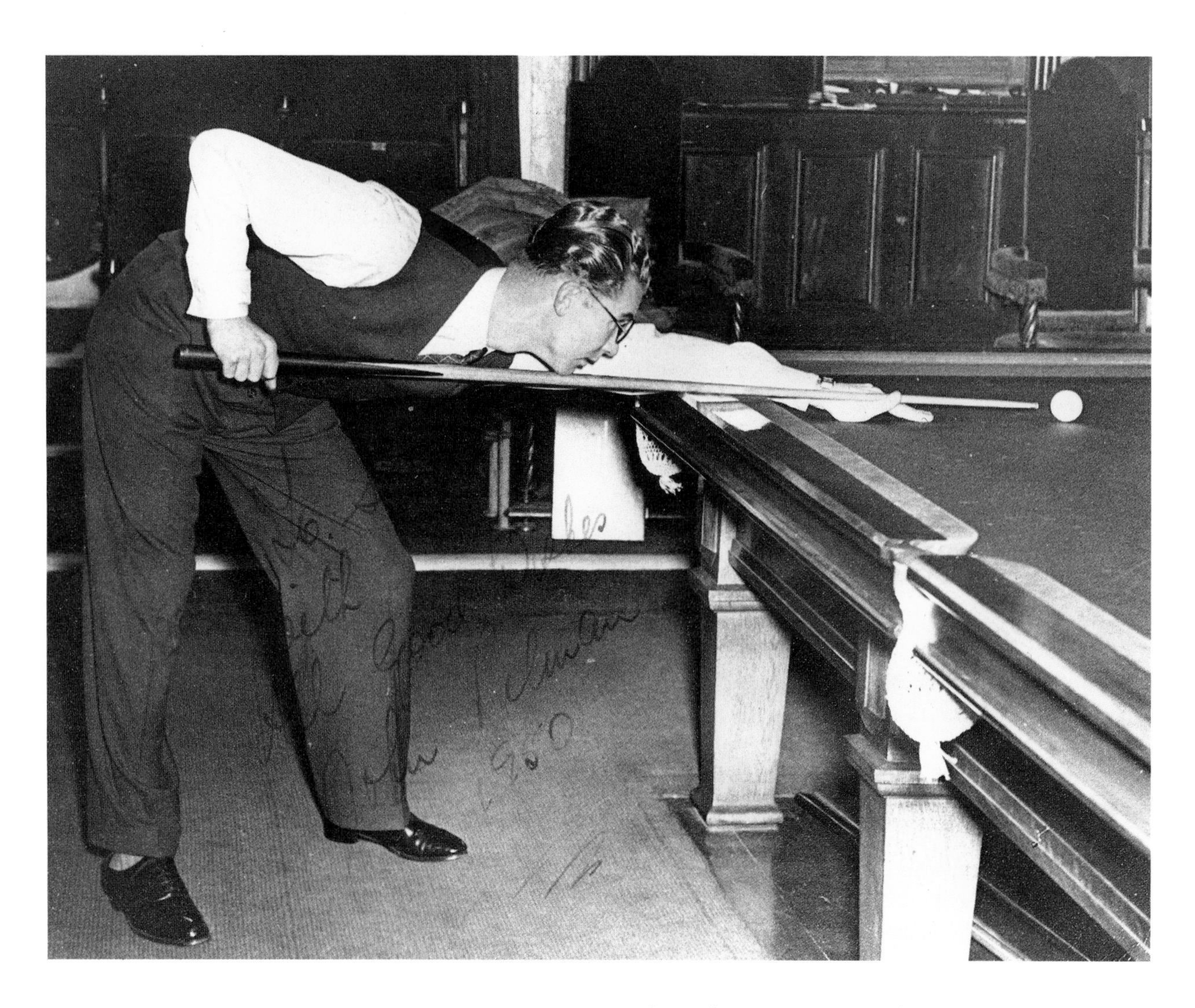

John Pulman in 1950. Pulman is now one of our most respected TV commentators.

play again'. The governing body objected to this and consequently refused to recognise any breaks made under such circumstances. Their difference with the players then spread to financial matters, resulting in a split in 1952, and the professionals going on to play in their own World Matchplay Championship.

However, before the split, the 1951 World Championship saw John Pulman beat Sidney Smith 38 – 33 in an early round, despite the cold room. Reports of the 'chilled cloth which often caused the balls to skid', at the St. John's Ambulance Brigade Hall in Accrington, give one the feeling that by the early 1950s some of the venues chosen for the early rounds often left a lot to be desired! Unfortunately, and probably because of the cold, Pulman had to pull out of the semi-final against Fred Davis due to ill-health, whilst in the other semi Walter Donaldson beat Horace Lindrum 41 – 30. In the final, again played at the Tower Circus in Blackpool, Fred avenged his previous year's defeat with a convincing 58 – 39 victory. The crowds exceeded those of any previous year in the history of the event, and Davis and Donaldson had both reached five successive finals. As Fred said at the time: 'I think it can go on a little longer'. It certainly did.

RESURRECTION OF THE BILLIARDS CHAMPIONSHIP

At this point it should be noted that in the following year, 1951, the World Billiards Championship was resurrected at the Leicester Square Hall, where Clark McConachy did battle with John Barrie from Wisbech. This was the first match for the world title since 1934, when Walter Lindrum had last won it before resigning in 1950. John Barrie was a late replacement for Fred Davis, and the result was an easy win for Clark by 6,681 – 5,057 points.

RIVAL SNOOKER CHAMPIONSHIPS

After the 1952 split with the professionals, the BA & CC held their own private World Snooker Championship in which Horace Lindrum and Clark

McConachy were the only contestants. Horace won a farcical match 94 – 49 at the Houldsworth Hall in Manchester. Although not recognised today as a previous world champion, Horace Lindrum's name is still engraved on the cup.

Prior to that match, McConachy made a maximum break of 147. Before this, only two other players had peformed such a feat – the Australian, E. S. O'Donoghue, in 1928, and Lee Levitt, a Canadian, in 1948. Unfortunately for McConachy, however, the table, upon official examination, proved to be slightly over-generous, so that Joe Davis' 146 made in March 1950 remained the official record.

In the Matchplay Championship of 1951, which was considered the real snooker Championship of the World by the general public, Fred Davis beat Walter Donaldson for the fourth time, 38 – 35. Meanwhile, in other events Joe Davis was still winning, even when giving his opponents starts, and in February 1953 he made his 500th century against the Irish pro, Jack Rea. (Interestingly, it was at this time that Rex Williams made his professional début. He was never to win the world title at snooker, but at billiards he was to prove more successful. In the resurrected World Professional Billiard Championship of 1968, he beat Clark McConachy 5,499 – 5,234 points, and through to 1980 he had successive victories over Bernard Bennett, Jack Karnehm and Eddie Charlton).

In 1952, Clark McConachy made a maximum break of 147. However, upon official examination the pockets of the table proved to be slightly over-generous, and thus Joe Davis' 146, made in 1950, remained the official record.

A LOW EBB IN THE 1950s

Snooker in the mid 1950s was at a low ebb, particularly the World Championship, which was losing credibility. After Fred had beaten Walter in 1953 by 37 – 34, and in 1954 by 39 – 21, Walter had had enough, and retired from the Championship. He later turned his billiard room into a cow shed, using the slates from his table to lay a garden path!

Walter Donaldson is watched by Fred Davis during the 1954 World Championships which Fred Won.

JOHN PULMAN

With Walter gone, this was the cue for John Pulman to challenge Fred in the world finals, which he did unsuccessfully in 1955 and 1956, losing 37 – 34 and 38 – 35 respectively. However, Pulman did have success in the 1954 News of the World round robin tournament, in which he finished top and collected a handsome prize of £500, beating Joe Davis into second place from a field of nine professionals. Joe was conceding to John 12 points per frame.

Giving starts to opponents at both billiards and snooker has always been a difficult problem, and sometimes only serves to re-enforce an existing advantage, as the following tale illustrates. In Australia, in the early 1900s, John Roberts encountered that well known 'young player' who is always ready to give his opponent a 30 point start. Roberts, in reply to the persistency of one particular precocious young man, told him 'I happen to be John Roberts – retired billiards champion'. 'Retired? Well in that case I'll give you a 50 start', came the generous reply.

FINAL MATCH AT LEICESTER SQUARE

On January 28, 1955, Joe and Fred Davis played the final match at the Leicester Square Hall. It was televised and viewers witnessed Fred making the last century at this old and famous venue. But if only the television cameras had been there six days earlier, they and the viewers would have witnessed the game's first televised 147. Joe had made the maximum break against Willie Smith, bringing a fitting climax to the closure of the Leicester Square Hall, and also to the professional playing career of Smith, who retired shortly afterwards.

THE RIFT IS MENDED

At the time of his record break, Joe was chairman of the Professional Billiard Players Association, and proof of how big the rift had become between the professionals and the BA & CC was again demonstrated when the governing body refused to validate the new record because of the 'Play Again' rule. Joe had to wait over two years, until March 20, 1957, before the Control Council's decision was reversed. And when it was, the relationship between the two bodies finally 'thawed', resulting in the acceptance of the 'Play Again' rule by the BA & CC in January 1958.

During the slump of the late '50s and early '60s, up-and-coming players such as Rex Williams complained to Joe Davis that professional snooker had become a closed shop.

DEMISE OF THE CHAMPIONSHIP

However, by 1957 the World Championship had really gone into decline. Fred Davis did not enter that year and the final was held in Jersey, where John Pulman beat Rex Williams 21 – 16 and then Jackie Rea 39 – 34 to gain his first title. That was the last Championship to be held until 1964.

Television was then well on the way to becoming the world's prime entertainment medium, but snooker, with its subtle interplay of colours against the green baize, did not lend itself to exposure on the black and white screen.

During this gap in the history of the Championship, interest was kept alive by events such as the News of the World Tournament, which still attracted the major stars, including Joe Davis, mainly because 'that was where the money was' – the all-important concern for the professional player.

NEW CONTROVERSY

The next controversy to affect the game occurred amongst the professionals themselves, when up-and-coming players such as Rex Williams levelled the charge at Joe Davis that professional snooker had become a closed shop. Their grievance was fuelled by Williams' omission from the News of the World Tournament. Joe's reply was that this tournament had run for ten years with six players on each occasion. However, due to lack of interest in the provinces the numbers had to be reduced to four and, as the one suitable hall in London was only available for three weeks, entries unfortunately had to be cut down.

Regarding the younger players, Joe went on to say: 'They must do more to help themselves. When I was a lad in Chesterfield I had to be my own promoter and I have paid players to be there and give me practice. I climbed the hard way. Too many youngsters nowadays expect everything to be done

Rex Williams (left) and Fred Davis are all smiles during their £3,000 Championship Series which travelled to clubs throughout the United Kingdom.

for them. All they do is wait for a postcard telling them where they will play and how much they will get. It is not good enough'. This was pretty strong stuff, and shows the extent to which Joe ruled the game – very much in the manner that John Roberts Junior did at the end of the last century.

HUSTLING

Certainly, Joe ran professional snooker virtually by himself. But in this he was partly motivated by a desire to keep the game clean, with its image intact. Yet despite these aspirations, many a 'hustle' took place in the country's halls and hotels – as the following stories illustrate.

Apparently, a few friends were having a four-handed game of snooker and just as the match had finished a young man entered the room and challenged any one of them to a game, which was taken up by the group's best player. The stranger then asked if they would like a bit of 'interest' on the match, which was agreed and several pounds were imprudently left, for the time being, in the hands of the stranger. He proceeded to break the pack, after which he took his jacket off, hung it up and asked for the whereabouts of the toilet. Informed of this, he went out and is still 'coming back' to this day!

Another example of 'bringing the game into disrepute' concerns the artful thief who, accompanied by several confederates, induced a trustful elderly gentleman into wagering that he could balance a billiard ball on his wrinkled brow for a period of three minutes. Unfortunately, whilst the old gentleman was bending back, he was quietly relieved of his watch, chain and wallet and the thieves disappeared leaving him still balancing the ball on his head.

NOVELTY TOURNAMENTS

Turning our attentions away from the unseemly behaviour sometimes found on the fringes of the sport, and back to the professional game, there are many examples over the years of novelty tournaments being introduced to entice the crowds back (especially during the lull of the 1950s). For example, a 'Snooker Plus' championship was held, and was played with two extra balls – a purple and an orange – which were valued at eight and nine points respectively.

PRESS

Billiards, too, has had its novelties – perhaps the most extreme involving a change in the size and shape of the table! The oval table was the most famous of these, around the turn of the century. As its name implies, it was oval in shape, and it created a boom which came within an ace of giving us two billiard games 'oval and rectangular billiards'. John Roberts Junior used to spend many hours on the 'The Oval' at London's Liberal Club.

1960 saw the novelty of a World Open Snooker Championship held in Melbourne, Australia. With Fred Davis being the only recognised professional present, his easy win was not altogether unexpected. And the innovation of a series of matches, each being the best of just nine frames, helped to establish the format of the tournaments that we see on television today.

EARLY TELEVISED MATCHES

During the early winter months of 1962, viewers could tune into ITV and watch four professionals play a handicap tournament against four amateurs. The matches were played at the National Liberal Club in London, and produced an unexpected final in which the the amateur, Jonathan Barron, beat the professional, Ron Gross, 4–3. In another match, an amateur had beaten a professional in two or three games, and this was remarked upon to the professional. 'Yes', he said. 'He has beaten me two or three times in a short match, but the table we played on was terrible. Let him turn professional and play me in a longer match on a true table and he'd be lucky to win the odd frame. 'Does this mean', said the inquisitor, 'that an amateur is a man who can only score on a bad table and a professional is one who can only score on a good one'?

The only other television snooker at this time was shown on the BBC, where Joe Davis would play regular matches against another fellow professional. We are fortunate that the BBC recently found a lost tape of Joe playing John Pulman, in which he makes a 100 break.

RESURRECTION OF THE CHAMPIONSHIP

In 1964 the World Professional Snooker Championship was resurrected, and conducted on

The Tower Ballroom, Blackpool is packed to capacity as John Pulman takes on Fred Davis in the 1956 World Snooker final. Davis won 38–35.

a challenge basis with each match carrying a £50 sidestake. The duration of the matches was decided between the two players concerned and the challenger was responsible for providing a suitable venue. Initially, Fred Davis and John Pulman were nominated by the Professional Billiard Players Association to play for the title.

However, before the Championship was due to start, two significant events had taken place. Firstly, John Pulman had won the first professional snooker tournament to be held for four and a half years. It was played under the new format of 12 five frame matches condensed into one week's play. Staging two complete matches each evening meant that peaks of excitement occurred far more often than in the old-style tournament – where each match lasted three days and tension was consequently more thinly spread. (It should be noted that this new system has been recently introduced into modern billiards – with games being just '150 up' over anything between 7 and 13 frames.) And secondly, whilst this professional tournament was taking place, the final of the English Amateur Snooker Championship was being fought for at the Central Hall, Birmingham. The two competitors, who were later to dominate the professional game in the '60s and '70s and, perhaps more importantly, as household names, usher snooker into the era of colour television, were Ray Reardon of Wales and John Spencer of England.

Novelties are part and parcel of snooker and billiards. This oval table proved so popular that it almost created a wholly new game.

Returning to the '64 World Championship, the match was played over three days at Burroughes Hall, in London. Over 37 frames, Pulman came from behind to romp to victory in the final session and beat Davis 19 – 16. Unfortunately, an incident again occurred in which an amateur rule spoilt a professional match. Fred was on a free ball and failed to nominate it, as was required then by the rules (which were not changed until 1976). After potting his intended ball the referee penalised Fred seven points, even though it was blatantly obvious which ball he had intended to play. Fred was furious while John remarked that it was a rule they (the professionals) had never observed. But the BA & CC were sanctioning the Championships again, and thus enforcing their rules. But there is no question that the dispute upset Fred and that it had an effect on the final result.

PROBLEMS WITH RULES

This incident supports the now widely-held view that the best rules of the game are those which require the referee to make an initial statement before a stroke is played – as when, for example, two balls are touching. However, even this is not foolproof! After all, as Dennis Taylor often asks when told two balls are touching: 'which one?' And then of course there will always be other, slightly more unexpected problems, as the following episode reveals. Sometime during the Edwardian era, the referee failed to turn up for a game between Charles Dawson and Fred Bateman, so a volunteer more familiar with boxing than with billiards stepped in. He smoked a pipe throughout the session, and Dawson, playing intricate close cannons, stopped and asked him if the balls were touching. In bending down to observe the situation, the referee allowed the ash from his pipe to fall on to the table exactly where the three balls lay. He immediately picked up the balls, blew away the ash, replaced the balls in a heap and declared them to be 'not touching'!

The 1965 Championship at Burroughes Hall produced one of the greatest finals of all time. John Pulman and Fred Davis played the best of 73 frames over six days, with John scraping through 37–36 to retain his title.

ONE OF THE GREAT FINALS

Later in that year of 1964, John Pulman fought another successful challenge, this time winning 40–43 against Rex Williams. Pulman, in accordance with the new system, had to be accessible to challenges from any of his professional colleagues at any time, and in March 1965, Fred Davis entered the Championship stakes again. It turned out to be one of the great finals of all time. Playing the best of 73 frames at Burroughes Hall, over six days, the match went the full distance.

The frame scores were level at 20–20 and 30–30, and it was a toss-up as to who would win. On the sixth and final day, Pulman won three of the first four frames in the afternoon, with Davis responding by winning three in a row to make it 33–33. It was the first man to 37, and when Fred took the lead at 36–35, the odds seemed heavily in his favour. One slip now and Pulman was an ex-champion. But Pulman scored an early 27, followed by a 23, and won the frame 69–40 on the pink. Thirty-six frames all, and the spectators were on the edge of their seats.

It was the final frame with Fred to break. There were two safety shots each before Fred made the first mistake by kissing a red near the blue spot. John made a 32 break off four blacks. Fred then made 10 and 14, but John got back in to score a splendid 33 which gave him a lead of 40 with just four colours left. That is how John Pulman escaped to retain his title with a final 37–36 scoreline. When asked many years later which match stood out in his career, he quoted this one as the most satisfying.

John Pulman at his peak in the early 1960s. Pulman won a long succession of World Championship Challenge matches from 1957 until he was beaten by John Spencer in 1969.

A RECORD BREAK

Another Championship held in 1965 was decided on a series of matches played in South Africa, with Pulman again victorious, this time against Rex Williams – the final score being 25–22. During the match, Williams took the Championship break record to 142, and soon after he became the second professional after Joe Davis to make an official maximum. This was achieved in a match against Manuel Francisco, in Cape Town. Then, in another challenge match in South Africa, John Pulman achieved his sixth successive Championship win by beating the South African Freddie van Rensburg fairly convincingly, 39–12.

THE PERILS OF PLAYING ABROAD

Of course, the modern professional travels to all corners of the world to play the game. But this is not a new phenomenon, as both John Roberts Senior and Junior travelled extensively – particularly the latter – as did most of the billiard professionals that followed them. However, some trips were obviously better than others. Melbourne Inman once played on Thursday Island, in the Pacific Ocean. When he arrived he found the shore full of wreckage. Inquiring the reason for the damage, he was informed that they had just had an earthquake on the island. 'Do you have them often?', enquired Inman. 'Oh yes, quite often', was the reply, as two coffins were being carried past him. The inhabitants also informed him that the lighthouse on the Island hadn't been seen since the previous earthquake, and for the same reason the billiard table was out of level. Inman duly fulfilled his engagement and was first on the ship leaving the following day!

And others were even worse . . . in the 1890s, according to one contemporary account, the worst of playing billiards in tropical Beira was that it was so hard to get through a game without being interrupted. 'If you are enjoying a temporary respite from the ever-present malaria yourself, it is almost certain that your opponent, or someone else in the room, will be suffering from it, and be taken with the 'shakes', and this sort of thing puts a man off terribly. On the seats surrounding the table are men of all shades of hue. Years ago they were white but yellow fever, jaundice and malaria have wiped out their original colour. Then someone gets a chill. The players utter a malediction and the victim stuffs a

In recent years the game abroad has been booming. But travellers for years have encountered billiards and snooker in the most unexpected places.

quantity of quinine down his throat or calls loudly for whisky. The climate of Beira destroys everything, even the tables deteriorate, and are not true after they have been set up for a year or so. When a regular of the room is missing from his accustomed seat, no questions are asked as to where he is. The doubt is expressed as to when he went in. The in, in this case, being hospital.

The rooms open at midday and keep open until midnight when closing-up time arrives. A stranger might be surprised to see the customers running at top speed as soon as they reach the street. He might imagine they were all hurrying away before they remembered to pay for the table. This would be incorrect. They are hurrying to escape the miasma which arrives from the marshy land at night, and which is laden with fever germs. As a consequence, first class billiards was the exception rather than the rule in the tropics'!

THE FINANCIAL PROBLEMS OF TRAVEL

Financial considerations as well as the club's location, had to be taken into account by the professional. Tom Aiken, who was a canny Scottish player back in the first half of the century, was asked to play in a certain remote village. Unfortunately, the fee demanded was considered by the committee to be too high. Eventually, Aiken happened to be working in the club's locality and offered a fee which was nearer the committee's original figure – to which they agreed. After the exhibition, having soundly beaten a local cueist, the chairman of the club turned to Aiken and said: 'You were lucky tonight'. 'How is that', replied Aiken. 'I only got shots I played for.' 'Yes', replied the chairman, 'but if it hadn't been for my casting vote, you wouldn't have been here at all'.

1966 TO 1969 – NEW BLOOD

On his return to England in 1966, John Pulman was challenged on a best of seven matches basis, again by Fred Davis, at St. George's Hall, Liverpool. But Pulman's constant matchplay was giving him the edge over Fred and he won the series of five frame matches by 5–2. The match scores were 3–2, 4–1, 4–1, 2–3, 3–2, 4–1.

After such a hectic spell of Championship challenges, 1967 brought a halt to the proceedings with the main focus of attention shifting to a 51-match series between Fred Davis and Rex Williams, to be played at any club which wished to book them. This was snooker at real grass roots level and Williams won by 26–25.

Ray Reardon, who won six world championship titles between 1970 and 1978.

Three other big events of 1967 were the announcements that Gary Owen, who received the MBE as the world amateur snooker champion, was to turn professional, as was John Spencer, the former English amateur champion. Owen's first competitive appearance was in a new professional tournament, the Willie Smith Trophy, in Leeds, during January 1968, and he signed a coaching and exhibition agreement with the manufacturers Riley Burwat. And last but by no means least, was the announcement that Ray Reardon, who was also a former English amateur champion, had decided to turn professional and, like Spencer, was available for exhibition engagements , either privately or on behalf of the National Spastics Society. Owen, Spencer and Reardon were the first new breed of professionals since Rex Williams' appearance way back in 1951.

The final challenge to John Pulman's reign came from Eddie Charlton in the early spring of 1968. The event again was played over the best of 73 frames at the Co-op Hall, Bolton, and was sponsored by the tobacco firm Player's, who had done much to foster interest in snooker that season. By the fifth day of the match, Pulman needed to win 3 of the last 13 frames remaining, which he achieved in the fifth frame of the afternoon session. With John winning 39–24, Eddie complimented his opponent's fine form and finished off by saying in his distinctive Australian accent: 'Now I know what's ahead of me, I'll know what lines to practise on when I get back to Australia'. And that he certainly did.

THE MODERN ERA BEGINS

The modern era of snooker can be said to have begun in 1969. After being run on a challenge basis for the previous four years, the World Professional Snooker Championship reverted to a knock-out format and, for the first time since 1952, the rift between the professionals and the governing body had more or less healed.

Moreover, unlike in the early 1950s, television suddenly had become a help rather than a hindrance. The introduction of colour brought the game alive, which was well demonstrated by the viewing figures of the first Pot Black series, and not surprisingly youngsters began to copy the new television stars. Indeed, the power of television was illustrated by the fact that many people thought the winner of Pot Black became world champion, simply because Pot Black was televised – while the real World Championship had to wait until the mid-1970s before it had comprehensive coverage.

JOHN SPENCER

This new era in snooker brought together two of the young professionals to the 1969 Championship finals – with Gary Owen starting odds-on favourite against the more stylish John Spencer. Spencer had won the English amateur title at his third attempt in 1966 – beating Marcus Owen 11–5 at Huddersfield. In that match he had made the first-ever century break in an amateur final, and had so impressed the organisers that he was invited to play in the World Amateur Championships to be held in Karachi, Pakistan – where he finished runner-up to Gary Owen. On returning home, John received an invitation from the National Spastics Society to turn professional and play exhibition matches around the country to help raise funds for them. Thus he entered the World Professional Championship for the first time in 1969.

On his way to the final he beat the reigning champion, John Pulman, 30–19, and dismissed Rex Williams, 55–18. In the final, played over 73 frames, he beat Gary Owen 46–27 at the Victoria Hall in London, and thus joined that exclusive group who have won the world title at their first attempt! His first prize was £1,500 from a prize fund of £3,500 sponsored by Player's No. 6.

Below: Pot Black *presenter Alan Weeks and producer Reg Perrin on the set at Pebble Mill in Birmingham. Right: A classic pose of John Spencer.*

Left: Alex Higgins becoming the game's youngest World Champion at 22 years 11 months in 1972. Above: Ray Reardon (left) and John Spencer who dominated professional snooker during the 1970s.

RAY REARDON

There were two World Championships in 1970. The first was held in April, and again sponsored by Player's. Whilst the second was in November, but this time with no sponsor. The former brought the third new professional to the finals in the form of Ray Reardon who beat the ex-world champion John Pulman 37–33 at the Victoria Hall, London, on April 11.

Then in November of that year the Championship was held abroad for the first time, in Australia. In the semi-finals John Spencer had his revenge over Ray Reardon, after losing to him at the same stage back in April, and went on to beat the Australian Warren Simpson 37–29 in the final – in the process making three centuries in four frames, the first time this had been achieved. With a total of nine entries, first prize was £2,500.

ALEX HIGGINS

There were no Championship finals in 1971 as, with entries increased to 16, it took most of that year to complete the earlier rounds. One of the finalists these produced for the following year, 1972, was the young Alex Higgins who was to win the title at his first attempt.

After a sensational career as an amateur, initially in Northern Ireland and later on in the North of England – where the whole area was soon humming with talk of four-minute century breaks and the nickname, 'Hurricane', first appeared – Higgins

There were two World Professional Championships in 1970. The second, in November, was held abroad for the first time, in Australia. John Spencer beat Warren Simpson 37–29 in the final, and made three century breaks in four consecutive frames – which had never been done before.

became Irish Professional champion in January 1972, beating Jackie Rea, who had held the title for the past 20 years, 28 – 12. Six weeks later he met Rea again in an early round of the World Championship and this time his winning margin was 19 – 11. He then went on to beat John Pulman 31 – 23 and Rex Williams 31 – 30, after being nine frames down at one stage. The scene was set for a thrilling final, and so it proved – Alex capturing the world title by beating John Spencer 37 – 32 on the 25th of February at the Selly Park British Legion Club in Birmingham.

It was a great final made no less so by the fact it was played during the miners' strike, and the consequent power failures. A makeshift generator had to be used for lighting and there was no heat at all in the packed club's concert room. But the action was so hot on the table, that customers were standing on beer crates for a better vantage point. Snooker had never seen anything like it and it was to change forever the format for the Championships, bringing it all under one roof over a fortnight's play.

The first Benson and Hedges Masters tournament was held in 1975. It was appropriate that the first final was between the two leading players of the '70s, Ray Reardon and John Spencer – the latter winning 9–8 in a very close match.

CHAMPIONSHIPS UNDER THE NEW FORMAT

The 1973 Championship was played at the City Exhibition Hall in Manchester. Park Drive were the new sponsors, putting up a prize fund of £8,000 for a field of 27 players – with the winner picking up £2,000. The matches were played on eight different tables – Wimbledon style – and in a classic match between Alex Higgins and Fred Davis, rain actually stopped play – Wimbledon style – because of a leaking roof!

In a first-round match, two future world champions of the 1980s first entered the Championship arena, with Cliff Thorburn beating Dennis Taylor, 9 – 8. In the semi-finals Spencer led Reardon 19 – 12 at one stage, but suddenly missed an easy black off its spot which led to one of the great recoveries in the history of the game, with Reardon eventually winning 23 – 22.

In the final Reardon beat Eddie Charlton 38 – 32. This was to be the first in a run of four titles for Ray. His second was at Belle Vue in Manchester when, apart from himself, all the favourites had fallen in earlier rounds to leave an unexpected final against Graham Miles. Ray won 22 – 12, with the number of frames being reduced to the best of 43 and the winner collecting a £2,000 cheque from a total prize fund of £10,000.

A RETURN TO AUSTRALIA

1975 was the inaugural year for a tournament which is still going strong today – the Benson and Hedges Masters. Fittingly, the first final was between the two masters of the 1970s, Reardon and Spencer – with Spencer winning by the skin of his teeth, 9 – 8.

In the World Championship of that year no sponsor came forward in the UK, resulting in the tournament returning to Australia – the seedings being based only on the previous year's Championship. This meant that Reardon was No. 1, while Spencer, because of his early defeat in 1974, was unfortunately seeded No. 8. Many considered their quarter final game, which Reardon won 19 – 17, to be the 'real final', and a tremendous match it turned out to be – with both players today agreeing that it was possibly their finest ever clash.

The final itself was an even closer affair, with Eddie Charlton leading 29 – 23 before Reardon made his customary burst of match-winning frames to finally attain victory at 31 – 30. If Charlton was to win his main prize in life, The World Professional Snooker Championship, then surely 1975 was the year. Unfortunately it was not to be.

EMBASSY SPONSORSHIP

Embassy's first sponsorship of the World Championship was in 1976 – a tournament bedevilled by all manner of problems resulting from the decision to split the event into two venues. The top half of the draw was in Middlesbrough, while the bottom half and finals were played at the Wythenshawe Forum, Manchester. In a match against David Taylor, Spencer made a 138 break, only to lose to Alex Higgins 15 – 14. However, Reardon's initial problems of having to adjust to a new venue were

Fred Davis who, even though in his 70s, is still an active player today.

THE Q WORLD

finally settled and he went on to secure his fourth win in a row by beating Higgins 27 – 16 – collecting £6,000 from record prize money of £15,000.

THE CRUCIBLE

The following year – 1977 – was another milestone in the Championship's history, as promoter Mike Watterson brought it to the now world famous Crucible Theatre, Sheffield, for the first time. There were 24 entries and the total prize money had been improved to £17,000. TV coverage increased and the fortnight's play attracted over 20,000 spectators. Reardon's winning sequence finished with a 13 – 6 second-round defeat by Spencer who was playing for the first time with a two-piece cue – and sporting a moustache. The two-piece cue stayed but the moustache didn't! In the final Spencer beat the Canadian Cliff Thorburn, 25 – 21, to become £6,000 richer.

There were a number of surprises in 1978, with both Spencer and Higgins being eliminated in the first round. However, Fred Davis was performing well and, under the watchful eye of older brother Joe, made the semis, losing narrowly to Perrie Mans – the first time a South African had made it to the final. In that final Mans met five-times previous winner, Ray Reardon, who in the semi-final had shaken off Eddie Charlton 18 – 14. However, this match obviously sharpened Ray for the final and he never looked in any real trouble, finally overcoming the spectacular potting of Mans to win 25 – 18. Sadly Joe Davis fell ill before the final and died a few weeks later.

A NEW BREED

If not exactly the end of the Reardon – Spencer era, 1979 saw the beginning of a new breed of player coming through when the Welshman Terry Griffiths captured the Championship at his first attempt. Griffiths, after winning the English Amateur Championship in 1977 and 1978, had turned professional in June '78 and had unfortunately experienced a truly traumatic first tournament. In the United Kingdom Championship he had led Rex Williams 8 – 2, seemingly invincible he then went seven frames without a win, eventually losing 9 – 8.

He had to qualify for the 1979 World Championship by beating Bernard Bennett 9 – 2 and Jim

Steve Davis with the 1980 Coral UK Championship trophy. It was the first major title to come his way. In the final Davis beat Alex Higgins 16 – 6.

Ray Reardon in action during 1979 – a year when snooker's 'new breed' started to make their big breakthrough.

1979 saw the beginning of a new breed of player coming through, with the Welshman Terry Griffiths beating Dennis Taylor 24–16 to take the world title at his first attempt.

Meadowcroft 9 – 6. And in the tournament proper, he reached the final by beating Alex Higgins 13 – 12 and Eddie Charlton 19 – 17 in two memorable televised matches. And so to the final, in which Dennis Taylor was his opponent. Terry duly won this as well, by a margin of 24 – 16 – his prize being £10,000 from a total pool of £35,000.

INCREASED MEDIA INTEREST

During the '79 Championship, Bill Werbeniuk made a 142 break to equal the tournament record established by Rex Williams in 1965. But, perhaps more significantly, late night snooker was featured on the radio, with up-to-the-minute reports on the marathon Griffiths/Charlton semi-final being broadcast after television had closed down.

This media interest increased for the 1980 World Championship, when the final was watched by 15 million viewers on TV, and a total coverage of 70 hours was allotted to the fortnight's play. Like the two previous winners at the 'Crucible Championships', Terry Griffiths went out in his first match, losing to a young man named Steve Davis. No relation of Joe's, but later to dominate the game in similar fashion. Steve got no further in this

In 1980, Cliff Thorburn beat Alex Higgins 18–16 in the final of the World Championship. For the first time the title had gone to an overseas player and 14.5 million viewers had watched the climax on television.

tournament, losing in the next round to Alex Higgins 13–9, who himself thereby made it to his third world final, where he met Cliff Thorburn.

Cliff, who had beaten Doug Mountjoy 13–10, Jim Wych 13–6, and Dennis Taylor 16–7, overcame Alex in the final, winning by 18–16. Thus the world title had gone to an overseas player for the first time, and the climax of the tournament had attracted 14.5 million viewers during a total television coverage of 70 hours.

A NATIONAL SPORT

By the end of the 1980 Championship it is clear that professional snooker had become a far cry from those matches played in the back room of Tom Dennis' pub all those years ago. With Steve Davis about to stamp his authority on the game, massively increased coverage in the media, including all-important prime-time television, spiralling audience figures and the consequent mushrooming of commercial sponsorship, the game has become a truly national sport. The players who have emerged during the 1980s have become superstars and the general public have followed their exploits both on and off the table. (Turn to pages 102–103 for profiles of the modern players, and to pages 156–157 for a view of the game today.)

What's more, the fortunes that are made today by the game's leading professionals make Herbert Spencer's quote: 'Proficiency at billiards (snooker) indicates a misspent youth', seem somewhat inaccurate. Another quote, attributed to King Edward VII, 'No 'gentleman' ever made a break of more than 25', would also appear to be equally wide of the mark. With so many 'rich gentlemen' in the game today it is clear that times have changed.

John Spencer after compiling a maximum at the Holsten Lager tournament in Slough. Unfortunately the TV cameras were not there to record this feat.

GREAT GAMES

SNOOKER HAS ENJOYED MANY HEART-STOPPING MOMENTS, OUTSTANDING SHOTS THAT WIN TITLES AND BREATHTAKING FINALES, SUCH AS DENNIS TAYLOR'S BLACK BALL, LAST FRAME VICTORY OVER STEVE DAVIS IN THE 1985 EMBASSY WORLD CHAMPIONSHIP. COME WITH US DOWN MEMORY LANE AS WE RECAPTURE ALL THE EXCITEMENT, HEARTACHE AND TRIUMPH GENERATED BY SOME OF THE GREAT GAMES.

The greatest game in snooker history – the 1985 Embassy World Championship final – featured Dennis Taylor (left) and Steve Davis. Taylor won 18–17 on the final black in the final frame.

ALEX HIGGINS V JOHN SPENCER

1972 WORLD CHAMPIONSHIP FINAL: BIRMINGHAM

Alex Higgins, the brash youngster already branded a hell-raiser by some, had been shouting it from the rooftops in Muhammad Ali fashion: 'I am the greatest. I will be the new world champion!' And those who saw the mercurial Higgins in action in the months throughout which the 1972 World Championship was spread could hardly deny he was the most exciting talent ever to emerge on the snooker scene. And yet, he had flirted with danger against Rex Williams in the semi-finals – scraping through by the tightest of margins, 31–30, to a final against the great John Spencer after coming within a blue ball of defeat!

Higgins' opponent in the '72 final, John Spencer, who had won the Championship in 1969 and regained it in 1971, had long been thrilling crowds with his dazzling long potting and outstanding ability to screw the ball. But for all Spencer's finesse around the table, Higgins, already dubbed the 'Hurricane' because of the speed with which he dispatched balls from all over the table, was a firm favourite to take the title and become the youngest-ever world champion at the age of 22.

The venue – the Selly Park British Legion, in Birmingham – was hardly conducive to world championship snooker. Instead of the plush seating and lighting of today, the fans who packed into the hall perched precariously on planks laid across tiers of empty beer crates. And what players today would put up with spectators wandering to and fro across the arena to replenish their glasses at the bar! But world final it was and, to add to the almost farcical conditions, it occurred during the power-cuts of the miners' strike.

Spencer brightened the opening day's play with a break of 101, made in the gloom of the emergency lighting switched on after a power cut before the start of the evening session. It cast a shadow over both ends of the table, but neither player seemed unduly affected as they set the scene for a sizzling encounter by sharing the day's 12 frames.

John Spencer (left) and Alex Higgins made light of a power cut during their classic 1972 World Championship final at the Selly Park British Legion.

Alex Higgins, the young man who took professional snooker by storm, came from behind to take the world title at his first attempt.

By the end of the second day, Spencer – recently returned from an arduous yet successful tour of Canada – had showed only flashes of his true class, but still managed to compile a 13–11 lead. And on day three, Higgins slipped three frames behind, 17–14, only to draw level again at 18–18 by the end of evening.

HIGGINS CUTS LOOSE

The players were still all-square after the first six frames of day four, and even when Higgins forged ahead 24–21 there was no hint of the explosion to come. But then, the Irishman suddenly cut loose. A quick-fire 65 put the next game beyond Spencer, and Alex, warming to his task, fired in breaks of 40, 33 and 31, to lead 27–21. The world champion could only watch as the Hurricane almost brought the roof down with his spectacular play. The tide had turned against Spencer, and those who witnessed a magical session were convinced they were in the presence of a genius.

After being stranded for 25 minutes in a hotel lift with his wife, following another power cut, Spencer arrived late for the start of play on day five. Clearly rattled, he soon went another frame down and had to call on all his experience to pull the next two back. However, Higgins himself was becoming unsettled by the pressure, and the champion was able to cut the deficit to three and stand 29–25 down by the end of the session.

Refreshed by the interval, Higgins came back to compile breaks of 57, 46 and 50 and go 31–25 ahead. But, with fame and fortune looming large, Alex's nerves began to show again, and Spencer took three of the next four games to trail 32–28 by the end of the evening.

Snooker was never to be the same again. But surprisingly, Higgins had to wait a full decade before he was able to lift the coveted world crown once again.

As the final day unfolded errors crept in on both sides, and though Higgins won the opening game, the title-holder came into his own with an immaculate 123. He also took the next two games as the tension became almost unbearable. At 33–32 he was still in with a chance of retaining his crown. But Higgins would not be denied, and promptly retaliated with breaks of 82 and 41 to go 35–32 ahead. And when a weary Spencer missed an opening in the next frame, Higgins swooped with a break of 94 – his highest of the match – followed by a 40 in the next, to clinch a memorable 37–32 victory.

STEVE DAVIS V CLIFF THORBURN

1981 EMBASSY WORLD CHAMPIONSHIP SEMI-FINAL: SHEFFIELD

One shot, one blue ball from the middle of the table to the top left-hand corner pocket was all that stood in the way of immediate fame and fortune for an emerging Steve Davis. And he wasn't even playing the ball! His opponent and defending world champion, Cliff Thorburn, was clinging on to his crown for all he was worth in the white-hot atmosphere of the Crucible Theatre. He had earlier tested the youngster, and found him wanting, but now, faced with a vital shot, was reeling under a fresh onslaught not only from Steve but his supporters as well!

The atmosphere was acrimonious to say the least as the fervent Romford supporters gathered to cheer their hero Steve Davis on to his first World Championship final. However, it wasn't the first time Cliff Thorburn had sampled the Romford Roar. Weeks before their eagerly-anticipated clash the Canadian had accepted a lucrative challenge from Barry Hearn – the man who had masterminded Steve's career almost from scratch – to take on Davis.

Professional opposition had seldom come to anything but grief at the shabby old Romford Matchroom, where Steve had honed his game to perfection over the years. But Thorburn, never one to shirk a challenge, looked on this one with anticipation – only to be thrashed 6–0 by Davis, who thus gained a handsome psychological advantage for the battle ahead.

Once at Sheffield, Steve gained in confidence, claiming the scalps of world amateur title-holder Jimmy White, making his championship début, and former champions Alex Higgins and Terry Griffiths. He was in sparkling form, but so was Thorburn, angered by his recent setback at Romford and determined to put Davis in his place.

There was little warning of what lay ahead as

Steve Davis, snooker's master cueman, has that steely-eyed look as he lines up another shot during an epic world championship semi-final against Cliff Thorburn – a match that he went on to win 16–10.

Davis opened a 6–4 lead, but when they resumed the following day he learned about world-class pressure for the first time. Thorburn, dubbed the 'Grinder' by Alex Higgins in the previous year, demonstrated just why as he stretched Davis to the limit with a superior brand of safety and tight play. Steve sat back, stunned, as the Toronto star put him on the rack, winning the final four frames of the session. The youngster simply couldn't cope. He looked up to the heavens, down at his feet and buried his head in a towel at one stage as if to blot out the nightmare. For a full 60 minutes he failed to pot a ball and at 23 years old and 8–6 down his vision of becoming the second-youngest world champion seemed remote.

A PHANTOM WHISTLER

However, with four major titles and a dazzling season behind him, Steve was able to gather his senses during the afternoon interval. At the restart, his noisy supporters, led by Hearn himself, draped a Union Jack over the balcony and with a cheery

Anticipating that his rival would concede, Steve turned to shake his hand but Cliff ignored it and moved back to his corner. He then made as if to carry on with a futile exercise. The spectators could see he was raging inside, and having made the gesture he left the arena.

wave to them, he set about repairing the damage. As he pulled back to 9–10, Thorburn's concentration wavered, but the Canadian fought back in the vital 20th frame to be within three balls of regaining a two-frame lead.

Three times he got down to play the last blue and three times his concentration was disturbed. A 'phantom whistler' put him off once, then a plastic cup crackled and finally someone struck a match. 'Not our doing', insists Hearn to this day, but whoever was responsible the distractions were enough to put Cliff off his stroke. Davis clinched the frame to draw level and thrust a defiant fist in the air at the Romford crowd, who voiced their approval with a roar never before heard at a snooker tournament.

Davis then took full advantage of Thorburn's

Cliff Thorburn, nicknamed the Grinder, stretched Davis to the limit with a superior brand of safety and tight play on the second day.

obvious discomfort to thunder into an overnight lead, clearing up to the pink in the final frame with a high break for a 12–10 advantage. Anticipating that his rival would concede, Steve turned to shake his hand but Cliff ignored it and moved back to his corner. He then made as if to carry on with what was now a futile exercise. The spectators could see he was raging inside, and having made the gesture he left the arena.

Backstage, Cliff's temper finally got the better of him. He snapped at Davis and then he stormed off saying: 'I'll see you tomorrow'. But Davis and Hearn were ecstatic because the ice man had definitely cracked, and when play restarted the next day Steve won all four frames to secure a momentous 16–10 victory. Whilst Cliff had the grace to apologise for his behaviour on TV after the match, it rankled with him for years afterwards.

CLIFF THORBURN V TERRY GRIFFITHS

1983 EMBASSY WORLD CHAMPIONSHIP SECOND ROUND: SHEFFIELD

Winning the Benson and Hedges Masters at Wembley some two months earlier had given Cliff Thorburn, who had been playing below his best snooker for some time, the impetus to impose his formidable game once more on the 1983 World Championship. Yet, when he missed his first attempt at the opening red in frame four of his second-round match against Terry Griffiths, saw the ball cannon into another red and send it across the top of the table and into the opposite pocket, he could hardly have dreamed he was on his way to a £10,000 jackpot as the first man ever to compile a World Championship maximum.

Cliff Thorburn achieved his record-breaking maximum on the second Saturday morning of the Championship, to the delight of fellow-Canadian Bill Werbeniuk, playing on the other side of the screen, and the capacity crowd in the Crucible – though the time of day meant that the television audience was relatively small. However, apart from Dennis Taylor's Championship-winning black against Steve Davis two years later, no shot or break has ever been repeated so extensively by the BBC.

Who could ever forget that spine-tingling moment when Thorburn carefully wiped his hands and composed himself for an assault on the final black – having methodically picked off black-red, black-red followed by the colours after outrageously fluking that first red. Who could ever forget commentator Jack Karnehm voicing the thoughts of everyone watching when he said: 'Best of luck mate'! And who could possibly forget Cliff's response to his perfect shot: kneeling on the spot as the black ball disappeared and giving a two-fisted victory salute to the audience.

Not surprisingly, the audience erupted. Big Bill Werbeniuk, who had long since abandoned his own game to cheer his pal on, gripped Cliff in a huge bear hug. Yet this was just one feature of a remarkable match which cracked record after record and, in fact, led to a change in the rules.

History in the making for Canadian Cliff Thorburn, as he becomes the first man to score a 147 maximum during a world championship match.

THAT LUCKY MOMENT

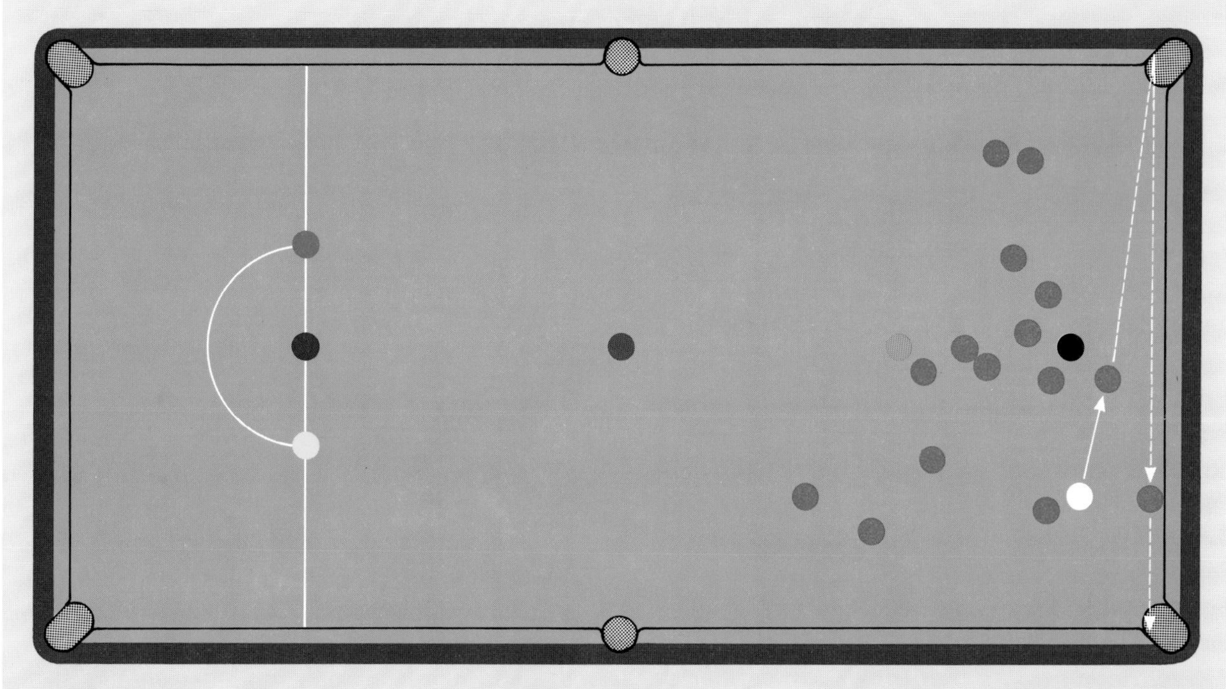

Cliff Thorburn's first shot on the way to his historic 147. He attempts a red which stays up, but travels along the cushion to hit another red which rolls slowly into the opposite pocket. The white stops perfectly for the black. The first shot was lucky, the rest of the break was pure genius.

With Thorburn and Griffiths acknowledged as two of the slowest players on the circuit, a lengthy match was always in prospect. What they supplied, however, was the *longest* in snooker history – the 25 frames spanning an amazing 13 hours 15 minutes. The final session alone took more than six hours (a record in itself) and by the time Cliff had struck the winning ball the clock registered a mind-blowing 3.51am – the *latest* finish ever to a professional tournament match!

To compound the problems for those covering and watching the event – especially the goggle-eyed cameramen and other BBC technicians – Eddie Charlton and John Spencer had crawled through a 12-hour match which spilled over into the evening session, forcing Thorburn and Griffiths to wait nearly 1½ hours just to get to the table! It was a nightmare for officials and players alike. As tournament director Paul Hatherell said in exasperation: 'How can I sort it out? Jimmy White and Tony Meo took just 50 minutes to complete four frames a few days earlier, while Terry and Cliff spent nearly four hours over the same number!'

After some deliberation, a new rule was introduced for the following season which prevented matches from going beyond 1am. Those which remained unfinished were to be continued the following morning, regardless of the state of play at the time. The rule has since been relaxed.

This epic, record-breaking, second round match also played a significant role in the outcome of the Championship. Obviously Cliff was emotionally drained going into the third round. But then he heard that his wife, at home in Toronto, had lost the baby she was expecting. Told to 'play on' by Barbara, Cliff showed he was one of the game's great professionals by making it all the way to the final. But two gruelling encounters with Kirk Stevens and Tony Knowles, after everything he had already been through, left Cliff exhausted in body and spirit, and he went down 18–6 to Steve Davis in the final – a rotten way to finish, but at least Cliff can look back with pride on that history-making maximum!

It was without doubt the most fortuitous shot ever played in the World Championship and 15 minutes later it enabled Cliff Thorburn to write another glorious chapter in the history of snooker.

ALEX HIGGINS V STEVE DAVIS

1983 CORAL UK CHAMPIONSHIP FINAL: PRESTON

Having lost the 1982 world title he won so proudly at Sheffield, to his chief tormentor, Steve Davis, the brilliant but controversial Irishman Alex Higgins went on to lose his wife, Lynn, and their two children during the stormy 1983 summer that followed. His play hit rock-bottom as the new season unfolded, and even though he managed to scrape together enough form to reach the Coral UK final at Preston in December, he was given little hope of avenging two solid years of defeats by the player who had plagued him more than any other.

As Steve Davis progressed without fuss to his third Coral UK final in four years, Alex Higgins was dodging searching questions from newshounds about the state of his marriage. 'No comment', was the only reply they succeeded in eliciting from an unusually cheerful 'Hurricane', whose wife had actually slipped in during one of the early sessions to give him moral support.

A convincing victory over Tony Knowles, then an even more satisfying 9–4 win against Terry Griffiths, who pipped him 16–15 for the previous year's crown, confirmed a return to form and set him up nicely for the final. That his daughter Lauren was due to celebrate her second birthday on day two of the final – at Alex and Lynn's luxurious ranch-style home in Cheadle – indicated that a semblance of order had returned to Higgins' life.

Yet nothing could have prepared him or his followers for what was to come. By the end of a scintillating first session Higgins was left reeling from Davis' onslaught. The world champion hammered home breaks of 78, 84, 82, 54, 64 and 67 to lead 7–0, and it looked as though Alex would be home in time to join his daughter's birthday party.

Instead, the Hurricane, a fighter on and off the table over the years, gritted his teeth and inch by inch began narrowing the gap. Those who witnessed the evening session just couldn't believe it, and

The calm before the Hurricane as Steve Davis builds up a 7–0 lead. But Alex 'Hurricane' Higgins was ready to pounce.

Looking for an opening as Higgins launches one of the most famous fightbacks in snooker history to beat Davis 16–15 and take the UK title.

neither could Davis, as Higgins won frame after frame. At the end of an amazing first day's play only a fluked yellow by Davis separated the two giants, with the Irishman just 8–7 in arrears.

There are no prizes for guessing who slept soundest on the Saturday night, although Davis, even at this relatively early stage of his career, had made a habit of starting well. Higgins, a notoriously bad day-time player belied that reputation when play resumed on the Sunday afternoon and he quickly wrapped up the opening frame to be level for the first time in the match.

ALL SQUARE INTO THE FINAL SESSION

But Davis, recovering steadily from his understandably dazed state of the previous night, managed to keep pace with the little Irishman after that and they were all square after 22 frames going into the break. With nine more to play the huge, raucous Guild Hall crowd, roaring their favourites on, couldn't wait for the action to start.

As they began the final session, neither player showed any sign of nerves. And Higgins, positively bubbling yet in full control of his game, actually matched and then outplayed Davis in the safety stakes, to edge in front for the first time at 13–12.

He took the next frame as well, to be within two of the title, but Davis responded like a true world champion, running off the next three frames to lead 15–14. Just one needed with two to play, but Higgins refused to perish after such a gallant effort and all his years of experience on the road were brought to bear as he launched himself into a grandstand finish.

The Ulsterman drew level to force a last-frame shoot-out, and he could hardly wait to leap out of his chair and get stuck in again. The bit between his teeth, Alex quickly took advantage of a miss by his opponent to sink a careful 21 and spelled out his intentions by snookering Davis with his next shot. Even the ice man from Romford was feeling the heat now, but Higgins remained cool and followed up with an unassailable 44 break to secure what for many was his greatest-ever victory.

Considering the traumas of the summer and his lack of form approaching the tournament, Alex's win must be ranked as snooker's second-greatest comeback – topped only by Dennis Taylor's famous black-ball world title victory over Davis 18 months later (see pages 80–81).

STEVE DAVIS V TONY MEO

1984 LADA CLASSIC FINAL: WARRINGTON

Tony Meo lined up against Steve Davis in the final of the Lada Classic, at the Spectrum in Warrington, as the complete underdog. His record of 'played 4, lost 4' to Davis meant history was against the young Londoner. What's more, Davis, the reigning world champion and world No. 1, had been in his usual dominant form earlier in the season, having already won the Langs Scottish Masters and the Jameson International. And, whilst the Coral UK Championship had eluded him, he had beaten Meo 9–4 in the quarter-final. However, Tony was also in fine form and had beaten Jim Meadowcroft, Rex Williams, Kirk Stevens and Mark Wildman on the way to the final. An exciting match was in prospect.

In a slow start Davis took the first two frames after two hours – the sort of lead he rarely gives away. But Meo, chasing his first ever title, was determined to hang on and produced a purple patch that had the world champion under pressure. He took the third with a break of 52, quickly added the fourth and fifth and then, remarkably, completed a run of four frames in row by winning the sixth with a break of 52, to lead 4–2.

The crowds were always good at Warrington and this final was no exception as a full house sat enthralled as the match turned into a tense, tight battle – Davis responding to the onslaught in the best way possible with a break of 122, to be 4–3 behind at the interval.

In the evening session Tony could not have made a worse start. Davis, cueing confidently, knocked in two breaks of 54 to take frame eight, and that was quickly followed by a 51 to wrap up frame nine and go into a 5–4 lead. In those two frames Meo had managed just six points, and he scored only nine more as Davis, warming to the occasion, fired in breaks of 35 and 49 to take the score to 6–4.

The 11th frame was vital to Tony, but he lost that as well – this time scoring just two points as a break of 58 secured the frame for Davis. At 4–7 in arrears, Tony was virtually at the point of no return. He knew he had to knuckle down.

Tony Meo was robbed of victory when a spectator called out in the final frame. Meo missed and a relieved Davis won on the pink.

THE FATEFUL SHOUT

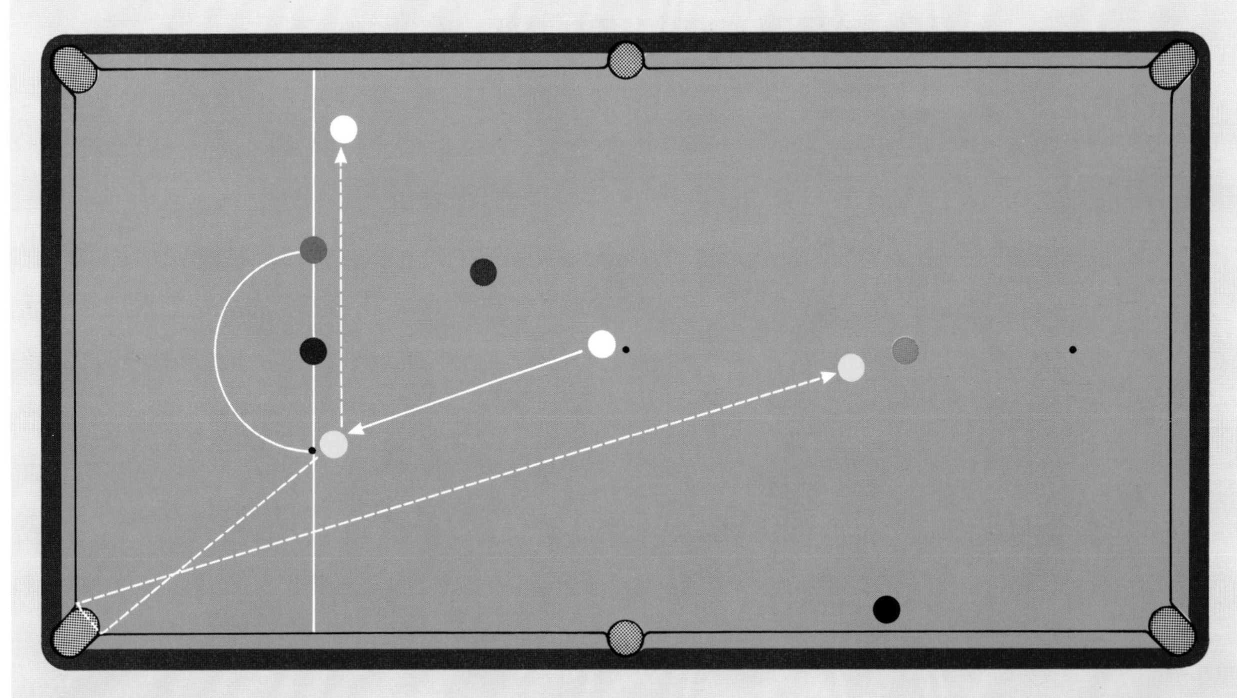

The final frame and Meo, level at 8–8, looked set to clear up for a famous victory as he lined up this yellow. But disaster struck as a misguided supporter yelled: 'Come on, Tony'. That shout was enough to upset Meo's concentration and the yellow stayed out.

This renewed effort produced immediate results. The 12th frame, despite a break of 43 from Davis, went Tony's way, and he pulled the score back to 6–7 by taking the 13th as well. Now the pressure was back on Davis – especially when Meo's 38 brought the scores level at 7–7 in frame 14.

BATTLING BACK

Meo was full of himself. From being almost down and out, he now believed he could win. Davis no longer seemed invincible, and to prove the point Tony didn't flinch when Steve went nearly 50 points in front in the 15th frame. Instead, he battled back, matched Davis for safety play and finally edged in front 8–7 by winning the frame on the black. It was a breathtaking display by Meo and now he needed just one frame for a famous, gutsy victory.

Deep down Davis might have been worried, but it didn't show. Ice-cool, he knocked in a break of 84 and won the frame 101–0, to make it 8–8 and set up a last frame decider. Steve, by far the more experienced in one frame 'shoot-outs', took an early lead. But by the time it got to the colours the match was in the balance, and Meo needed to pot from yellow to pink to win.

Then came one of those moments, one of those sickening events in sport, that turn a game inside out. Both players were totally immersed in the game, the crowd was hushed and expectant – that is apart from one man, who was to change the face of a gripping final. As Meo prepared to play the yellow, one of his fans screamed: 'Come on, Tony'. That was it. Meo, so composed up to then, missed the yellow by a mile and Davis was back at the table.

Tony couldn't believe it. He'd had victory in his grasp, his first title nearly wrapped up and his first win over Davis in his sights – but it was not to be!

Steve would later feel sorry for his snooker pal, but now there was a job to be done. Working his way through the colours, he finally won it on the pink – and went on to condemn the idiot who had shouted out. But poor Tony couldn't believe it. He'd had victory in his grasp, his first title nearly wrapped up and his first win over Davis in his sights – but it was not to be!

JIMMY WHITE V KIRK STEVENS

1984 BENSON AND HEDGES MASTERS SEMI-FINAL: WEMBLEY

It wasn't so long ago that Kirk Stevens, a flamboyant youngster with a *penchant* for white suits, was being hailed as a prospective world champion. Having won the Canadian national championship he had followed his compatriot and mentor Cliff Thorburn on to the tough British pro circuit, and all that remained for him to prove his pedigree was to win a ranking tournament. But by the time Kirk arrived at Wembley for the 1984 Benson and Hedges Masters, he had another target to aim for. Nine months earlier, Thorburn had compiled a record 147 break in the World Championship – only the second player, after Steve Davis, to do so in a major televised tournament.

Thorburn's maximum break was hardly uppermost In Kirk's mind when he stepped into the Conference Centre arena to do battle with his pal Jimmy White – who at 21 was four years his junior – for a place in the final of snooker's most prestigious non-ranking event. Both players, exciting, instinctive and attractive to watch, had been searching for the form that had made them instant crowd-pullers, and fortunately, before a capacity audience of 2,700, they were to be inspired as never before.

Stevens was 'hot', having celebrated the finest win of his life in the previous round – a 5–3 victory over world champion Davis after trailing 3–1 at the interval. But he was to get even 'hotter' as, in one of the most dazzling matches ever staged at Britain's largest snooker arena, both players set the place ablaze with their quick-fire break-building and open play. True, each made the odd mistake, but it didn't seem to matter as the sparks flew in an electric, but good-natured, atmosphere.

By the time eight of the eleven scheduled frames had been played – almost in a flash – White was 5–3 ahead and looking for the one game he needed to clinch his first Wembley final. But unfortunately for Jimmy, Stevens (temporarily) spoiled the script, and for the next few minutes he had to sit impassively whilst an enthralled crowd

Jimmy White (at table) watched in admiration as Kirk Stevens compiled his memorable 147 break but it was White who had the last word.

OPENING SHOT

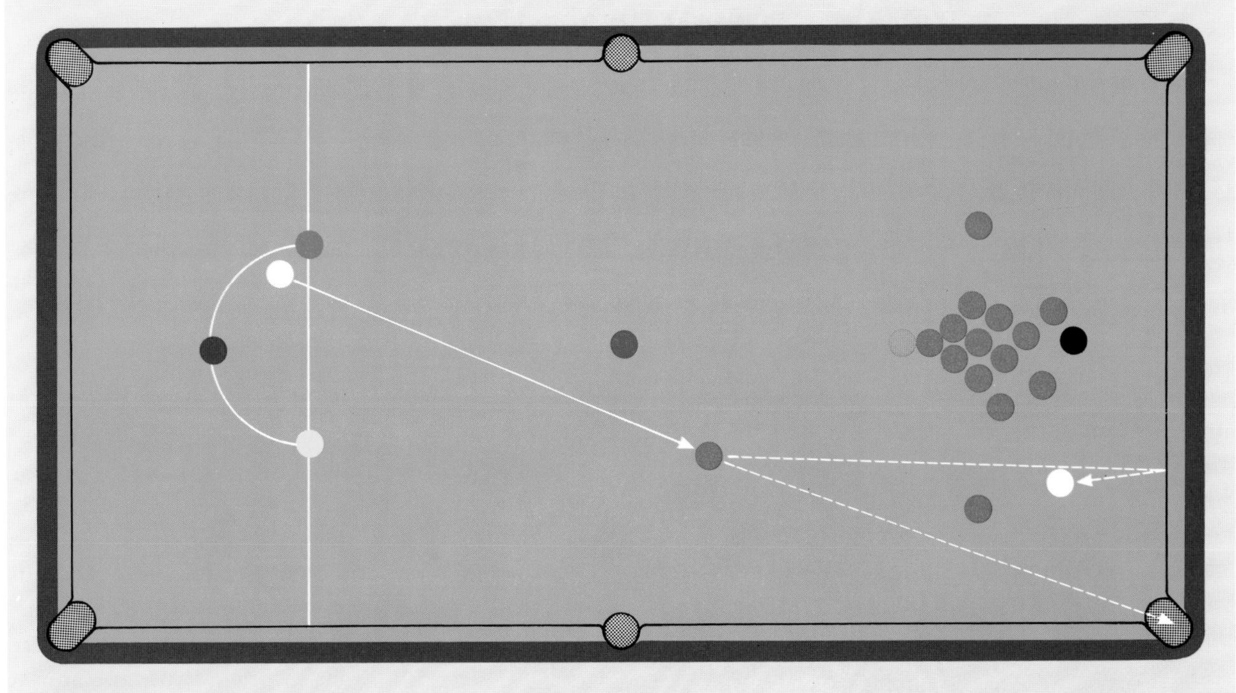

Kirk Stevens' first shot in his startling 147 break – a long, bold red from the D, from which the cue ball returned perfectly for the black. White was only one game away from the final, but Stevens was able momentarily to steal the spotlight.

held its breath as the young Canadian carved out a spellbinding maximum break. In an earlier game White had knocked in a 113, but for all the excitement nothing had prepared them for this.

When Jimmy broke-off in frame nine and left a long red on, Kirk's confidence was such that he didn't hesitate for a moment. The white had returned to the left-hand side of the D and from there he began his break with a perfect shot on the red, holding the cue ball to leave himself with the black.

MAXIMUM BREAK

Eleven reds and ten blacks later – all polished off with precision – Kirk encountered his first dilemma after sinking the eleventh black and drifting slightly out of position for the next red, which lay a foot or so off the left-hand cushion and about a yard from the top pocket. A slight screw shot would have left him comfortably on the pink, which had drifted towards the centre of the table. That would have been fine for the high-break prize, but, with the frame won, Stevens had only one thought and he conjured up his finest shot of the night to edge ever nearer his goal. Employing check side he potted the red and come off the left-hand cushion at a narrow angle – the white travelling across the table into the perfect position for his 13th black.

Unlucky 13? Not likely! His heart may have been turning somersaults by this time, but the Canadian appeared to be the coolest person in the arena as he potted his way relentlessly on – finishing off the remaining reds and blacks and then negotiating the colours with the air of a man knocking a few practice balls around.

The final black disappeared to a tremendous roar and Stevens' beaming smile seemed to light up the arena. Indeed, such was the euphoria that the evening's main business was temporarily forgotten . . . but not by Jimmy White. Once the fuss had died down, he strode to the table at his first opening in the next game and proceeded to fire home a match-winning 119 to complete a quite astonishing 6–4 success.

Almost unbelievably, in their World Championship semi-final only months later, the two players provided a similar feast of attacking snooker (though without a maximum this time), which left them both limp with exhaustion. Sadly for Kirk, he again finished on the wrong end of a classic match. His world title ambition virtually expired that night and personal problems were to haunt and hound him for the next few years.

STEVE DAVIS V JIMMY WHITE

1984 EMBASSY WORLD CHAMPIONSHIP FINAL: SHEFFIELD

Jimmy White, the boy who conquered the amateur snooker world in the most emphatic manner by taking both the English and World Championships before his 19th birthday, was hunting a far bigger prize when he competed in the 1984 World Professional Championship. Victory for White in the final against defending title-holder Steve Davis would have made him the youngest-ever champion – overtaking the proud record set by a tenderfoot Alex Higgins 12 years earlier, shortly before his 23rd birthday.

The Irishman had, in fact, two years earlier come back from the dead in their semi-final to break the heart of the teenager who, as a schoolboy, had modelled his game on the Hurricane, and had befriended his idol while still an amateur. Yet, in the true spirit of friendship Higgins wanted, more than anything, for White to beat Davis and claim his long-standing record.

There was no such closeness between Davis and White – just mutual respect. Yet the combination of their different styles was tailor-made to provide a great Crucible final. At least that's the way it seemed as White displayed the finest form of his career to date on his way past Eddie Charlton and Cliff Thorburn and into his second semi-final. There he was caught up in a sizzling, high-speed match with Kirk Stevens. It spanned 30 breathtaking frames and left the South Londoner absolutely shattered with only a night's sleep to prepare himself for the most important match of his career.

How the mighty Davis cashed in when they squared up the next day – exploiting a weary Whirlwind's every mistake to build a 12–4 lead without ever needing to produce the formidable form which had swept all his opponents aside time and again. It all looked depressingly familiar, because only 12 months earlier he had trounced Cliff Thorburn 18–5 a full session early. But if he thought

Jimmy White, playing the best snooker of his young career, sizes up another shot against Steve Davis as he begins a dramatic fightback from 12–4 behind.

he was in for another early night, the world champion was in for the biggest shock of his life because White, now fully recovered from his semi-final ordeal, came out refreshed and raring for battle on the final day.

For luck, Jimmy wore a suit loaned for the occasion by Higgins himself, and millions of viewers watched enthralled as he cut deeply into the deficit – winning frame after frame with his own special brand of attacking play until Davis, with the aid of a fluke, halted his charge. Even so, White had taken seven out of the eight frames of in the session, to trail just 13–11 with all to play for that night.

DAVIS REGAINS HIS COMPOSURE

Unfortunately for Jimmy, the interval came at the wrong time, while for Davis it couldn't have arrived soon enough. When they next appeared in the Crucible arena it was Steve's turn to be composed. He won three of the first four frames and Jimmy's bold tactics – all the effort he had poured into the afternoon session – appeared to have been of no avail. But then, from 16–12 down and only two games from defeat, the Wimbledon Whirlwind launched another counter-attack with breaks of 64, 72 and 53 taking him to only 16–15 behind, and with everything to play for.

Davis became the first player to win the world title in successive years at the Crucible Theatre. But he had to scrap all the way.

Davis took the next, but when he missed a match-winning blue in frame 33, White again seized his opportunity and pulled back to 17–16. Alas, the strain of coming from behind had finally taken its toll on Jimmy, and Steve, back in control after one of the most nerve-racking days of his career, was able to clinch the 34th frame for an 18–16 victory.

The Ginger Giant from Plumstead thus became the first player to win the title in successive years at the Crucible, but after the match he was quick to lavish praise on his beaten opponent: 'What Jimmy did was devastating and he nearly pulled it off . . . he played his brains out and he's got to be disappointed because he potted more accurately than me'.

A dejected White, beaten on his first appearance at the Crucible three years earlier by the same player, conceded: 'I just gave up on the first day because my semi-final with Kirk took it all out of me. I know that's what cost me the match but I also know I am about to win the world title very shortly. I can't say it's the best I've ever played but the crowd seemed to enjoy it'. They certainly did, but sadly for Jimmy, some four years on, he has still to capture that world crown.

WILLIE THORNE V CLIFF THORBURN

1985 MERCANTILE CREDIT CLASSIC FINAL: WARRINGTON

For all the hundreds of centuries, all the practice maximums and all the promise, Willie Thorne had been labelled the 'Nearly Man' throughout his nine-year career because, when it came to the crunch, his nerve inevitably went. Yet Thorne knew he had a championship inside him, and what better way to prove it than in front of his beloved Leicester Crazy Gang – a collection of characters from his native town who rejoiced in names such as Racing Raymond, Relentless Reg, Bill the Dip and Creamcake!

Even Willie's loyal followers must have thought his bid for a championship would be thwarted when he had to face the almost-invincible Steve Davis in the semi-final of the Mercantile Credit Classic. But this time he kept a tight grip on his nerves. Willie just couldn't control the tears of emotion after his greatest-ever win – yet there was another lethal problem ahead, for facing him in the final was snooker's No. 2 hard man, his great friend Cliff Thorburn, whom he had partnered to the world doubles final the previous month.

The question everyone was asking was: could Willie possibly break the toughest two players on the circuit in successive matches? Indeed, could he even find any sort of rhythm against a man capable of slowing even the quickest of players down to a snail's pace? He certainly could, and to the delight of the capacity crowd at the Spectrum Arena in Warrington, both men put on a potting spectacular good enough to grace any venue and any championship in the world – indeed, seldom had Thorburn thrown his cue with such abandon!

Willie set the ball rolling with a break of 72, only for Cliff to bounce straight back with a 77, He also took the next game despite a 52 break being scored against him, and then, having got that early skirmish out of the way, they both proceeded to blitz the balls. Thorne started it with an 88, added a 105,

Willie Thorne reads a 'Good Luck' message before the start of his Mercantile Credit Classic final with Cliff Thorburn which he won 13–8.

Errors crept into Thorburn's play as he tried to pull back the deficit against his opponent and good friend, Willie Thorne.

then followed with a 118 clearance after a first-red fluke, which brought a wry smile from his rival. Willie shrugged his shoulders apologetically, but Cliff responded: 'That's okay, I scored a 147 from the same position'!

The Canadian himself was quick to join in the fun, rattling home a 40, then a 75 and a 48 in one frame. He followed those with a 72 and a 66, and ended a magnificent day's play with a 100 clearance to be just one frame behind at 8–7. Veteran TV commentator John Pulman, one of the game's legends, said admiringly: 'That was the highest-quality snooker I've ever seen in a final'!

GRINDING THE GRINDER

Could there really be a Sunday afternoon encore? Thorne, still on a high from the previous night, couldn't wait to restart and said so, adding: 'I didn't really play that well (yesterday)'. Thorburn, content to pass the time of day with him at breakfast, just smiled. Willie got straight back into the groove – not with spectacular potting this time, but with a cautious approach which had been seldom seen in his game before.

They shared the opening two frames and, as the tension mounted, Thorne imposed his will with his finest display yet, forcing Thorburn into cat-and-mouse safety exchanges and actually grinding down the Grinder. Errors crept into Thorburn's play, particularly over the top left-hand pocket, where he was to miss numerous shots.

Slowly but surely, Willie crept towards the winning post, taking frame after vital frame with a clever mixture of attack and defence. At 12–8 he needed just one more. Would he collapse as he had done so often in the past? Not this time! Scenting the success he had yearned for over years of heart-break Willie was not about to let this one slip. He compiled a magnificent break of 53 – created from nothing. It was a break which left his adversary needing three snookers.

'I felt there were only five pockets out there today', said Thorburn after the game.

True to character, Thorburn fought for all he was worth to keep a fingerhold on the game, but to no avail. This time there were no tears as Thorne triumphantly held the Classic trophy aloft after one of the most memorable matches of our time – though sadly, it was a feat Willie was unable to repeat regularly in the years ahead.

DENNIS TAYLOR V STEVE DAVIS

1985 EMBASSY WORLD CHAMPIONSHIP FINAL: SHEFFIELD

It was, quite simply, the greatest snooker match ever played. There had been tremendous matches before and there will be tremendous matches in the future, but nothing can compare to that night in Sheffield in 1985. World champion Steve Davis was the odds-on favourite to collect yet another title. And in some people's eyes, Irishman Dennis Taylor was there just to make up the numbers. So, as the match began there was little sign of the dramatic finale that was to grip the packed audience in the Crucible Theatre and keep 18.5 million people watching on BBC2 until 12.23 in the morning.

At the start of the match there seemed little but humiliation in store for Taylor, as he rapidly went 8 – 0 behind. But the No. 11 seed just knuckled down and got on with the job – winning seven out of the eight frames, to finish 7 – 9 down at the end of the first day's play. Dennis said later: 'I knew I was behind on that first day but because I had made such a comeback I was thinking I had ended up a winner'. Not surprisingly, Davis went to bed shattered, hardly believing what had happened.

The next day saw Davis forging ahead, only for Taylor to fight back to 11 – 11. Davis then won the next two frames on the black, taking the score to 13 – 11 by the end of the afternoon and edging ever nearer to his title dream. Then, when the evening session began, Steve quickly knocked in a break of 86 to give himself a three-frame lead. Surely Taylor would now cave in and concede the title. But that was the last thing on his mind as his breakbuilding just got better and better as scores of 61, 70, 57 and 79 gave him four frames out of the next five to square the match at 15 – 15.

Davis responded by taking two more frames in succession to make it 17 – 15. But as Dennis said afterwards: 'Even though Steve needed just one more frame I was telling myself I could do it because I could sense he had put himself under pressure'. Cheered on by the unbelieving audience, the under-

An ecstatic Dennis Taylor after potting the final black in the final frame to take the world crown by 18 – 17.

BLACK MARK

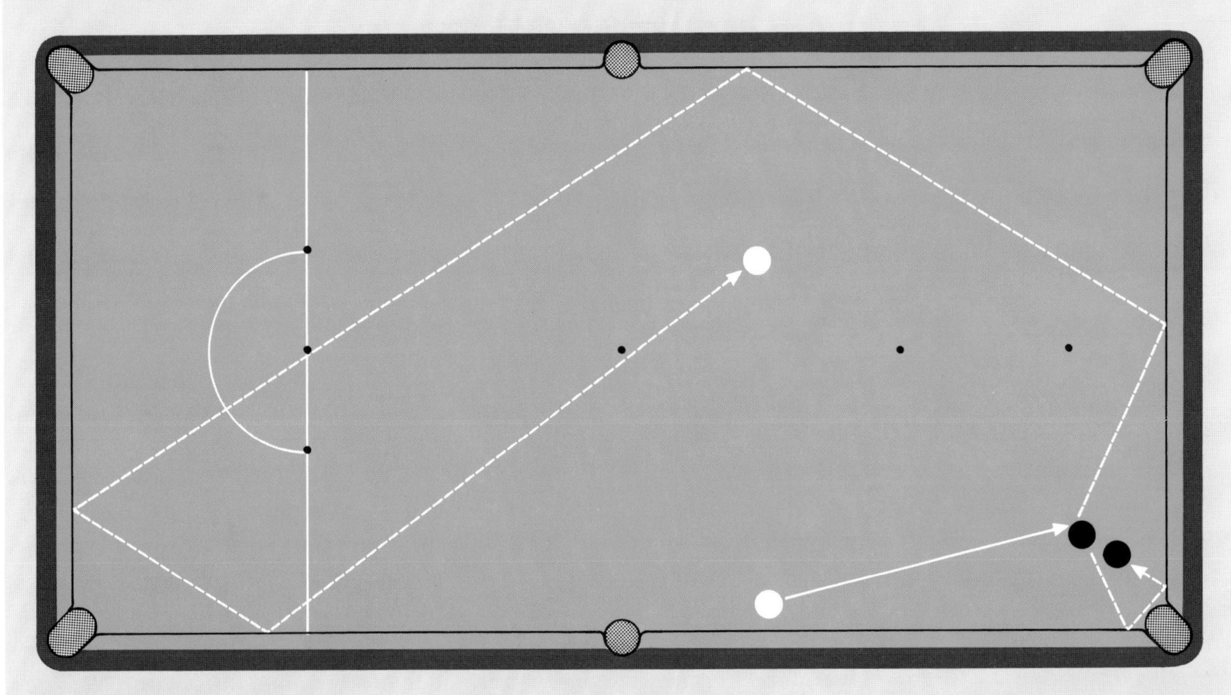

The most famous miss in snooker history. Three attempts had already been made on the final black of the final frame. Davis then tried to cut it in, but he overdid it and turned away in horror. Taylor was to return to the table to pot the black and take the title.

dog took the next two games to tie score at 17 – 17 and set the match up for a last frame decider.

That final frame lasted 68 minutes and was the longest of the entire championship – though the level of tension and excitement was such that time seemed to fly by as they battled it out for the game's greatest prize and a £60,000 winner's cheque.

ALL ON THE BLACK

Taylor forged into a 29 – 19 lead, but then went in off a red, and Davis, despite missing a blue, came back to squeeze in front at 59 – 44. With just the colours to go, Steve took the green but then presented Dennis with the chance he needed on the brown. It wasn't that easy but it went in and blue and pink finally followed to leave Taylor just three points behind at 62 – 59. It was now all on the black – and the black was safe. Both players knew that one error could cost them the match.

Taylor had a go at a double and missed, Davis missed, and then Taylor went for a long attempt that also failed. Dennis returned to his seat not daring to look were the ball had finished. He said later: 'I guessed it was going to be sitting over a pocket'. He was right. It was near a pocket, but not as easy a shot as the world No. 1 would have liked. Davis went for it, missed and turned away in anguish. Taylor returned to the table, hardly believing that he had another chance, and powered the black into the pocket, raised his cue two-handed above his head and celebrated the most memorable triumph in snooker history.

The crowd went totally wild and millions of late-night viewers could hardly believe what they had just witnessed – one of the greatest sporting moments of all time. But as Taylor hugged his family, his future now secure, Davis was gutted, having failed to make it three World Championship wins in a row. 'I have never felt worse after a match', he admitted afterwards. 'Even at 8 – 0 up I knew I still had a fight on my hands but I just never believed I could lose . . . that last black will stay in my mind for ever . . . in the end I just overcut it . . . but it was a great game and Dennis played some magnificent snooker.' He certainly did!

'I have never played in a greater match and I don't suppose I ever will' said Taylor.

STEVE DAVIS V WILLIE THORNE

1985 CORAL UK CHAMPIONSHIP FINAL: PRESTON

If things hadn't gone the way Willie Thorne had planned since his first championship breakthrough, in the Mercantile Credit Classic at the start of the year, he certainly made up for lost time at the Coral UK in Preston's Guildhall, where he bounced back with a vengeance. The tall, balding Leicester star had already taken care of a trio of world champions – Cliff Thorburn, Terry Griffiths and current title-holder, Dennis Taylor – when he launched into his third major final of the year. This time, however, his opponent was the formidable Steve Davis.

Having already beaten Steve Davis on his way to victory in the Mercantile Credit Classic, Willie Thorne was convinced he had the beating of him again. So, even though Davis took the opening frame, Willie hit back immediately with a break of 112 to win the second, and only lost the third after being put off by a spectator in his line of vision. It was obvious that Willie was on song, and he lashed in breaks of 49 and 41 to draw level, then adding a further 70 and 69 to lead 4–2.

When Davis levelled at 4–4, Willie's response was to fire home another century – Davis replying in kind as the action grew hotter. But the Leicester man found yet another gear and raced into a 7–5 lead with more razor-sharp potting. Indeed, a 67 in the next frame ought to have given him a three-frame cushion, but Davis took advantage of a missed red to come back with a decisive clearance of 43. Only for Willie to wrap up the first day with a break of 63, to lead 8–6 overnight.

Davis was the first to strike when play resumed in front of a packed Guildhall the next day. However, his 50-point lead failed to unsettle Thorne, who quickly extended his lead to 9–6. Then, from 56–0 adrift in the next game, the 'Great W.T.', as he is known to his friends, rocked the champion with a 68 clearance, and followed that up by firing in breaks of 115 and 61 to extend his lead to 12–6.

Steve Davis looked down and out as he trailed 13–8, but he took full advantage of an appalling miss by Willie Thorne in frame 22.

A HORROR SHOW

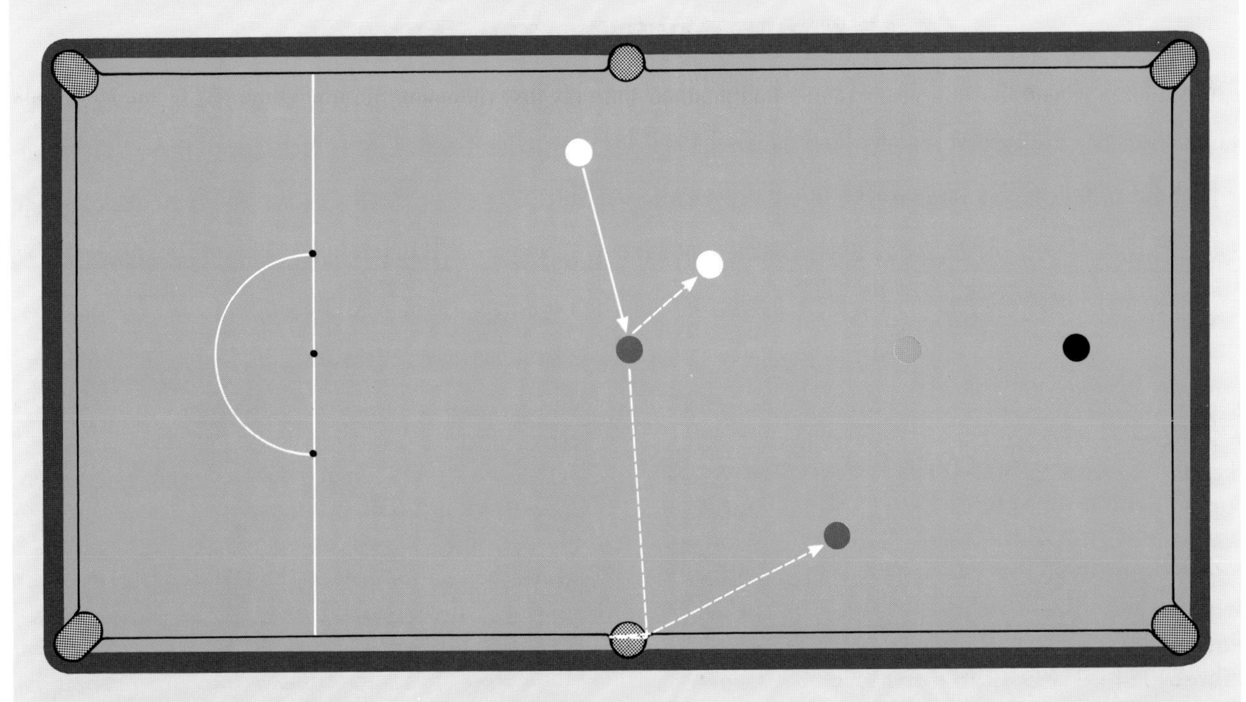

The moment that haunted Willie Thorne for years. The Leicester pro led 13–8 and the blue and pink looked formalities to go 14–8 ahead. But the blue wobbled in the jaws and stayed out. Thorne was already moving towards his next shot but could only stare in anguish as the blue stayed on the table.

Thirteen to play and only four wanted for victory . . . could the world champion really be humbled in a manner never seen before?

'I wasn't worried at that stage because no-one could possibly have stayed with Willie the way he was playing', said Davis later, and he added, 'I wasn't playing that badly so it was just a matter of waiting for him to burn out.' Despite Willie's reputation for doing just that – it seemed more than unlikely because, even though Steve took the next two frames to be 12–8 in arrears, Willie responded yet again with a 49 in the final game of the afternoon, to be within touching distance of the title he so badly wanted.

A VITAL BLUE

Davis began the final session with a big break, but Willie immediately settled down to chipping away at the deficit, as he had done so many times before during the match. The remaining reds disappeared, as did the yellow, green and brown, leaving him with a simple blue off the spot and an equally simple pink for game. From the perfect position Willie played the shot and was just about to move up for the killer blow when, to his horror, the blue wobbled in the jaws of the middle pocket and stayed out!

In that one moment he had blown his chance – not only of the match, but of imposing himself on snooker for perhaps years to come. His look of disgust said everything as he went, almost numbed, back to his seat – it was as if he knew what was going to happen. Davis was also shocked, hardly daring to believe he had been given a last-minute reprieve. He sat, collected his thoughts, then took a deep breath and proceeded to dispatch the remaining three balls to take the frame.

And so began the finest recovery of Davis' career as, with a glint in his eye, he slowly but surely edged nearer and nearer to his target, while Willie's confidence drained away with each game. Four frames later and, incredibly, they were all-square at 13–13, with Davis looking every inch a winner.

Blessed with the finest break-building gift in the world, Willie somehow dredged up a 96 to regain the lead. But it proved short-lived, as Steve carefully drew level and then destroyed him with two more frames to run out a most unlikely 16–14 winner. 'If he'd potted the blue, I would have been resigned to losing 16–8', admitted Davis afterwards. Sadly for Thorne, the new found 'bottle' which saw him to victory against Davis on their last outing had deserted him in his hour of need!

JIMMY WHITE V CLIFF THORBURN

1986 MERCANTILE CREDIT CLASSIC FINAL: WARRINGTON

If reputations were won and lost on just one shot then Jimmy White could have staked his on the stunning snooker he laid against Cliff Thorburn in the final game of the 1986 Mercantile Credit Classic. The climax of an epic match, it gave the Whirlwind his first ranking title and revenge over Cliff, who some months earlier had come back to beat him 12–10 in the one-off Goya Matchroom Trophy after initially trailing 7–0. That loss had been especially disappointing for Jimmy who had, according to Cliff, been 'playing the best snooker there's ever been' during those first seven games. But this time the young Londoner was determined not to lose his grip.

Having beaten Steve Davis in the quarter finals of the tournament, and with Cliff below par in his semi-final against Doug Mountjoy, the omens looked good for the young Londoner. And sure enough, armed with a new cue tailor-made for his power play, Jimmy began the 25-frame final by taking the first four frames – only to see Thorburn painstakingly fight his way back to take the next three frames of the session.

At 7.15pm, as the match was scheduled to restart, there was no sign of White. Delayed by a traffic jam he arrived, breathless, two minutes late and was penalised a frame. Just sixty minutes later Thorburn had opened up a 6–4 lead, leaving Jimmy with that same, awful feeling he'd experienced in their previous encounter. 'I couldn't believe it', he said later. 'One minute I'm in front and feeling confident for the evening session. Next minute I'm behind and right out of it.' However, although Cliff went 8–5 ahead, the Londoner took the last two frames of the evening to draw back to 8–7.

Cliff won the first game of the following afternoon, to lead 9–7. But back came White with a 56 break and he scrambled the next frame as well to tie things up at 9–9 with seven to play.

Now it was Thorburn's turn to get the jitters and a poor safety shot in frame 19 allowed White to seize the initiative. White promptly celebrated with

Jimmy White got the snooker he needed with just pink and black remaining in the final frame. Thorburn faulted and White took the title.

Cliff Thorburn can only reflect on the chance that was lost in the final frame. It was a memorable final but one that the Canadian was destined to lose.

a sparkling 117 clearance to go 11 – 9 ahead and, just two games away from the the first ranking tournament success of his career, eked out a 54-point lead in the 21st frame. But having lost the lead Cliff seemed to relax slightly and he clawed his way back to win on the final black.

LAST FRAME SHOOT-OUT

Things got worse for Jimmy in the following game, when a howling error allowed his opponent to clear up the colours and snatch an equalising frame, again on the last ball. Jimmy responded by taking the next and moving into a 12 – 11 lead – only to see the Canadian draw level and force a dramatic last-frame shoot-out.

Cliff seized the initiative at the start of the final frame by opening up a 49-point lead. But with the black ball 'safe' along the top cushion, the game's greatest percentage player gambled his all on potting it – knowing the black and one more red would put White in dire trouble. But the black stayed up and rolled into the open – allowing Jimmy to clear the remaining reds and narrow the deficit to 25 points with all the colours, worth a total of 27 points, still available. Unfortunately, he missed the yellow, Thorburn sinking it and fluking the green to leave Jimmy needing a snooker.

When Jimmy potted the brown and blue in quick succession he seemed to have miscalculated – it left him needing 17 points with only 13 (pink and black) remaining. But the Whirlwind's thinking was crystal clear, even though he failed to lay a snooker with the pink and left the Canadian an awkward angled shot into the middle pocket.

Cliff missed his chance and, under intense pressure, Jimmy returned to the table for a do-or-die effort. This time he played the shot of a lifetime, tucking the cueball firmly behind the black on its spot and pushing the pink into the centre of the table. There wasn't a sound in the previously noisy arena when, with great deliberation, Thorburn played but missed by a fraction. It left White a none-too-easy shot on the pink but the jubilant Londoner cracked it home without fuss and followed up by potting the final ball of the match for a memorable triumph.

'I couldn't believe it', said White. 'One minute I'm in front and feeling confident for the evening session. Next minute I'm behind and right out of it.'

JOE JOHNSON V TERRY GRIFFITHS

1986 EMBASSY WORLD CHAMPIONSHIP QUARTER-FINAL: SHEFFIELD

The only ambition Joe Johnson nurtured when he arrived at Sheffield's Crucible Theatre for the 1986 World Championship was to win a match there. Ranked in the world's top 16 for the first time, thanks to a series of fine performances in other events, the Bradford player had never displayed his best qualities in the Championship, nor indeed whenever he had to perform in front of the television cameras. So, tradition was against him, and it didn't help, either, when he developed a nasty back ulcer just before the tournament began.

Despite the back trouble, Jolly Joe was as confident as he could be, having made all the right preparations, and his relief at getting past Geordie Dave Martin in his opening match was clearly evident. That 10–3 success was the perfect platform from which to launch an attack on the next round, where he faced Mike Hallett, who had pulled off the shock of the year by toppling defending champion Dennis Taylor in the second round.

Hallett, still on a high, found Johnson a much tougher nut to crack. The 13–6 scoreline in favour of Johnson was a fair reflection of play and it pitched him into the quarter finals against seasoned campaigner Terry Griffiths, the man who had taken snooker by storm when he won the world title at his first attempt in 1979.

Griffiths had also experienced setbacks since that memorable victory – often at the hands of stablemate Steve Davis – so he must have been delighted to find himself in the opposite half of the draw to the world No. 1. Terry was a firm favourite to beat the Yorkshireman, but when Joe won the opening three frames, then later led 6–3, he must have had a few doubts. However, Griffiths – one of the game's great battlers – held his opponent to 9–7 overnight and could count himself a little unfortunate not be on level terms, because in the last frame Johnson had covered the final red with the

Joe Johnson, despite suffering from terrible back trouble, lines up another shot in an astonishing fightback against Welshman Terry Griffiths.

Terry Griffiths contemplates his next shot as he attempts to press home his advantage against Joe Johnson, but it was Johnson who kept his nerve.

black after it had been left over a baulk pocket.

There was no such good fortune for Joe the following morning, when he missed a straightforward black, allowing Griffiths to take the first frame. Terry won the next as well, to level the scores at 9–9, and then shattered Joe by winning three more on the trot to take a 12–9 lead. With only one frame needed for victory, it now seemed a formality for the softly-spoken player from Llanelli, but he made an error in the following frame which was to cost him dearly. Having potted an early green he screwed up the table for a choice of reds, only to fluff the shot.

SHELL-SHOCKED

Relieved and reprieved, Johnson promptly hit back with a magnificent 102 break to recapture his confidence. And from that point on he found that special gear most players can only dream about. A frame-winning break of 43 came next and he followed that with a spectacular 110 to draw level. No wonder Griffiths looked shell-shocked!

Joe then ran in a swift 54 to open the final frame, and even though an unfortunate in-off when he was in sight of victory offered his rival an outside chance, it was not to be. The dazzling Yorkshireman completed an amazing four-frame burst with a 33 break, to clinch his semi-final place 13–12. What a session! Five in a row from Griffiths, then four in 52 minutes from the man who, until a week earlier, had never tasted victory at the Crucible. 'I've never felt like that before on television', said the now jubilant Johnson.

Joe could have been forgiven for thinking that this was to be the highlight of his career. But, in one of the most emotional journeys ever undertaken in snooker, he roared past Tony Knowles 16–8 in the semi-finals dismantled the overwhelming favourite, Steve Davis, 18–12 in the final itself.

'When you feel you can't miss you go for them' said an ecstatic Joe Johnson.

The 150–1 outsider had claimed his place in snooker history in the most emphatic manner, and to prove it wasn't a fluke he almost staged an action-replay 12 months later. This time he reached the final, again despite all the odds, only for Davis to gain revenge and his fourth world title. But it was that 1986 quarter-final devastation of Griffiths which put Johnson on the road to fame and fortune.

STEVE DAVIS V JIMMY WHITE

1987 MERCANTILE CREDIT CLASSIC FINAL: BLACKPOOL

With ever-increasing standards of play, the results of modern-day snooker matches are often decided by a deluge of high breaks. But at the end of the 1987 Mercantile Credit Classic, in Blackpool, between Steve Davis and Jimmy White, it was just one brilliant snooker that settled the outcome of an outstanding game. Davis and White are always guaranteed to play in front of sell-out crowds, and this time there was a record ITV audience of 15.2 million tuned in to watch the superstars battling it out over 25 frames. It was a classic encounter that always threatened to go the whole distance.

Jimmy White, who had not beaten Davis in a final for six years, started well. He took the first frame 61 – 51 and followed that with a break of 46 to take a two-frame advantage. The safety play was good, but not excessive, and the potting was of the highest calibre – with breaks of 31, 43, 42 and 70 earning Davis three frames in a row. The players then shared the final two frames of the session, to give Davis a 4 – 3 lead going into the break.

By the end of the first frame of the second session, White had drawn level – only for Davis to move ahead by winning the ninth. In turn, Jimmy brought the match once more back to all square, at 5 – 5, with a break of 49. Steve responded by producing what turned out to be the highest break of the match – a 119 – to take the eleventh. Yet, for all his experience, the world champion could not pull away from his determined young rival, and by the end of the first day's play Steve had only just squeezed into an 8 – 7 lead – and that was after an outrageous slice of luck had enabled him to pot the pink in the 15th frame.

White knew that one spell of brilliance could turn the game his way, and an epic struggle ensued. The first four frames were played at a cracking pace and settled in less than fifty minutes! With two apiece, the scoreboard confirmed Davis still holding on to a slender 10 – 9 lead. The way things were going,

Time to reflect for Steve Davis, a man whose face only rarely betrays what is going on inside his computer-like brain.

A MATCHWINNER

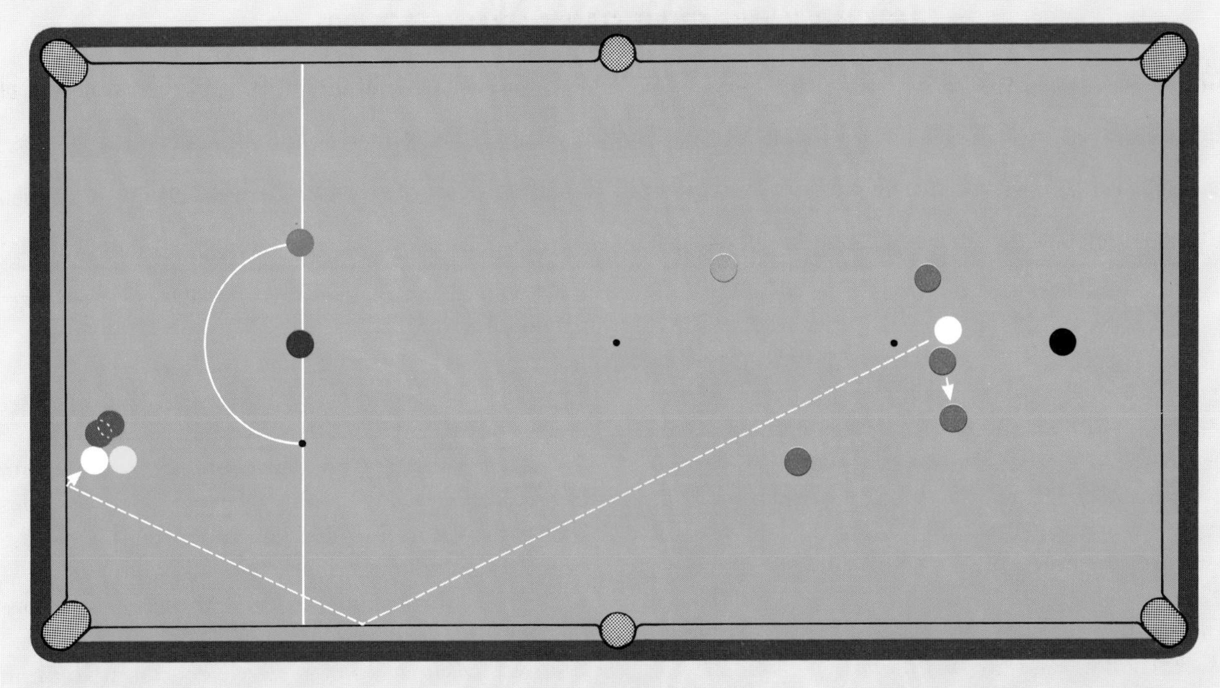

Steve Davis doesn't quite get the position he needs and looks to snooker Jimmy White in the final frame. The cue ball comes off two cushions and nestles in sweetly behind blue and yellow. After White's failure to escape, Davis stepped in with a break of 33 to win the title.

it would have taken a brave man to put any money on the final outcome, especially when White drew level once again at 11 – 11.

THE PRESSURE BEGINS TO TELL

With the pressure on the players increasing by the minute, Davis renewed his attack and put together a break of 47 to take the 23rd frame and go 12 – 11 ahead. However, requiring only one frame for victory, the pressure began to tell, and he missed an easy-looking red despite being well placed for the shot – allowing Jimmy to return to the table and take the frame 80 – 55 after a break of 44.

With the score now standing at 12 – 12, it was suddenly White who, for the first time since the opening frames of the match, seemed to be in the driving seat and on his way to the £50,000 first prize. But, having taken a 35 – 0 lead, he went for a long red, missed, and allowed Davis a chance to repair the damage.

Steve paced around the table, also eyeing up the possibility of a long red. He examined and re-examined the shot, knowing that if he missed he could present the match to Jimmy. After much deliberation, the world's No. 1 took a deep breath, lined up his shot and the red flew into the pocket.

The subsequent break reached 36 before it broke down, and then came the snooker that was to tie up the game. Drawing on all his experience, Davis played the cue ball off the final red and brought it back, via two cushions, the length of the table, to

It was a brilliant shot, leaving Jimmy no safe route back to the red. The Whirlwind looked around the table in despair to try and find an escape from his predicament.

finish perfectly behind the blue and yellow. It was a brilliant shot, and left Jimmy no safe route back to the red. The Whirlwind looked around the table in despair to try and find a way out of his predicament. But there was no escape, and after the foul, Davis mopped up with a break of 33 to take the title 13 – 12.

It had been a titanic duel between the two best players in the world. And whilst the majority of viewers were probably willing on White, the underdog, to win, in the end they could not fail to admire the outstanding skill and sheer professionalism of Steve Davis.

STEVE DAVIS V JOHN PARROTT

1988 MERCANTILE CREDIT CLASSIC FINAL: BLACKPOOL

John Parrott made no secret of his admiration for world champion Steve Davis as he prepared for their clash in the Mercantile Credit Classic at Blackpool's Norbreck Castle Hotel. It was to be Parrott's first ranking tournament final and he adopted a positive attitude: 'If you can't look forward to playing Davis then you can't look forward to playing anyone. I certainly won't be overawed – I am just going out to enjoy the match'. However, John left no doubt that he was fully aware of the magnitude of his task: 'Steve is the best player that has ever been born', he said.

Davis seemed to be proving the point as he went to the table in the very first frame and knocked in a break of 99. He followed up with a 33, to take the game 139–0. But Parrott, as he had promised, wasn't overawed. He took the next frame 72–31 and added a break of 69 on his way to establishing a 3–1 advantage. Predictably, Davis fought back immediately to level at 3–3, only to see John go ahead again 4–3 by the interval.

After the restart, lack of concentration cost Parrott the eighth frame. This seemed to upset him and it allowed Davis to take control. Breaks of 79, 35, 60 and 34 helped Steve race into a 9–4 lead, and in two of those frames Parrott didn't pot a ball! John knew he had to take the last frame of the day, which he did, despite the pressure, by a margin of 64–28. Even so, he went to bed knowing that missed chances had cost him dear, and that he would have to be a lot sharper on the second day, otherwise Davis would easily retain his title.

However, at the start of play the next day, Parrott's Liverpudlian supporters had plenty to cheer about, as John knocked in the first century break – a 103 that reduced the deficit to 9–6. But, despite a break of 38 from John in the next frame, Davis hit back straight away to make it 10–6. Surely, knowing that he needed just three frames for victory, the world's No. 1 would now complete the formalities

Steve Davis found himself under early pressure from John Parrott in the latter's first ranking tournament final, but then Davis took control.

WHAT A MISS!

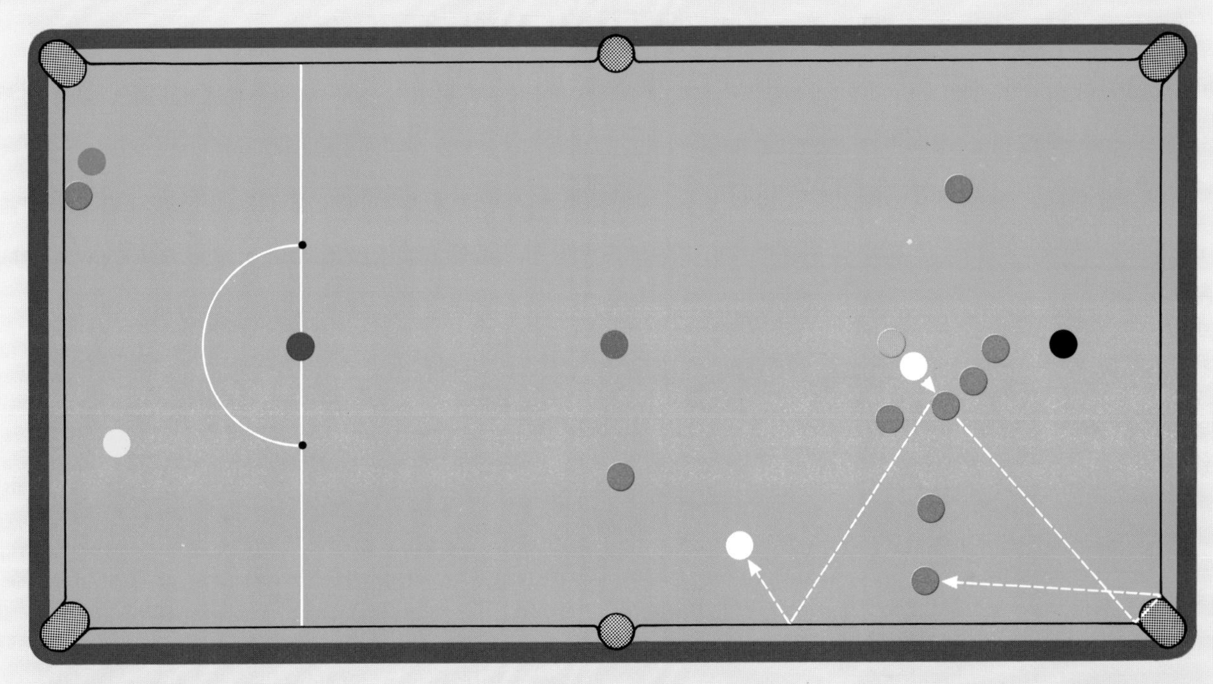

The shot that turned the game: Parrott, 11 – 10 ahead, takes on what should have been a straightforward red. But the red stayed out and Davis came back to the table to fire in a break of 83 to level at 11 – 11. 'I threw Davis a lifeline' admitted Parrott.

and collect the £50,000 first prize.

As it happened, nothing could have been further from the truth! Parrott took the next two frames, to trail by just 8 – 10 at the interval. And after the break he returned much the sharper player. The crowd could scarcely believe it as Steve missed a couple of easy shots and John compiled breaks of 44, 56, 38 and 58 to take the next three frames and lead 11 – 10. But then the match changed.

THROWN A LIFELINE

Leading 31 – 16 in the 22nd frame, and looking well on the way to his first title and his first win over Davis, Parrott lined up a red. It wasn't that easy a shot – but not that difficult for a man who had hardly missed a ball all day. However, the ball stayed out, giving Steve just the spur he needed. As Parrott was to admit afterwards: 'I threw Davis a lifeline and he took it. It was most probably the only ball in the match I hadn't played 100 per cent'. But the damage was done and Steve, with a new spring in his step, returned to the table and knocked in a break of 83 to level the match at 11 – 11.

Davis, after sitting and watching for so much of the day, looked across the see Parrott in despair. With that further incentive, he fired in a break of 68 to make it 12 – 11 – Parrott conceding the frame with four reds still left on the table! Steve was virtually home and dry – and he knew it. Davis captured the 24th and final frame with an outstanding break of 99, to collect the title 13 – 11.

Afterwards, Parrott, who picked up the runners-up cheque for £30,000, was quickly back to his chirpy self, telling the assembled press: 'When I was 9 – 5 down I won six of the next seven frames and I have got to be proud of the way I played. Not many people do that against Davis'. This was the 37th title of Steve's magnificent career and he had been successful in his previous nine finals! But it might have been a different story, as Steve admitted: 'In the earlier stages of day two I felt like I was going to lose because John was playing so well. But then he gave me that one chance I needed'.

As John cracked afterwards: 'That miss on the red will go straight out of my head, as soon as I collect my pension book!'

MIKE HALLETT V JOHN PARROTT

1988 BENSON AND HEDGES MASTERS SEMI-FINAL: WEMBLEY

John Parrott, even if he goes on to be the most celebrated player in snooker history, will never forget the truly disastrous shot he played when in a seemingly invincible position during the last frame of the 1988 Benson and Hedges Masters semi-final against Mike Hallett. The match itself was a gripping encounter and a minor snooker classic. But that last frame really had everything – drama, excitement, mistakes and an unbelievable conclusion – and will linger in the memory for a long time to come.

Hallett began the match with breaks of 53, 38 and 46, and then 46 again, to establish a 3–2 lead. But Parrott quickly levelled the scores, producing a break of 45 to take a close sixth frame. Parrott then slightly lost his grip as Hallett fired in breaks of 46 and 62 to go 5–3 up (taking the eighth frame 93–0) with only three to play. But John Parrott is a fighter and he pulled back the next two, to set up a last frame decider.

Clearly now in charge, John established a lead of 65–22 and it seemed a certainty that Hallett, despite those early leads, was on his way back to Grimsby a beaten but wiser man. But how wrong can one be! Parrott, the world No. 13 from Liverpool, had sunk the final red and it seemed an impossible task for Hallett to recover with only the colours left. But then fate stepped in and handed him a lifeline he could never have expected.

Parrott was buzzing – delighted to be going through to the final. Having sunk that final red he opted for an easy green, before, or so he thought, breezing through the formality of potting the colours! But then, instead of simply rolling the green in, he went for the showman's finish and hit it with tremendous power. It flew into the pocket, straight out again and off the table – leaving Mike requiring three snookers and the rest of the colours. Even so, the odds were still heavily in Parrott's favour.

Mike Hallett looked like a no-hoper in this Benson and Hedges semi-final, but he produced one of the most exciting comebacks ever seen.

SUPERB PRESSURE SHOT

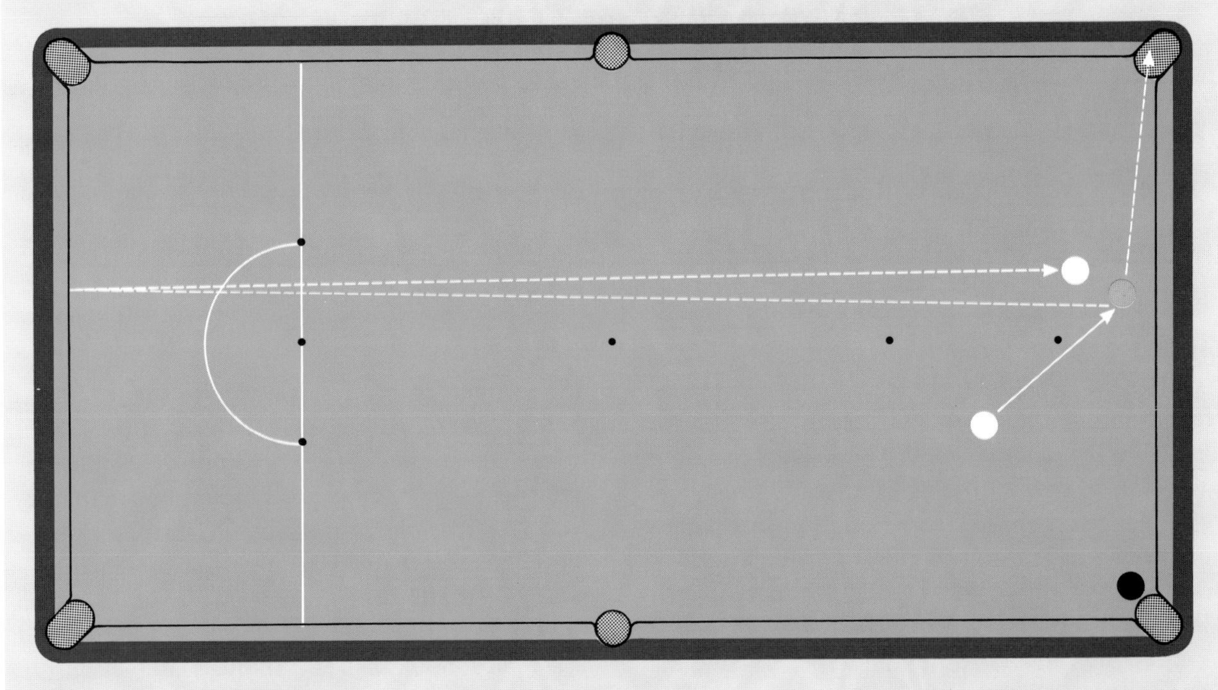

In an amazing final frame, Mike Hallett, let in through the back door by John Parrott, found himself with a very tricky pink. He executed a superb cut, however, after which the black was a formality. It was a suitably emphatic end to an extraordinary game.

Afterwards, John explained: 'I looked at Mike and knew he was ready to call it a day. I hit the green at 100 miles an hour and after that it was just a nightmare'. It certainly was, as Hallett just gritted his teeth and got on with the job in hand while Parrott visibly wilted under the pressure – especially when giving away four more points during the 14 minutes spent trying to pot the yellow!

NO ESCAPE

Eventually, Hallett pocketed the yellow, but poor Parrott made mistake after mistake. He went in off the green and then failed to escape from a snooker, hitting the pink in the process. That reduced the deficit to 65–46, which meant that Hallett, to the amazement of the crowd, could now win a match in which he had apparently given up all hope.

Parrott looked around as if begging for help from some unseen agency, but none was forthcoming and he just had to sweat it out as Hallett finally put away the green. Mike followed up with the brown and screwed the cue ball back for the blue – which he potted to make the score 65–58 to Parrott.

Everything had been going Hallett's way and it seemed almost illogical that he could lose from this position. But suddenly it was Mike who was under pressure. The pink was pottable – but only just! If he missed the fine cut he would probably leave it open for Parrott. The crowd were marvellous and, despite the stress of the situation, they kept perfectly quiet as Hallett went for the pot rather than safety – he was on a high and knew that he had to keep it going. The pink duly disappeared and the cue ball returned to provide him with the formality of an oh-so-simple shot on the black.

Mike admitted in the pressroom: 'If John had potted the green I would have probably called it a day. But that gave me the slim chance I needed'.

The crowd gave the exhausted players a standing ovation. As Hallett said afterwards: 'My character shone through out there. It's got to be the greatest frame I have ever won'. (Though he went on to be whitewashed 9–0 by Steve Davis in the final!) But Parrott was gutted – he had gone for the big finale and had paid dearly for it.

JIMMY WHITE V STEPHEN HENDRY

1988 EMBASSY WORLD CHAMPIONSHIP SECOND ROUND: SHEFFIELD

When snooker's young guns, Stephen Hendry and Jimmy White were seeded to meet in the second round of the 1988 Embassy World Championship at Sheffield, it was on the cards we were in for a classic encounter. What could be better: the game's two hot shots playing the best snooker of their lives and vying for the No. 2 slot behind Steve Davis in the new world rankings. It turned out to be a cracker with White, approaching his 26th birthday, in the unaccustomed role of 'veteran' and 19-year-old Hendry, favourite with the bookmakers.

When the two young warriors stepped out to do battle in the Crucible arena, both went straight for the jugular. The first eight-frame session, containing as many 50-plus breaks in 92 minutes, was breathtaking from the moment Hendry opened the proceedings with a 78. White hit back immediately to take three games in a row, but faltered twice on vital balls and a relieved Hendry accepted his chances to trail just 5–3 overnight.

When play resumed the following morning White quickly extended his lead with a 59 break, but there was no hint of the explosion to follow. Hendry suddenly found the inspiration to take control of the match with the most inspired hour ever seen at the Crucible. From 6–3 down he blew White aside with six magical frames, beginning with breaks of 52 and 35 in frame ten. He followed those with a 79 and then a 125 to draw level. White could do nothing to put the brakes on, and Hendry continued his avalanche with another two breaks of 50 to take the lead. As if that wasn't enough, Stephen edged through the next game and then finished his golden hour with a 101 break, to be 9–6 ahead with one to play that day.

A shell-shocked White displayed his own class by climbing off the ropes with breaks of 31 and 47 to keep within touching distance of the young superstar. But television commentators John Virgo

Jimmy White survived a devastating spell from Stephen Hendry, and retaliated to win one of the greatest games seen at the Crucible 13–12.

and Jack Karnehm were in total agreement that Hendry had produced the finest six frames they had ever witnessed! 'Don't blink or you'll miss it', they said the following morning.

TRUE SPORTSMANSHIP

The final day began with an incident in the first frame that revealed the truly sporting nature of this epic contest. White, struggling to stay in touch, found himself snookered behind the last brown. He played the shot with perfect weight, struck the green at the other end of the table, and rolled to safety. But to the astonishment of everyone, referee John Street included, Jimmy called a foul stroke on himself, saying: 'I touched the brown with my cue'. What a time for honesty, with your Championship dreams slipping away! Not surprisingly, Hendry went on to win the frame and take a 10–7 lead.

However, far from having an adverse effect, the incident acted as a spur to White, who promptly ran off four frames in a row to regain the advantage he had lost so spectacularly the previous evening. Hendry then demonstrated his own resolve by levelling again with his third century of the match. In response, Jimmy put in a 64 to go 12–11 ahead, but a missed red ended a break of 48 in the 24th game, when it seemed he was home and dry. That enabled Hendry to hit back with a 43, to send the match into a final-frame shoot-out.

Hendry, one of the game's oustanding talents, had to give second best to White as the Whirlwind knocked in a break of 86 to win the match.

Now the nerve-ends began to show – especially Hendry's – and when White spurned a safety shot and instead sank a brilliant long red, the writing was on the wall for his gallant opponent. To deafening applause, ball after ball disappeared as the Whirlwind forged a break of 86 to win the contest.

When the dust had settled on a superlative contest featuring 21 breaks of 50 or more, a relieved White paid tribute to Hendry, saying: 'It took me six years to do what he has done in six months!'

As a hugely impressed Jack Karnehm said afterwards: 'I could have watched them all night long. They both emerged winners from the best match I've ever seen as a spectacle'. This was an opinion which was echoed by referee Street, who should have the last word: 'I was privileged to have a grandstand seat for the most exciting encounter I've ever seen. We've had some classics at the Crucible but I can't believe two players have ever hit such a peak at the same time!'

DOUG MOUNTJOY V STEPHEN HENDRY

1988 TENNENTS UK OPEN FINAL: PRESTON

After half a decade in the doldrums, and faced with the despair of slipping out of the top 16, 46-year-old Doug Mountjoy had turned to the coaching 'guru', Frank Callan. Callan, who recognized Mountjoy's natural ability, set about painstakingly re-fashioning the Welshman's game to put his once-illustrious pupil back on the title trail. However, he insisted in his blunt Lancashire brogue, it would be 'another year or two' before all the hard work paid off. And Doug was equally realistic, telling the press that 'a couple of top eight finishes is all I hoped for'. So, to reach the final of the Tennents UK Open a few months later must have been beyond his wildest dreams!

Doug Mountjoy's improving form at the Rothmans Grand Prix earlier in the year, where he beat Stephen Hendry 5 – 1, had gone largely unnoticed. And yet it was not until he crushed compatriot Terry Griffiths 9 – 4 in the semi-final that his resurrection commanded the attention it deserved. But even then he was only meant to be cannon-fodder for the all-conquering Hendry, who had justifiably hogged the headlines already by drubbing Steve Davis 9 – 3.

And so the Scot was the odds-on favourite when play began on the Saturday afternoon. Mountjoy opened with 35 and took the first frame after the youngster missed a black on its spot – but a Hendry century in the next levelled the scores. The Welshman scrambled the third and fourth frames for a useful 3 – 1 lead, but another century – a 113 – by the young Scot silenced any premature alarms. In a scrappy encounter that did not even hint at the drama to come, Mountjoy then won the sixth, despite missing an easy pink and miscueing a free black ball, before finishing the first session with a 74 and the undeniable bonus of a 5 – 2 lead at the interval.

Hendry may have sensed things were slipping inexorably away from him when a fluked red set his opponent on the way to a 98 in the first frame of the evening. However, as Doug was within one ball

The end of a barren spell as Doug Mountjoy holds aloft the Tennents UK Championship trophy. Mountjoy's last major win had been in 1979.

Doug Mountjoy displays the new-found confidence from sessions with coach Frank Callan. It was sufficient to withstand the challenge from Hendry.

of a 7–2 lead, he missed the pink on its spot and allowed Stephen back in. Reprieved, the young man started to flow again and was soon level at 6–6. And despite missing a plant in the penultimate frame of the day, he followed up with a clearance of 129 to level the scores again, at 7–7, and put himself in line for the highest break prize.

SUBLIME SNOOKER

In a continuation of the first day's sketchy exchanges, Mountjoy collected the first two frames of the following afternoon and then, inexorably, began to ease himself into the form of his life. He would go into the interval having scored 222 points without reply, and, more significantly, with a lead of 11–7! The odds had swung dramatically in the Welshman's favour, as he made it 12–7 and then followed up with two consecutive centuries – a 131 and a 106.

Incredibly, there was more to come straight after the interval, as Doug compiled a 124 for a record-breaking, third consecutive century. With only one frame required, surely there was no stopping him now? But Hendry had other ideas. With nothing to lose he leapt from his chair and had soon pulled back the next three frames. After he had won a fourth with a break of 51, the audience were on the edge of their seats. And the tension became almost unbearable as for some eighteen minutes both players executed a series of superb safety shots with the black, surrounded by reds, hanging over a bottom pocket.

Although Hendry eventually won that frame, Mountjoy had been able to ease the tension with light-hearted banter. And that may have been all he needed. When Hendry finally made a mistake – a jawed red in mid-frame – Doug was sufficiently composed to put together a modest 39 for the match, the title, and a place in snooker folklore.

Amid scenes that evoked memories of Dennis Taylor's unforgettable win over Steve Davis in the 1985 World Championship, the tears and tributes poured out for both Doug and his 'guru', Frank Callan. And it was left to Doug to put his achievement into perspective: 'Reaching the final was like swimming the Channel', he insisted when the game was over, 'but winning it is like swimming the Atlantic!'

STEVE DAVIS V JIMMY WHITE

1988 NORWICH UNION GRAND PRIX FINAL: MONTE CARLO

Jimmy White went into the final of the Norwich Union European Grand Prix, held in the luxurious setting of the Beach Plaza Hotel in Monte Carlo, knowing that world champion Steve Davis could be beaten. Just a couple of months earlier he had thrashed Davis 9–4 in the final of the BCE Canadian Masters, in Toronto. That was White's first ranking tournament win for 18 months, and the first time he had beaten Steve in a final since his 11–9 win in the Northern Ireland Classic in 1981. So, it was not surprising when he told the press after his Masters win: 'I owed Davis that one – in fact, I owed him about 20'! Indeed, but could he do it again?

With the waves of the Mediterranean gently lapping just 50 yards away, the dinner-jacketed celebrity audience took their seats in the Beach Plaza Hotel's Sea Club to witness what would turn out to be one of the great finals of our time. Forget the fact that it wasn't a ranking tournament, forget the fact that there were only eight players competing – this was the world's No. 1 playing the world's No.2 for a £50,000 first prize, with no quarter expected and none given. What's more, whilst White had recently triumphed over Davis in Canada, Davis had beaten White in the final of the Fidelity Unit Trusts International earlier in the season. Now it was time to see who was boss.

Potting with precision, White matched Davis in safety play, and established a 4 – 1 lead. Davis, on the other hand, had scant opportunity to show this new snooker audience the skills of which he is capable – except for a brilliant 136 break in the third frame (the highest of the tournament).

However, White started to falter. And whilst both players struggled to put breaks together in the sixth frame, it was Davis who eventually took it and followed up with a confident 60, to trail by just 4 – 3. Not surprisingly, Steve was now itching to get to the table but White, desperate to make it two final wins

Steve Davis with yet another trophy – this time after beating Jimmy White 5 – 4 in the Norwich Union European Grand Prix in Monte Carlo.

MOMENT OF TRUTH

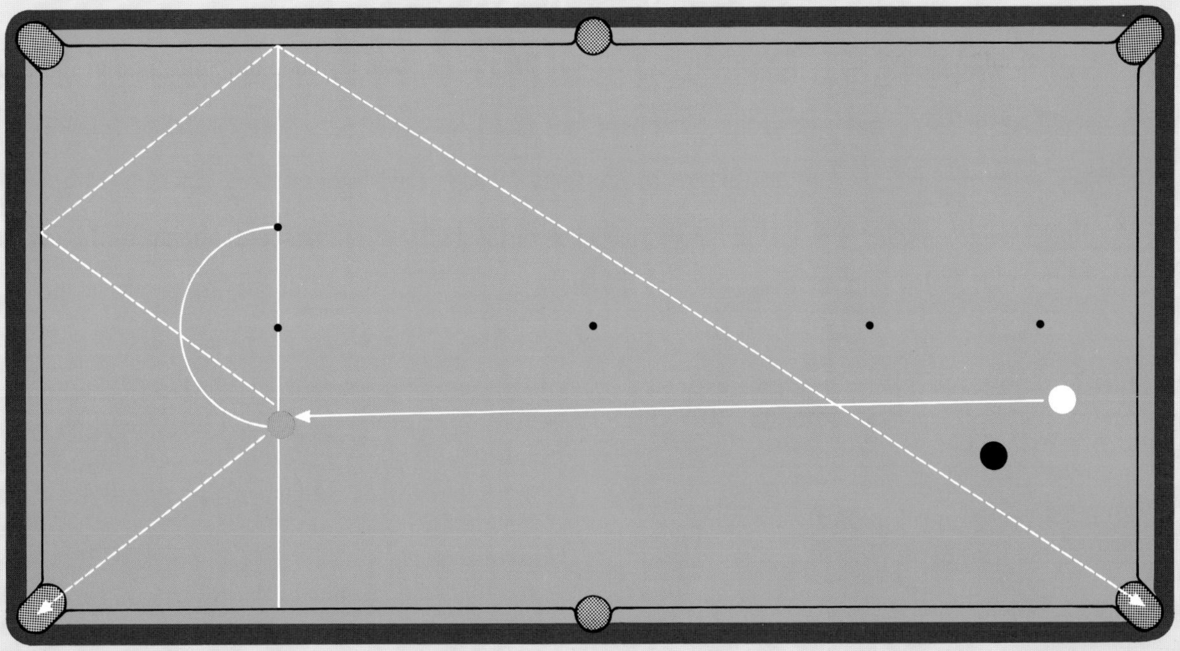

Jimmy White, 4–3 and 55–40 ahead, needed this pink for the match. He potted, but the applause was silenced as the cue ball rolled slowly back down the table and dropped into a corner pocket. Davis, predictably, took this frame and the next to snatch victory.

in a row over Davis, moved into a 55–40 lead in the eighth frame – and with pink and black on the table that meant Steve required a snooker.

WATCHING IN AGONY

The crowd were loving every minute of this intriguing duel and on three occasions Davis played superb snookers to leave White in serious trouble. But Jimmy kept his cool and three times escaped. Someone had to make a mistake, and eventually it was Davis who left a long pink that could give White the game. Jimmy examined the angles and must have realised there was a chance of an in-off, but bravely he finally went for the shot. A sell-out crowd rose to acclaim him as the winner as the pink went into the pocket, but he could only watch in agony as the white came off two cushions and travelled diagonally, and ever-so-slowly, the length of the table, to drop into a corner pocket. Jimmy looked away in total disgust, while Davis, having been thrown an unexpected lifeline, potted pink and black to take the match into a last frame decider.

As if that wasn't enough, there was more excitement to come. White quickly regained the initiative to take a 41–25 lead. However, with the pink perfectly positioned for him to sink and then get on to the next red, the Wimbledon Whirlwind got a terrible 'kick'. The pink stayed out and Davis, for the second frame in succession, was back in a match he was convinced he had lost.

In those circumstances Steve is the most dangerous player in the world. A break of 35 gave him the match 5–4 and left White shattered and unable to comprehend how he could have lost. As Davis said afterwards: 'That was a snooker miracle. I was finished and Jimmy should have buried me. I had no right to win this match. Even so I did well to get back into it and it must rank as the second most exciting match I have ever played in' – the audience in Monte Carlo certainly thought so, and the French TV station, Canal Plus, were delighted with such a sensational final. But poor Jimmy White could only think of what might have been!

White could only say: 'Don't ask me what went wrong. I must have had that match won four times over'.

ENGLAND V REST OF THE WORLD

1989 FERSINA WINDOWS WORLD CUP FINAL: BOURNEMOUTH

The World Cup has, traditionally, been treated as one of snooker's 'lesser' events, but it finally arrived as a tournament of major importance in 1989. And deservedly so, because fans and television viewers enjoy the short frame format, with the opportunity of seeing six top class players in the same session. They were certainly not to be disappointed this time, when England, represented by the top three players in the rankings, Steve Davis, Jimmy White and Neal Foulds, and favourites to repeat their title success of the previous year, met a Rest of the World side in the final.

England had no trouble in taking their expected place in the final, having beaten the Republic of Ireland 5 – 1, and then Canada 5 – 2. Whilst in the other half of the draw the Welshmen put out Scotland 5 – 3 but then came unstuck by the same score against the Rest of the World – a team rated as 25 – 1 outsiders before a ball had been struck.

The Rest of the World were a 'genuine' United Nations side, consisting of South African Silvino Francisco, Tony Drago of Malta and Dene O'Kane of New Zealand. Drago, the 23-year-old from Valletta, was the most consistent player of the tournament thus far, having won all his seven previous frames, and he extended his record run by beating Steve Davis 67 – 25 in the opening frame of the final, after compiling a break of 51. Davis immediately retaliated to make the score 1 – 1, and then Foulds handed out a 2 – 0 defeat to O'Kane. At 3 – 1 ahead, the final looked to be going England's way.

Silvino Francisco, plagued by personal problems, had not been in the best of form but that all changed in the last four frames of the afternoon session. He won three of them against his opponent, Jimmy White, who had also been suffering a series of bad results, to bring the scores level 4 – 4 at the interval.

Neal Foulds, Steve Davis and Jimmy White after their second successive victory in the Fersina Windows World Cup. England beat the Rest of the World 9 – 8.

POINT OF NO RETURN

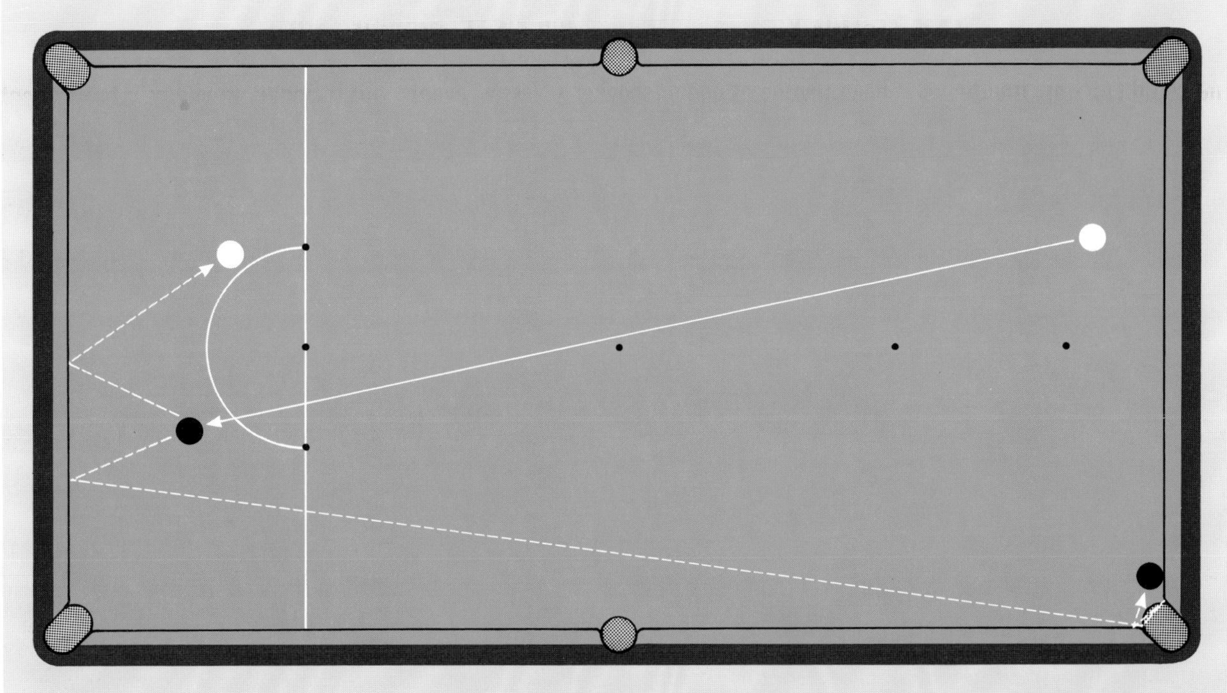

Dene O'Kane knew he could end up as a hero or a villain with this one shot in the shootout frame against Steve Davis. O'Kane took a gamble and bravely went for a long double on the respotted black. He missed however and found to his horror that he had left the black hanging invitingly over the pocket.

White returned in the evening session, and could not have had a tougher opponent than the in-form Drago. England's fears were realised when Drago scored breaks of 30 and 39 to take the first frame 75–0, and put the Rest of the World in front at 5–4 – only to concede the next frame on the black and allow England to level the scores again at 5–5.

Davis, who had won four frames in a row to give England the title over Australia the previous year, then returned. He quickly beat the luckless O'Kane 2–0, and when Foulds took his first frame against Francisco the result looked inevitable as England led 8–5. However, Francisco knocked in a 96 break against Foulds – the best of the tournament – and pulled one back to make it 8–6.

Foulds remained at the table to face Drago, the Maltese Tornado. But the Englishman didn't pot a ball as Tony won the frame with a break of 75. And there was worse to follow for the English supporters in frame 16, Drago taking that as well to set up a last frame decider between Davis and O'Kane. Drago's record was quite staggering – 11 frame wins out of 13 – but even more importantly it had give the Rest of the World a chance of that attractive £43,200 first prize!

Over nine frames Davis would be expected to beat O'Kane quite easily, but over one frame anything could happen. And everything did! With so much at stake both players were very nervous, missing clear chances to build a break, but finally Davis started to edge in front at 46–31. O'Kane would surely cave in, thought those looking on, but amazingly, the New Zealander stuck in there, fluked a snooker to make it 46–35, potted a green and then Davis went in-off to make the score 46–42 to England.

With the tension at fever pitch, Davis took the brown and blue to leave the Rest of the World trailing 55–42, and O'Kane needing a pink and black to force a re-spotted black. Incredibly he took them both to level the scores at 55–55. We were about to witness the first-ever re-spotted black finish to a major final in the history of the game! Sadly for Dean, he played the black the length of the table, but the ball wobbled in the jaws and stopped virtually over the pocket for a relieved Davis to step in and win the frame 62–55, giving England a remarkable 9–8 win.

Afterwards Davis was shell-shocked and eased the tension by joking: 'I was in total control of myself out there. It was no trouble!' But it was a desperately close shave, and an especially heartbreaking experience for Drago who had played like a genius throughout the tournament to give the rank outsiders a real chance of the title.

PROFILE OF THE PROS

PROFESSIONAL SNOOKER PLAYERS LIKE STEVE DAVIS, ALEX HIGGINS AND RAY REARDON, HAVE, THANKS TO THE ALL-SEEING EYE OF TELEVISION, BECOME NATIONAL FIGURES AND HOUSEHOLD NAMES. IN THE FOLLOWING PAGES WE TAKE A CLOSER LOOK AT THE CAREERS AND LIVES OF THESE AND OTHER LEADING PLAYERS WHO DOMINATE THE INTERNATIONAL SNOOKER CIRCUIT.

The face of the future, Stephen Hendry, who became the youngest winner of a major professional tournament when he took the Rothmans Grand Prix title in 1987.

EDDIE CHARLTON

Eddie Charlton, born in 1929, began playing snooker at his father's club in Newcastle, New South Wales when he was just nine years old. Just two years later he appeared in a billiards exhibition with the incomparable Walter Lindrum, and he has been a sporting phenomenon ever since. Whilst snooker and billiards have always been the love of his life, he spent more than ten years playing First Grade soccer, and in 1950 he was a member of the winning team in the Australian Surfing Championship. As if that wasn't enough, he has been a top class boxer, tennis player and runner and, just for good measure, he even carried the Olympic torch when the Games came to Melbourne in 1956.

Eddie Charlton, once a miner, turned professional in 1960 and made his first trip to England for the World Championship eight years later. In those days the title was played for on a challenge basis, but Charlton failed in his bid to take the crown when he lost to John Pulman.

Eddie had to wait until 1970 before his next World Championship attempt, when the tournament was held in his native Australia. Again he was unsuccessful, losing this time to his fellow countryman, Warren Simpson, 27 – 22 in the semi-final.

However, Charlton has always been a fighter, a trier who stayed the course whatever the challenge. Thus two years later, 'steady Eddie' was in the World Championship semi-final again, this time going down 37 – 32 to John Spencer.

By then Eddie had virtually become a snooker commuter between Britain and his native Australia. 'They should have given me a season ticket between Sydney and London. I made that flight so often I lost count', he once said. This perhaps explains why the one major disappointment in his distinguished career is that he has never won a major title in the UK.

However, there have been many close shaves and heartaches and none more so than in 1973. In that year's World Championship Charlton beat Perrie Mans, Graham Miles and then Alex Higgins – the Irish Hurricane having taken snooker by storm when winning the world title at his first attempt a year earlier. Higgins was dispatched 23–9, leaving Eddie lined up against the incomparable Ray Reardon over 75 frames in the final. Charlton went into a 7–0 lead but could not maintain his momentum, and the Australian's dream faded and finally died as Reardon came through to win 38–32. Two years later (1975), Eddie was through to the final again. However, the ending was the same with Reardon winning one of snooker's epic matches 31–30, and Eddie hasn't contested the final since.

Throughout his career Charlton has been one of the game's greatest servants – spending his life globe-trotting to spread the snooker word. He has played in more than 25 countries, including exotic spots like Papua New Guinea, China, Japan and Hong Kong. 'I was going to these places years before the new professionals started visiting them', says Eddie.

COMPETITIVE INSTINCT

Of course Charlton has won many titles over the years. He has been Australian professional champion on numerous occasions, and won the World Matchplay event in Melbourne in 1976 when he beat Ray Reardon 31–24. And whilst other players have come and gone, Eddie has kept plugging away – his competitive instinct never swaying. Although he has slid out of the top ten and down the rankings – to No. 26 by the start of the 1987/88 season – Eddie has refused to buckle under. Indeed, outstanding performances in the Fidelity Unit Trusts International and the Rothmans Grand Prix of that year saw him move back up the rankings to No. 19.

WORLD RANKINGS FROM 1983–4

SEASON	WORLD RANKING
1983–4	6
1984–5	6
1985–6	12
1986–7	25
1987–8	26
1988–9	19

In fact the '87–'88 season held a number of proud moments for Charlton. He became a father again at the age of 57, when wife Robyn presented him with a son, Andrew. (Eddie already has three grown-up children from a previous marriage). And he helped Australia go all the way to the final of the Fersina World Cup in Bournemouth. Opponents England were the red-hot favourites but, with the score at 1–1, Charlton went out and whipped Jimmy White 3–1. Australia, suddenly, were in with a chance of the title and Charlton could hardly contain his excitement as the proud Aussies looked like causing one of the upsets of the season. But it was Steve Davis, the all-time great of the 1980s, who ruined Eddie's day by the seaside as he won the last four frames – two against Charlton and two against Warren King – to give England the trophy by a 9–7 margin.

This strongly-built Aussie is still a keep fit fanatic and tries to get out for a jog every day. He has no thoughts of retiring. Eddie loves the game too much to contemplate 'hanging up his cue'.

FACT·FILE

NAME: EDWARD FRANCIS CHARLTON AM

DATE OF BIRTH: OCTOBER 31, 1929

BIRTHPLACE: MEREWETHER, AUSTRALIA

TURNED PROFESSIONAL: 1960

FIRST MAJOR WIN: NONE

BIGGEST PAY DAY: £8,333 AS RUNNER UP IN THE FERSINA WINDOWS WORLD CUP, 1988

FRED DAVIS

Despite winning the World Championship from eight out of ten appearances in the final – the earliest being in 1947 and the last in 1966 – lovable Fred Davis always had to live with the fact that he remained in older brother Joe's shadow throughout their prime years. Yet he can never speak highly enough of Joe, and it is a remarkable tribute to today's Grand Master of snooker that more than a decade after his illustrious brother's death, in 1978, Fred is still an active pro, still carries the family name with pride and still retains his enthusiasm for the game.

Now well into his seventies, Fred may no longer have the stamina of today's young bloods, but he still negotiates the table with all the panache of a teenager, and is quite capable of handing out a lesson in potting and safety to anyone who treats him too lightly – just ask 1988 newcomer Steve Campbell, beaten by Fred in his first professional outing!

What's more, whilst Fred may not be a television fixture these days, the smile which caused his brother to complain, during their younger days in the family's Chesterfield billiard hall, that Fred wasn't serious enough about the game is still evident. The pace may have slackened somewhat with the passing of time, but the sense of humour and twinkling eyes which made Fred snooker's first Housewives' Choice in the 1970s have never dimmed.

Always the gentleman, it takes a rare occurrence for Fred to lose his cool, and even when asked to appear before the WPBSA for failing to attend a 1988 ranking tournament qualifier, Fred merely smiled and shook his head in disbelief. In fact, after playing in two of the rounds he had been forced to withdraw because of arthritis, and had made this quite clear to officials before leaving the venue. No wonder he smiled ruefully at the mix-up!

EIGHT WORLD TITLES

The Norbreck Castle Hotel, setting for the modern game's qualifying rounds, is exactly three miles from the scene of Fred's greatest triumphs: the Blackpool Tower Circus. It was there that for eight years – during the late '40s and throughout the '50s – he contested the world final with Walter Donaldson. Huge crowds congregated at the Tower Circus each April for snooker's premier event, seemingly unconcerned that the same two faces had become almost permanent residents there following brother Joe's retirement from competition play after a 20-year unbroken reign.

Reardon says of his 1969 World Championship clash with Fred: 'He beat me 25–24 after some of the greatest safety play I can ever remember in one match. Fred taught me new dimensions to the game and I absorbed more then than I had learned in 20 previous years. I was amazed at how he could stop you seeing any of the reds when they were all on the table'.

Fred was triumphant on all but two occasions against Donaldson, and when John Pulman emerged as his leading challenger in 1955 and 1956, Fred saw him off as well – the narrow victories completing his eight-title haul. But, sadly, snooker went into decline after that, and Fred decided to curtail his 20-year professional career and retire to his wife's Llandudno hotel.

Fred returned from exile in 1964, just as the game was beginning to stir itself again, but the edge had gone from his play and he was beaten by Pulman three times in head-to-head challenge matches for the world title. And whilst the revival of a proper knockout tournament served to whet Fred's appetite, after a decade of easy living he found life much tougher against the new breed of pros.

WORLD RANKINGS FROM 1983–4

SEASON	WORLD RANKING
1983–4	28
1984–5	46
1985–6	56
1986–7	47
1987–8	61
1988–9	83

Thanks to his vast experience Fred was able to pip débutant Ray Reardon in the 1969 championship, only to be thumped by Gary Owen in the following round. In 1970 he suffered the first of two heart attacks, and was able to play in only one of the two championships held that year. Yet four years later, quite amazingly, Fred won the last three frames to edge out wonder-boy Higgins in the 1974 quarter-finals. As if that wasn't enough, he reached the 1978 World Championship semi-finals at the Crucible Theatre and the last eight the following year.

More was to come from the man who, as long ago as 1937, hid the fact that he was short-sighted, and who eventually took to wearing revolutionary swivel-lensed spectacles. In 1980 he returned to billiards, his first love. To his surprise, and that of Rex Williams, he beat the defending world champion in a nail-biting battle over four days. So Fred, the only player to beat his brother off level terms in competition, had at last matched Joe's achievement by becoming only the second — and almost certainly the last – player to hold both snooker and billiards world titles.

FACT·FILE

NAME: FRED DAVIS

DATE OF BIRTH: AUGUST 14, 1913

BIRTHPLACE: WHITTINGHAM MOOR, DERBYSHIRE

TURNED PROFESSIONAL: 1930

FIRST MAJOR WIN: WORLD PROFESSIONAL SNOOKER CHAMPIONSHIP v WALTER DONALDSON, 1948 (84–61)

BIGGEST PAY DAY: £3,117 FOR REACHING THE 3rd QUALIFYING ROUND OF THE EMBASSY WORLD CHAMPIONSHIP, 1988

STEVE DAVIS

Steve Davis is, in the eyes of many people, the greatest player ever to pick up a cue. Certainly he has dominated the 1980s with a skill and authority that has made him a sporting superstar and a household name. From being a raw teenager whose only real talent was to play snooker, he has developed into one of this country's finest sporting ambassadors. Personally honoured by Her Majesty the Queen with the MBE, a reward that was greeted with incredulity in some media quarters, his 'gong' was a tribute to the game itself – an acknowledgment that snooker is now as significant a part of our sporting heritage as soccer, cricket or athletics.

When he first emerged, as a long-haired teenager, at Barry Hearn's snooker club in Romford, a legend was about to be born. Up until then Davis' only job had been working one day a week in a local supermarket, and he had never been a junior champion of any note. But Steve had talent, dedication and a deep love of snooker. Separately those assets might have been insufficient, but Davis put them all together to devastating effect.

Alex Higgins was the first man to feel the real weight of Davis' power – in the final of the 1980 Coral UK Championship, an event that Davis was to turn into a one-man show throughout the 1980s. Higgins was hammered 16–6. Just a year later Davis arrived at the Crucible Theatre, Sheffield for the Embassy World Championship. Jimmy White,

Higgins, Terry Griffiths and Canadian Cliff Thorburn were all dismissed as Davis reached the final. There he faced Welshman Doug Mountjoy. The outcome? 18 – 12 to Davis.

Big-time professional snooker was never to be the same again. Title after title fell to Davis in an orgy of success that left other players as also-rans. By 1988, Steve had amassed five world titles, won the UK Championship four times in a row, and taken every major trophy the sport had to offer. What's more, in 1982 he scored the first 147 to be seen on television, and in 1988 he became the first player to score three successive century breaks in tournament play.

LUCRATIVE CONTRACTS

Fame has naturally brought financial reward: Davis regularly earns more than £1m a year from his tournament successes, his lucrative sponsorship and advertising contracts and his personal appearances. But no sportsman works harder at the game and no player spends more time away from home. Yet he remains a down-to-earth individual. As manager Barry Hearn says: 'Steve doesn't know how much money he has got'!

Steve Davis is one of the wealthiest sportsmen in Britain. He owns a 300-acre farm in Essex, has a forest in Scotland and property in the West End. Yet, he doesn't drive a car – he relies on the company Lincoln and taxis!

What he has got is property in the West End of London, a forest in Scotland and an investment portfolio that means he will never have to work again. Yet beneath all this, there remains his deep, deep love of the game. Steve says: 'I will carry on playing as long as I enjoy practising. When I lose a match, I don't go away and sulk, I just get straight back to the practice table with my dad, Bill. I know some people don't believe it, but I really enjoy spending hours at the practice table'. It's that single-minded approach that has seen him win title after title.

There is another consuming passion – rhythm and blues and soul music. He likes nothing better than shutting himself away to listen to some of his 5,000 records. He is even managing director of a soul magazine – 'Voices from the Shadows'.

WORLD RANKINGS FROM 1983–4

SEASON	WORLD RANKING
1983–4	1
1984–5	1
1985–6	1
1986–7	1
1987–8	1
1988–9	1

There have been memorable matches, memorable moments and deep heartache during Steve's illustrious career. But nothing will ever compare with that amazing last frame black ball finish against Dennis Taylor in the 1985 Embassy final. Davis, the defending champion after his 18 – 16 defeat of Jimmy White 12 months earlier, could only turn in anguish as Taylor potted the black, lifted his cue high above his head and claimed the world title 18 – 17.

That epic moment occurred at 12.23am and it proved what a grip snooker has on the British nation as 18.5 million people stayed up to watch every pulsating moment. It was the highest ever BBC2 viewing figure and the highest for any programme after midnight.

Today, Davis is recognised wherever he goes. He can't travel by tube, go to the cinema, or visit Macdonalds without stopping and signing autographs. But he does it all with a smile. After all, he knows that without the fame there could be no fortune. Yes, Steve Davis MBE has been in the right sporting place at the right sporting time. And, just for good measure, he's a hell of a nice bloke!

FACT·FILE

NAME: STEVE DAVIS

DATE OF BIRTH: AUGUST 22, 1957

BIRTHPLACE: PLUMSTEAD, SOUTH LONDON

TURNED PROFESSIONAL: 1978

FIRST MAJOR WIN: CORAL UK CHAMPIONSHIP v ALEX HIGGINS, 1980 (16–6)

BIGGEST PAY DAY: £100,000 FOR WINNING THE EVEREST WORLD MATCHPLAY CHAMPIONSHIP, 1988

TONY DRAGO

At the start of the 1988/89 season, Tony Drago, the Maltese Tornado, lived up to his nickname when he fired his way into the snooker record books. Drago met Worksop's Danny Fowler in a third round match in the Fidelity Unit Trusts International at Stoke-on-Trent and won 5–2. One of the frames lasted just three minutes – the fastest in the history of the sport. As Fowler said afterwards: 'I was playing okay but Tony was just a blur in that frame'. And that's the way Drago has always approached the game – the breathtaking speed of his potting delighting snooker audiences everywhere he plays.

At the 1985 Embassy World Championship both Steve Davis and Dennis Taylor finished their semi-final matches a full session early, leaving the organisers to fill an embarrassing gap for television and, more importantly, the paying customers who had been expecting to see the world's great players in action. So John Virgo, whose comic impressions of fellow players had made him a great favourite, stepped into the breach. So too did beaten semi-finalist Ray Reardon, who donned a false grey beard. And making up the trio was a young newcomer, Tony Drago, showing no hint of nerves despite the clowning from the two superstars in a session of fascinating exhibition play.

It should have been the most daunting of tasks for the tall, slim, curly-haired youngster. Yet Drago,

Malta's amateur champion, seemed perfectly at ease in the awesome surroundings of the Crucible Theatre. Having made an impressive impact on the amateur scene in Britain – earning nearly £10,000 in just 18 months – Tony now thrilled the watching millions with his lightning break-building.

However, it is quite possible that Drago might still be playing the one-table clubs of Malta, had it not been for Vic Harris, the Essex professional who was first to discover the exceptional talents of Steve Davis. Harris had been chosen for a London Select Team to play against Malta's finest prospects in Valetta, which is where he first set eyes on Drago. 'I played a frame against him and won easily', recalls Vic. 'He was so nervous, I suppose because I was a pro, but he played one particular shot in such a way that I knew he had talent'.

Tony Drago holds the record for completing the quickest frame in snooker. That was during the Fidelity Unit Trusts International in 1988 during a match with Danny Fowler. The frame lasted just three minutes.

QUICK POTTING

The following night, Harris called in on the youngster and played with him again: 'He was still very much on edge so I decided to smash the pack up and see what he could do. All of a sudden he snapped into gear and started slamming balls down all over the place', says Vic. 'He lacked discipline but I'd never seen anyone pot balls so quickly, not even Jimmy White or Alex Higgins'.

It was obvious to Harris that the 16-year-old needed to play in Britain to gain experience, and with the help of Maltese tour operator Carm Zerafa, Drago quickly became established on the circuit, returning home to win his national amateur championship from the great Paul Mifsud.

His long-striding action and sure-fire potting made him a great favourite in London, where he was now based. Yet he suffered disappointment when, as favourite, he failed to win the 1984 World Amateur Championship. Although consolation came in the form of a world-record 132 clearance in just over four minutes.

Drago's English improved rapidly and he turned

WORLD RANKINGS FROM 1983–4

SEASON	WORLD RANKING
1983–4	–
1984–5	–
1985–6	–
1986–7	37
1987–8	32
1988–9	20

professional in September 1985. However, like so many of today's youngsters in the professional ranks, he found it difficult to adjust to the pace. Even so, he did claim the notable scalps of Eddie Charlton and Mark Wildman in his first season.

In 1986, however, Tony came into his own with a spectacular run in the Tennents UK. He tore up the form book at Preston by toppling Rex Williams, John Virgo and Willie Thorne to earn a quarter-final tie against Steve Davis. It should have been easy for Davis, but Drago raced into a 3–0 lead, then held on as the defending champion took control. At 8–7 down Drago looked out of it, but he fired home a winning break to take a thrilling match to the last frame – only to miss a crucial final yellow which would almost certainly have carried him to victory.

That miss haunted him for nearly two seasons and it wasn't until the 1988 World Championship that he burst back into the limelight, hammering former champions Alex Higgins and Dennis Taylor to reach the quarter-finals. But Steve Davis proved too solid for the excitable 23-year-old Maltese player, who will need to curb his attacking ways if he is to make the most of the unpredictable talent which makes him such an exciting player to watch.

FACT·FILE

NAME: TONY DRAGO

DATE OF BIRTH: SEPTEMBER 22, 1965

BIRTHPLACE: VALETTA, MALTA

TURNED PROFESSIONAL: 1985

FIRST MAJOR WIN: NONE

BIGGEST PAY DAY: £14,250 FOR REACHING THE QUARTER-FINALS OF THE EMBASSY WORLD CHAMPIONSHIP, 1988

NEAL FOULDS

Neal Foulds is still in his mid-20s, but already the likeable Londoner has experienced both the ups and downs of life as a professional sportsman. Foulds, who turned pro in 1983, could do no wrong for two seasons as he leapt 20 places to No. 3 in the world rankings. After joining Barry Hearn's Matchroom team, he won his first major title in September 1986, beating Cliff Thorburn 12–9 in the final of the BCE International. 'I was delighted to repay the faith Barry had shown in me. Being a member of such an élite squad, I felt I had to do my bit', said Neal.

Neal Foulds was one of the most consistent players on the professional circuit during the 1986/87 season. He finished runner-up to Steve Davis in the Tennents UK Open, beaten 16–7 in the final, and runner-up to Jimmy White in the Dulux British Open, losing 13–9. He was also a semi-finalist in the Rothmans Grand Prix and Embassy World Championship.

But at Sheffield his superb season turned sour. He became embroiled in a drugs controversy after admitting he had been prescribed a type of beta-blocker by his doctor for a heart complaint. Beta-blockers may have been banned by the International Olympic Committee but Foulds was not breaking the rules of snooker as they stood at the time. Nor, as some suggested, was he seeking to gain an unfair advantage. On the contrary, he was merely protecting his own health.

'This Sick Joke', shouted the banner headline in one national newspaper. Doctors, MPs and the

Sports Council all had their say and it was claimed that players who took beta-blockers were cheating. Not surprisingly, the injustice of the situation and the adverse publicity that followed it, have had a lasting and detrimental effect on Foulds, who is a shy, retiring person.

Despite reaching the final of both the English Championship and Benson and Hedges Irish Masters, and earning £135,560 prize money, Foulds failed to live up to expectations in the 1987/88 season. His enjoyment of snooker had been tarnished by the controversy.

HEART PROBLEM

'What's more important – what people think, or your health? I didn't worry about snooker when the doctor told me I had a heart problem and needed to take tablets', he explained. The whole issue 'made me question whether it was (always) worth succeeding at something. Snooker is only a game – your family and home life have to come first. I have realised that there is more to life than snooker. It's still very important to me but it's not everything. I owe a debt to the game, but it's a job we all do', said Neal.

He went on to explain: 'I never dreamt I could play the level of snooker I did two seasons ago. Now I have come to terms with the fact that I may not be able to play so consistently well again in the future. But hopefully, after the bad times I have had, I will emerge as a better player and a better person for it'.

Sharing in both his triumphs and his torture has been father, Geoff, who has helped Neal cope with the pressures both on and off the table. Indeed, fellow professional Geoff had neglected his own game to help Neal reach the top, and father met son in the third round of the 1986 English Championship, with pupil beating tutor 9–4.

Neal Foulds practises at the Ealing Snooker Centre in West London – when he's not on the the telephone! British Telecom's best customer has been nicknamed 'Buzby' for the amount of time he spends on the phone. Away from the table, Foulds' favourite hobby is greyhound racing. He spends many an evening watching his dogs run at Wembley Stadium. Not surprisingly he has two different types of ambition – to win the World Championship – and the Greyhound Derby!

After winning his first major title in September, 1986, Neal said: 'Everyone says to themselves "I can win a tournament". But there's a big difference between thinking it and actually doing it'!

Neal Foulds and dad, Geoff, are the game's only father and son professionals. Geoff virtually forsook his own career to concentrate on getting Neal to the top.

Neal Foulds first started playing as an 11-year-old at Greenford Conservative Club. He used to wear glasses but now plays in contact lenses.

WORLD RANKINGS FROM 1983–4

SEASON	WORLD RANKING
1983–4	–
1984–5	30
1985–6	23
1986–7	13
1987–8	3
1988–9	3

FACT·FILE

NAME: NEAL ROBERT FOULDS

DATE OF BIRTH: JULY 13, 1963

BIRTHPLACE: PERIVALE, LONDON

TURNED PROFESSIONAL: 1983

FIRST MAJOR WIN: BCE INTERNATIONAL v CLIFF THORBURN, 1986 (12–9)

BIGGEST PAY DAY: £42,000 AS RUNNER-UP IN THE FINAL OF THE DULUX BRITISH OPEN, 1987 (INCLUDING A HIGHEST-BREAK PRIZE OF £6,000)

SILVINO FRANCISCO

As an unknown, Silvino Francisco reached the quarter-final of the Embassy World Professional Championship at the first attempt in 1982. Despite whitewashing Chris Ross and then beating Paddy Morgan 9–1 in the qualifying rounds, he was still quoted at 250–1 to win the title. Once at the Crucible he beat the seasoned campaigner Dennis Taylor 10–7, and then put out Dean Reynolds 13–8 before losing by the same score to Ray Reardon, that season's surprise finalist. But Francisco had done enough to make the leading players take note of his name.

Silvino's father was a Portuguese fisherman who moved to South Africa. He later bought a restaurant which had on the premises a couple of snooker tables on which the nine-year-old Silvino and his older brother Mannie (father of current professional Peter Francisco) spent many hours practising.

Both Mannie and Silvino became leading amateurs at biliards and snooker, and Mannie reached the final of the World Amateur Championship in consecutive years, 1971 (billiards) and 1972 (snooker), finishing second on each occasion. Silvino, on the other hand, never managed to reach such heights – his best World Amateur Championship result coming in 1976 in Johannesburg when, after beating Mannie 5 – 1, he went on to the semi-final before losing to the eventual winner, Doug Mountjoy, 8 – 2.

However, Silvino had ambitions of turning professional, which he did in 1978 shortly after winning his fourth South African amateur title, while Mannie turned his attentions away from the billiard table to the bowling green.

MOVE TO BRITAIN

Eventually, Silvino made the decision to quit his job with an oil company and move to Britain in order to play snooker full-time. He did that during the 1982/83 season and, after his tremendous performance in reaching the quarter-finals of his first World Championship, he got a job the following summer working the Pontin's circuit, which enabled him to play snooker and get paid for it. It was something he had always dreamed of!

In his early days as a leading amateur in South Africa, Silvino worked as a table fitter for Thurston's. There can't be many current professionals capable of erecting a table and then knocking in a century break on it!

Silvino Francisco, away from the snooker table, enjoys scuba diving and fishing and he once sold oil for a living.

Based in the Chesterfield area, Silvino started making significant inroads into the professional game. He reached the semi-final of the Jameson International in 1984, where he lost to Tony Knowles. And later that season he made it to his first ranking final, when wins over Jimmy White, Tony Meo and Alex Higgins pitched him in the Dulux British Open final against Kirk Stevens. Both men were looking for their first major success and the honour fell to Silvino, who won 12–9. The win earned him a £50,000 first prize, a perfect wedding present for the South African and Denise, his bride of less than two months. But sadly, the final left a sour taste in the mouths of both players and generated considerable adverse publicity for the game itself.

After the match, Silvino accused Stevens in the tabloid press of having played whilst under the influence of an illegal stimulant. For such a claim he was fined a record £6,000 by the WPBSA and had

WORLD RANKINGS FROM 1983–4

SEASON	WORLD RANKING
1983–4	21
1984–5	17
1985–6	13
1986–7	12
1987–8	10
1988–9	12

two ranking points deducted, although Stevens later admitted he was addicted to cocaine, and the fine was reduced.

Francisco proved that he is strong enough to evercome the enormous media attention thrust upon him. A large part of his Dulux winnings was spent on building an extension to the Francisco household. The extra space was needed to house Silvino's own snooker table, and the many hours practising on his own helped Silvino develop a part of his game which he felt was weak – that is his safety play. Gradually he became an extremely tough competitor and a very hard player to beat.

It was the Dulux win that elevated him into the top 16 for the first time, and his new-found consistency has kept him there ever since – although he is still awaiting another major final. Unfortunately, the Stevens affair affected his game for some time, but in 1986/87 he enjoyed one of his best seasons ever, moving up the rankings to No. 10 after a semi-final appearance in the Rothmans Grand Prix and a quarter-final appearance in the Mercantile Credit Classic. Undoubtedly, there is much more to come from this talented South African.

FACT·FILE

NAME: SILVINO FRANCISCO

DATE OF BIRTH: MAY 3, 1946

BIRTHPLACE: CAPE TOWN, SOUTH AFRICA

TURNED PROFESSIONAL: 1978

FIRST MAJOR WIN: DULUX BRITISH OPEN v KIRK STEVENS, 1985 (12–9)

BIGGEST PAY DAY: £50,000 FOR WINNING THE DULUX BRITISH OPEN, 1985

TERRY GRIFFITHS

Terry Griffiths had set his heart on taking part in the 1979 World Amateur Championship in Malta, but Steve Newbury put paid to those plans by beating him in the Welsh Amateur Championship. So instead, Griffiths turned professional. In his first major professional tournament, the Coral UK Championship, he led Rex Williams 8–2 and needed just one more frame for a major upset, but the occasion got the better of him and he lost 9–8. However, in the next tournament, the World Championship at the Crucible, he took the snooker world by storm and, instead of capturing the world amateur crown as he had dreamt of, he became professional champion of the world.

Terry Griffiths had to get through the qualifying competition before beating three former finalists on his way to the 1979 World Championship final against Dennis Taylor. First he disposed of Perrie Mans 13–8, then Alex Higgins 13–12, followed by Eddie Charlton 19–17 – the latter in a tense and hard-fought semi-final clash that went on until the early hours of the morning. After which, Terry, when asked how he felt about his victory, uttered those immortal words in that broad Welsh accent of his: 'I'm in the final now, you know'!

In that final, Griffiths overcame his current Matchroom stablemate, and the man who was to win the Championship six years later, Dennis Taylor, 24–16, to capture the title at the first attempt – and all because Steve Newbury had knocked him out of the

Welsh Amateur Championship a few months earlier!

Although a former school mate of Welsh international rugby players Derek Quinnell and Phil Bennett, it was to the green baize that Terry turned his attentions. He started playing snooker in his home town of Llanelli, and soon captured the local under-16 championship. But he didn't take up the game seriously until he was 25, and that was only after a succession of jobs as a postman, miner, bus conductor and insurance agent.

However, as we have already seen, the decision to turn professional was quickly vindicated, and before 1979 was out Terry had added a second world title when he was in the Welsh team, along with Doug Mountjoy and Ray Reardon, which won the inaugural World Cup.

BEATING THE BOGEYMAN

Further success was soon to follow, with Terry completing a Benson and Hedges double in 1980, when he won the English and Irish Masters – beating Alex Higgins 9–5 and Doug Mountjoy 9–8 respectively. Then in 1982 Terry won the Lada Classic when he beat Steve Davis 9–8 in a great final. Victory was particularly sweet for Griffiths because up until then Davis had been his bogeyman. The two men had been deadly rivals, but the best of friends. And later that year they were to become team mates when Terry joined Barry Hearn.

Terry, wife Annette and the two boys, Darren and Wayne, still live in Llanelli. In 1987 Terry opened his own luxury snooker club in the town. Seen regularly practising on one of the tables is son Wayne, who in 1987 won the Llanelli Championship. Griffiths said afterwards: 'I've never been so chuffed in all my life, not even winning the World Championship'.

If 1979 was Terry's first memorable year then 1982 was certainly the second. First he beat Steve Davis 9–5 in the final of the Benson and Hedges Irish Masters, and then in the final of the Coral UK Championship he was involved in one of the sport's great matches – finally overcoming Alex Higgins 16–15 at the Guild Hall in Preston.

After a leaner period, Terry went on to win the Welsh Professional Championship in 1985, and in 1986 he beat Kirk Stevens to capture the BCE Belgian Classic.

WORLD RANKINGS FROM 1983–4

SEASON	WORLD RANKING
1983–4	9
1984–5	8
1985–6	8
1986–7	10
1987–8	6
1988–9	5

The snooker world then saw a revitalised Griffiths in 1988 – notably at the Crucible, where he came so close to emulating his performance of nine years earlier. But it was that man Davis once again who proved to be too great a stumbling block. After beating Lancastrian Steve Longworth 10–1 in the opening round, Griffiths then eliminated Willie Thorne, Neal Foulds and Jimmy White before losing 18–11 to Davis in the final.

Having been knocked out of the Embassy by Davis five times in eight years, Griffiths was quick to point out that: 'It takes the pressure off a bit when Steve's in the other half of the draw'. But in the end there was no avoiding him, and Davis made it six wins in nine years!

Today, Griffiths is one of the most consistent players on the circuit and he acknowledges the emergence of youngsters in the game. 'I'm going to be a threat next year', he said after reaching the 1988 Embassy final, but added: 'Then again, a hell of a lot of players are going to be a threat'.

FACT·FILE

NAME: TERENCE MARTIN GRIFFITHS

DATE OF BIRTH: OCTOBER 16, 1947

BIRTHPLACE: LLANELLI, DYFED

TURNED PROFESSIONAL: 1978

FIRST MAJOR WIN: EMBASSY WORLD CHAMPIONSHIP v DENNIS TAYLOR, 1978 (24–16)

BIGGEST PAY DAY: £57,000 AS RUNNER-UP IN THE EMBASSY WORLD CHAMPIONSHIP, 1988

MIKE HALLETT

Mike Hallett has emerged as a player to be reckoned with in recent seasons. But he has also found it hard to shake off that 'Nearly Man' tag. Hallett, who turned professional in 1979, earned a reputation for upsetting the big name players but failing to follow it through. Thus he beat Steve Davis 5–2 in the second round of the 1983 Professional Players Tournament, shocked defending champion Dennis Taylor 10–6 in the first round of the 1986 Embassy World Championship, and put out Tony Knowles 10–6 at the same stage in Sheffield the following year. But it wasn't until 1988 that he broke through to win his first singles title.

Mike Hallett took up snooker at the age of ten and went on to win many amateur tournaments, including the 1978 British Junior Championship. A shipping clerk when he left school, Mike also collected a string of pro-am titles, played for England on many occasions and in 1978, as a senior, reached the quarter-finals of the English Amateur Championship.

In 1987, the Grimsby pro, partnered by Stephen Hendry, won the Fosters World Doubles by defeating Dennis Taylor and Cliff Thorburn 12 – 8, having lost to Davis and Tony Meo in the final the previous year. Yet that first individual success still eluded him, something with which Steve Davis had a lot to do.

The world No. 1 hammered Mike 9 – 3 in the semi-finals of the 1987 Fidelity Unit Trusts International, then whitewashed the hapless Hallett 9–0 when he reached his first major final, the 1988 Benson and Hedges Masters. It was a nightmare ending to a dream Wembley début for Hallett, who had beaten Dennis Taylor in the first round, Alex Higgins in the quarter-finals, and then pulled off an incredible 6–5 semi-final victory against John Parrott – Mike having required five snookers during the deciding frame, still leaving him 41 points behind with only the colours remaining!

Hallett had the misfortune to come up against Davis again in the second round of the 1988 Embassy World Championship. He managed to win a frame this time – but only one – as he crashed to a 13–1 defeat.

NO MERCY

Stephen Hendry, Hallett's Cuemasters stable-mate, showed him little more mercy in the final of the MIM Britannia British Open, romping home to an easy 13–2 victory. It was another shattering blow to the confidence Hallett had built up by reaching four finals – the Australian Masters and New Zealand Masters being the other two – and confidence is a key part of his game.

A brilliant potter and fluent break-builder, Hallett said as he started the 1988–89 campaign: 'I had such a good 1987–88 season, I just expected the ball to keep rolling. I probably didn't put as much work in. I expected to get through a few matches on ability alone and it didn't turn out that way. I find it very difficult to motivate myself on the practice table'.

Despite that admission, Hallett has become more professional on and off the table since linking up with Ian Doyle, the shrewd businessman who also manages Stephen Hendry and John Parrott. 'Before I joined Ian, I would go home and play golf for a few weeks whenever I got knocked out of a tournament early on', he said. 'Now the golf clubs are gathering dust in the garage. I have such a busy schedule that there is no time to sulk about the last tournament. That's a compliment to Ian'.

Hallett earned close on £150,000 in prize money during the 1987–88 season – more than treble the amount he won the previous season. Little wonder then that he lists Doyle as the man he most admires! And his more professional approach is beginning to pay off in other ways: Mike finally captured his first singles title in 1988 – even if it was only in the Fosters Professional Tournament, a four-man invitation event. He beat Stephen Hendry 8–5 in the final and there was a wide smile of relief as he established himself as a winner for the first time.

Mike Hallett left school to work as a shipping clerk before becoming a snooker professional in 1979.

Mike Hallett had to wait ten years before winning his first major title – the English Professional Championship – with a 9–7 defeat of John Parrott in 1989.

Mike Hallett won the very last Foster's World Doubles title together with his great friend Stephen Hendry.

WORLD RANKINGS FROM 1983–4

SEASON	WORLD RANKING
1983–4	32
1984–5	25
1985–6	28
1986–7	27
1987–8	16
1988–9	9

FACT·FILE

NAME: MICHAEL WILLIAM HALLETT

DATE OF BIRTH: JULY 6, 1959

BIRTHPLACE: GRIMSBY, HUMBERSIDE

TURNED PROFESSIONAL: 1979

FIRST MAJOR WIN: FOSTER'S WORLD DOUBLES (WITH STEPHEN HENDRY) v DENNIS TAYLOR AND CLIFF THORBURN, 1978 (12–8)

BIGGEST PAY DAY: £36,000 AS RUNNER-UP IN THE MIM BRITANNIA BRITISH OPEN, 1988

STEPHEN HENDRY

20-year-old Stephen Hendry has not changed much since winning his first major championship. As a kid en route to the Rothmans Grand Prix title in 1987, he played conkers – but now it is the cueball that seems to be on a string! Undoubtedly, the Bonnie Prince of the green baize was born to be a snooker king. Since notching up a 50 break within weeks of his dad buying him a mini-table, some eight Christmases ago, young Stephen has seldom ceased to make men gasp at his prodigious talent – or women want to cuddle him!

Even now, as he challenges the great Steve Davis for the top spot on one of sport's toughest ladders of supremacy, there is still enough of the cherub in Stephen Hendry to suggest that conkers might be the limit of his combativeness. But as false appearances go that one takes some beating! Looking the innocent in this cruel game has undoubtedly lured many an unsuspecting opponent into believing they could teach the wee Scots laddie a thing or two about a man's game. Yet it has been the boy from South Queensferry who has invariably dished out the canings.

At 18 he was the youngest player to win a professional title – the 1987 Rothmans – and this was followed by the coveted British Open crown in 1988. But perhaps even more memorable was the drubbing he gave Steve Davis in the semi-final of the Tennents UK Open later that year. Displaying a sublime blend of the champion's precision and Jimmy White's panache, Hendry barely allowed

Davis a visit to the table in a brilliant exhibition that had some observers swearing they had witnessed snooker's act of succession.

And though it is really still too early to be absolutely sure – complacency brought about his downfall in the UK final against Doug Mountjoy two days after his victory over Davis – there are a few around who doubt that when snooker's undisputed crown is eventually passed on, it will be placed on the fair head of the Scot. The belief that Hendry has long ceased to be the young pretender was given further substance by his victory in the Benson and Hedges Masters, in January 1989.

Since first appearing on Junior Pot Black, as a tiny 14-year-old barely able to see over the table, the burden of 'infant prodigy' has inevitably been thrust upon his slender shoulders. In winning the Scottish Under-16 title the same year, the weight of those expectations increased, but did not prevent him becoming the youngest Scottish amateur champion the following season.

Stephen Hendry became the youngest winner of the Scottish amateur title at 15. At 16 he was the sport's youngest professional.

Astutely managed by Ian Doyle, a Stirling entrepreneur, Hendry has paced his rise to the top in the same meticulous manner with which he builds his breaks – quietly and without fuss, but with a lot of style.

Doyle has always believed in letting Stephen take a few knocks 'in order to learn', and it was from one of these that Hendry probably learned the most important lesson of his career. After a 6–0 series whitewash at the hands of Steve Davis, in January 1987, Doyle wondered if he had made the greatest mistake of his life. 'I knew Stephen would lose', he recalls, 'but I had not allowed for his attitude – he had really wanted to win and was very down when he lost. I was a bit concerned, but then he said to me, quite matter-of-factly: 'I know how to beat Davis'. Not even Doyle would argue with him now.

WORLD DOUBLES TITLE

Stephen leapt up the rankings, so that at the start of the 1987/88 season he was No. 4 – behind only Davis, White and Foulds – and had managed to avoid most of the pitfalls that all too frequently ensnare aspiring sportsmen. That is a tribute to the Doyle discipline, the help he has received from his pal and Cuemaster colleague, Mike Hallett – with whom he won the World Doubles title in 1987 – and to Stephen's own ability to be Mr. Cool in the cauldron of a televised tournament. 'It's strange', says the Scot, 'I don't feel the pressure at snooker yet I shook like a leaf at my driving test'.

As controlled in the press conferences as he is with his cue, Hendry shows a maturity beyond his years and, if his personality is still to blossom, it must be remembered that he has had to handle the break-up of his parents' marriage in addition to having fame and fortune thrust upon him at a tender age.

That 'Spike' is accepted as 'one of the boys' on the circuit is not only down to his pure genius on the table. Statements like: 'Whoever the next world champion is, he won't reign as long as Davis', suggest modesty and an equilibrium still intact – which is something for a young lad of whom coaching guru Frank Callan says: 'I can teach him nothing – the lad's got it all'. Indeed – and he's pretty good at conkers too!

WORLD RANKINGS FROM 1983–4

SEASON	WORLD RANKING
1983–4	–
1984–5	–
1985–6	–
1986–7	51
1987–8	23
1988–9	4

FACT·FILE

NAME: STEPHEN GORDON HENDRY

DATE OF BIRTH: JANUARY 13, 1969

BIRTHPLACE: EDINBURGH

TURNED PROFESSIONAL: 1985

FIRST MAJOR WIN: CANADA DRY SCOTTISH CHAMPIONSHIP v MATT GIBSON, 1986 (10–5)

BIGGEST PAY DAY: £68,000 FOR WINNING THE BENSON AND HEDGES MASTERS, 1989 (INCLUDING A HIGHEST-BREAK PRIZE OF £6,000)

ALEX HIGGINS

Alex Higgins, the mercurial Irishman who changed the face of snooker after winning the World Championship in 1972, can do no wrong in the eyes of his legion of admirers. Domestic dramas, public rows and punch-ups – they seem never ending, but Higgins takes them all in his stride and carries on with what he does best. Whilst that best comes sporadically these days, Alex remains a prime attraction on the circuit, and tournament sponsors are always grateful when the Hurricane blows into town looking for action on the green baize.

From the moment he went to live in Blackburn in the late '60s it was obvious Alex Higgins was something special. Brash, money-match challenges to the great John Spencer, then regarded as the finest player around, were accepted, and the skinny Irish kid soon built up a following.

Even as a raw amateur he attracted big crowds to the Benarth Club in Blackburn. 'Kids would come up to the hall simply to watch him play', recalls one of the partners in the club. 'He was their hero because they'd never seen anyone pot balls so quickly'. Neither had John McLaughlin or Jack Leeming, the men destined to be his first managers. When they saw him galloping around the table, potting balls in a blur, they promptly dubbed him 'Hurricane' – and the legend was born.

Higgins turned pro in 1971, and promptly won the Irish Championship from Jack Rea. From that platform he launched his first assault on the World Championship, beating such greats of the day as

John Pulman and Rex Williams, before going on to topple John Spencer 37–32 in a titanic 1972 final.

For all his brilliance, however, the flamboyant Ulsterman was to spend another decade battling for snooker's richest prize. When he did regain it, in 1982, amid scenes of tears and laughter, he declared: 'Now I can die happy' – though he actually followed up with a spectacular 16–15 success against Steve Davis in the 1983 Coral UK final, coming back from 7–0 down! But more recently Higgins hasn't really hit the headlines for the right reasons.

A HEAVY FINE

Alex's first world title earned him just £480 – a fraction of the £12,000 he was fined for, among other offences, head-butting tournament director Paul Hatherell during the 1986 Tennents UK Open at Preston. This incident also earned him a five-tournament ban, and even he would admit that his game has never been quite the same since then.

Higgins very nearly died after toppling some 22 feet from a flat window in January 1989. But, just as he has done on the snooker table so often in his turbulent career, Alex made a remarkable recovery, and was hopping about after a few days with nothing more than a fractured ankle and stitches in his head!

When he turned up for the 1986 Mercantile Credit Classic at Warrington, sporting a black eye and spouting a cock-and-bull story about falling off a horse, the press and public laughed it off. Then, a day later, when he came clean and confessed that he'd actually been socked by a fellow-pro during a private argument, it merely added to the legend.

When his private life, including the break-up of his six-year marriage to wife Lynn, was laid bare to the public in the pages of the popular press, it inspired a greater degree of sympathy than criticism. And when, in October 1988, he found a glimmer of his best form to battle his way through to the Rothmans final, the crowd loved him even more. That he went down to Davis mattered little, and Alex even went on to rescue the after-match banquet following the departure of the world champion in an incident sparked off by a domestic dispute between the sponsors and the Matchroom group.

So, controversy is never far away. But what makes him tick? Who knows? He is highly-strung, fuelled by nervous energy and remains, despite his decline in world snooker, the most popular player of all. That's not to denigrate Steve Davis, Dennis Taylor and the sport's other gentlemen. They will always provide high class, value-for-money entertainment. But with Higgins, the fans don't necessarily want to see century breaks – although they are always welcome!

Some may be misguided and come to see him lose his temper, perhaps pick a fight or even storm out in a huff. But it doesn't happen – Higgins is the supreme entertainer. He doesn't do trick shots like Steve, tell jokes like Dennis or do impressions like John Virgo. 'My job is snooker and that's what I give them', he says. Which perhaps best explains his rapport with the crowd: when he twitches, so do his fans; when he misses a vital pot, so do they, and when he wins, they can't wait to share victory with him.

WORLD RANKINGS FROM 1983–4

SEASON	WORLD RANKING
1983–4	5
1984–5	9
1985–6	9
1986–7	6
1987–8	9
1988–9	17

FACT·FILE

NAME: ALEXANDER GORDON HIGGINS

DATE OF BIRTH: MARCH 18, 1949

BIRTHPLACE: BELFAST

TURNED PROFESSIONAL: 1971

FIRST MAJOR WIN: WORLD CHAMPIONSHIP v JOHN SPENCER, 1972 (37–32)

BIGGEST PAY DAY: £39,000 AS RUNNER-UP IN THE ROTHMANS GRAND PRIX, 1988

JOE JOHNSON

There's a saying in boxing: 'Nice guys don't win fights'. If the same applied in snooker then Joe Johnson would never have been world champion in 1986. But he was, and what's more his win over Steve Davis gave heart to many other professionals. Born and bred in Bradford, Johnson has never forgotten his roots. He loves the people of the West Yorkshire city and they love him – his World Championship success coming at a time when, following the Bradford City Football Club fire, the city was nearing the end of the worst 12 months in its history.

Joe Johnson was a good player long before he stunned Steve Davis and won the world title. He had reached the final of the World Amateur Championship in 1978, before losing to current Welsh professional Cliff Wilson. And for many years Joe was the holder of the world record break by an amateur player, after compiling a 140 at the Middlesbrough TUC in 1978.

This latter achievement was covered by Tyne Tees television cameras although, funnily enough, playing in front of the TV cameras always seemed to hold a mental block for Joe. He maintained that the lights put him off, and appeared to confirm that when he beat such eminent players as Tony Meo, Jimmy White, Eddie Charlton and Cliff Thorburn to reach his first major final, the Professional Players' Tournament at Bristol's Redwood Lodge in 1983 . . . it was not a televised event!

In that final, against Tony Knowles, Joe came back from 6 – 1 down before finally losing 9 – 8, but not until he had compiled a championship best break of 135. Some time after that, he reached the semi-final of the 1985 Mercantile Credit Classic, before losing 9–2 to Cliff Thorburn – a performance that helped to lift Joe into the top 16 for the first time.

WORLD CHAMPION

At the end of the 1985/86 season, after only twice reaching the Crucible stage of the World Championship, but never progressing beyond that point, Johnson became the new darling of the Sheffield fans – his spats were also a big hit! First- and second-round wins over Dave Martin and Mike Hallett were followed by a classic 13–12 quarter-final success over Terry Griffiths, and in the semi-final he disposed of Tony Knowles 16–8 with relative ease. The final itself was easier than Johnson could have imagined, as he ran out an 18–12 winner over Davis – this down-to-earth Yorkshireman celebrating his success with a pint of lager with his friends at the Morley Snooker Centre near Bradford. There was no champagne and caviar for Joe Johnson!

Less than a week before the first anniversary of the appalling Valley Parade fire tragedy, Joe Johnson warmed the hearts of West Yorkshire people by lifting the world crown. It was little consolation for those who had lost loved ones in the tragedy. But those who know Joe knew that his win was not for himself, but was for the people of Bradford.

Joe was a great world champion, but sadly his success looked like being his downfall. Keen to share his glory with the many people who helped and supported him over the years, he undertook dozens of exhibitions and attended numerous charity functions. But this had disastrous consequences. His game fell apart, and the following season he suffered one defeat after another. By the time the World Championship came around again, Johnson was the last person pencilled in as a title contender.

But how wrong the pundits were. After a nervy 10–9 win over Eugene Hughes in the first round, life was slightly easier against Murdo Mcleod. But then came Stephen Hendry. The young Scot was favourite, despite Johnson being the defending champion. What a battle it was: Johnson led 8–1 but Hendry came back at him before Joe clung on for a terrific 13–12 win.

After that the semi-final against Neal Foulds was much easier, Johnson winning 16–9, and suddenly he found himself in the Crucible's first ever repeat final. Sadly for Joe, what was not repeated was the result, but at least he had the consolation of taking more frames off Davis – 14 – than Davis had taken off him the previous year.

Generous in defeat, he said afterwards: 'At 13–14 I was in with a chance but it would have been a travesty if I'd levelled and somehow gone past him'.

The up-and-coming Steve James ended Johnson's ambition of a hat-trick of final appearances in 1988 but, despite that, Joe managed to maintain his position amongst the élite top 16 of the game.

Success has never gone to his head. He remembers the days when he used to be a trainee mechanic and then a pipe layer. To be able to play snooker and get paid for it – Joe will always be the first to tell you what a great feeling that is.

WORLD RANKINGS FROM 1983–4

SEASON	WORLD RANKING
1983–4	23
1984–5	19
1985–6	16
1986–7	8
1987–8	5
1988–9	11

FACT·FILE

NAME: JOSEPH JOHNSON

DATE OF BIRTH: JULY 29, 1952

BIRTHPLACE: BRADFORD, WEST YORKSHIRE

TURNED PROFESSIONAL: 1979

FIRST MAJOR WIN: EMBASSY WORLD CHAMPIONSHIP v STEVE DAVIS, 1986 (18-12)

BIGGEST PAY DAY: £70,000 FOR WINNING THE EMBASSY WORLD CHAMPIONSHIP, 1986

TONY KNOWLES

Tony Knowles looked every inch a world champion when he thrashed defending title-holder Steve Davis 10–1 in the first round of the 1982 World Championship, before going on to reach the quarter-finals of the competition. It was regarded as the biggest upset in snooker history and when the Bolton player, who turned professional in 1979, clinched his first major title, the Jameson International, a few months later, his future seemed assured. Tall, dark, handsome and with skill in abundance, Tony had all the qualifications to be snooker's No. 1 pin-up . . . but controversy was to follow.

Just twelve months after that astounding 10–1 win, it seemed almost certain that Tony Knowles would again have the opportunity to impose his will on Steve Davis – this time in the World Championship final. But in the semi-final, when in a very strong position, Tony missed a simple, vital pink which allowed Cliff Thorburn to save the frame and go through at his expense. However, undaunted by this disappointment, Knowles went on to secure the now-defunct Professional Players' Championship six months later, and the jigsaw began to fall into place once more.

But then he spoiled it – or rather, a colourful account of his lurid womanising in a national newspaper did, just before the 1984 World Championship. It hardly enhanced his reputation as a snooker player . . . although the legion of female admirers he had already built up were made of tougher stuff!

The WPBSA, furious that televison's fastest-growing sport had been cheapened, fined him a record £5,000. Compared to today's scandals, the kiss-and-tell memoirs of an unattached youngster in the public eye seem tame. But they served as a severe blow to his pride and to his game, which evaporated.

From world No. 2, he slipped down the rankings, yet managed to earn enough points each season to retain a top ten position. Then the second bombshell dropped. A jilted girlfriend joined the list of those ready to sell their secrets, but Knowles was vigorous in his denials and, sensibly, maintained a discreet profile for the next 12 months.

FURIOUS ROW

Gradually, through sheer hard work, he regained the cutting edge that his game had been lacking. It was not enough to get back on the title-winning trail, but it was good enough to beat all but the best. And he certainly displayed his maturity in the 1988 Benson and Hedges Masters at Wembley when his stablemate Alex Higgins picked a furious row during their match.

Knowles had been in full control, holding a 3–1 lead, when the Irishman complained to the referee that his opponent was putting him off by standing in his line of vision. Knowles regarded the move as sheer gamesmanship, and when the row spilled over into the interval, the Wembley tournament director was called in to act as peacemaker. Unfortunately, Knowles fell apart, losing 5–4, but confined his remarks to saying: 'You all saw what happened out there'. Later, in private, he admitted: 'I should have taken him straight out of the arena and put a stop to his antics there and then, but it all happened so quickly that I was caught off guard'. Nevertheless, for the first time in his career, Knowles became seen as the aggrieved party, and his stock went up considerably, both inside the game and with the fans.

Tony Knowles displayed exceptional ability from an early age – twice winning the British Junior Championship. And when he won the still-prestigious Pontin's Open, and was voted Player of the Series while appearing for England in the Home Internationals at Prestatyn in North Wales, a place among the professionals seemed his for the taking.

The founder-member of Howard Kruger's Framework organisation, Knowles is still regarded as snooker's top pin-up, but these days he keeps his private life just that. And for all the scandal, he has done exceptionally well from snooker. The likeable Lancastrian has a snooker centre in the middle of Horwich, on the outskirts of his native Bolton, as well as several properties, including a beautifully-appointed house on the banks of Lake Windermere where he indulges in his twin passions – the great outdoors and water-skiing.

Today his snooker house is in order and Tony is convinced that there are many good years left in him at the top. Season after season be confounds his critics by securing valuable ranking points with his fast, fluent potting style. He cares very deeply about the game – and has an uncanny ability to replay shots and incidents years after they have taken place – and the only ambition left to him is that elusive world title. With his renewed hunger for snooker, who is to say he can't pull it off?

WORLD RANKINGS FROM 1983–4

SEASON	WORLD RANKING
1983–4	4
1984–5	2
1985–6	3
1986–7	4
1987–8	7
1988–9	8

FACT·FILE

NAME: ANTHONY KNOWLES

DATE OF BIRTH: JUNE 13, 1955

BIRTHPLACE: BOLTON, LANCASHIRE

TURNED PROFESSIONAL: 1980

FIRST MAJOR WIN: JAMESON INTERNATIONAL v DAVID TAYLOR, 1982 (9–6)

BIGGEST PAY DAY: £21,000 FOR REACHING THE SEMI-FINALS OF THE EMBASSY WORLD CHAMPIONSHIP, 1986

TONY MEO

The words of the master of ceremonies rang out around the Spa Grand Hall in Scarborough – 'Please welcome Tony Meo, British Open champion'. The applause was warm and prolonged as the little left-hander emerged, smiling, from behind a curtain to take on Terry Griffiths in a Matchroom League fixture on the evening of March 6, 1989. On the surface, it was a routine sort of occasion – a bread and butter League fixture away from the pressures of the big-money, televised ranking tournaments. But it was a moment to cherish for Anthony Christian Meo. After nine-and-a-half years on the switchback of professional snooker he had finally arrived as a true champion.

Just 24 hours before his match against Terry Griffiths, the dapper South Londoner with the Italian name was drowning himself, his family and friends in a sea of champagne and tears in a Derby hotel, as he savoured the sweetest moment of a career which had up to then seen far too many sour disappointments. Indeed, Meo had made his great breakthrough just as he appeared to be on the slippery slope to oblivion. After sliding out of the top 16, he was standing a lowly 31st in the rankings when he burst back into the frame in a memorable fortnight of snooker that will live in his memory for the rest of his life.

After seemingly hitting rock bottom just a few weeks earlier, when an administrative mix-up led to him arriving late for his match against David Roe in the European Open at Deauville, being penalised two games and 'inevitably' losing 5–1, Tony managed to turn fortune on its head by playing like a man inspired at the championship in Derby. He convincingly knocked out the holder Stephen Hendry, came back from the dead to pip Mike Hallett 9–8 in the semi-final and then crushed Dean Reynolds 13–6 in the final, to take his first major ranking title.

The £70,000 winner's cheque from the sponsors, Anglian Windows, was easily the biggest pay day of Meo's career. But the money was incidental. What mattered was the glory, plus the recognition and respect that he earned from everyone inside and outside the game.

RECOGNITION AT LAST

Recognition is something Meo had been striving to achieve for what must have seemed like an eternity. Despite winning more than his fair share of trophies over the years, there always seemed to be a catch. He was supposed to have a brittle temperament, a lack of confidence and was short of 'bottle'. And it must be said that Tony had made some statements which he bitterly regrets – notably his 'I'm a born loser' comment after losing to John Parrott in the 1986 World Championship. That, and his infamous miss on the yellow as he was clearing the colours for what would have been a glorious 9–8 victory over Steve Davis in the 1984 Lada Classic final at Warrington, gave his critics just the ammunition they were looking for.

When Tony won the Australian Masters he heard the murmurs: 'Well, it's only a little overseas tournament'. Then, when he won the World Doubles, the talk was: 'Well, of course, he was partnering Davis and the great man carried him'. And when he won the English Championship for the first time in 1986, beating Davis in the semi-final and Neal Foulds in the final, it was said: 'Well, it's not a ranking tournament and anyway, Davis probably wasn't trying'. Even after retaining the English title in 1987 – by beating outsider Les Dodd in a scrappy final – a couple of journalists gave him some stick!

When Tony failed to deliver in ranking events and paid the price, those who knew him well did not doubt his ability. The young man who had grown up with Jimmy White and used to match him, long pot for long pot, in their tearaway teenage days, had not suddenly become a bad player – he had just lost his confidence.

Significantly, Barry Hearn had been quick to defuse any doubts about Meo's future with the success-orientated Matchroom team when he lost his top 16 spot, declaring: 'When you sign a player – and a friend – nothing changes, whatever happens'. The grin on Hearn's face when Meo collected the magnificent Anglian Windows British Open trophy stretched from ear to ear.

On the flight back from the debâcle in Deauville, Tony wondered if it was possible to get any lower. 'Sitting on that plane, I really thought about packing up', he recalled. 'I felt terrible. But no doubt my manager Barry Hearn would have talked me out of it. Now I've got everything to look forward to, including the most important thing of all, belief in myself.'

WORLD RANKINGS FROM 1983–4

SEASON	WORLD RANKING
1983–4	15
1984–5	10
1985–6	10
1986–7	11
1987–8	20
1988–9	31

FACT·FILE

NAME: ANTHONY CHRISTIAN MEO

DATE OF BIRTH: OCTOBER 4, 1959

BIRTHPLACE: HAMPSTEAD, LONDON

TURNED PROFESSIONAL: 1979

FIRST MAJOR WIN: HOFMEISTER WORLD DOUBLES (WITH STEVE DAVIS) V TERRY GRIFFITHS AND DOUG MOUNTJOY, 1982 (13–2)

BIGGEST PAY DAY: £70,000 FOR WINNING THE ANGLIAN WINDOWS BRITISH OPEN, 1989

DOUG MOUNTJOY

Doug Mountjoy does not believe in reincarnation – not in snooker, anyway. Not even the overwhelming 'evidence' of his two consecutive titles after half a decade in the doldrums can convince him. 'I am rebuilt rather than reborn', he insists, as he pays yet another tribute to the man responsible for the reconstruction. After dropping out of the world's top 16 in February 1988, Mountjoy was willing to admit that: 'My game was in pieces'. But then he went to Frank Callan, who has done for the 46-year-old Welshman what Superglue might have achieved for Humpty Dumpty.

By the winter of 1988, the future for this former miner looked as gloomy as that of a disused coalfield, and he had already begun to contemplate life in one of the sport's lower seams. 'I was starting to wonder if I could live at the other end of the ladder', Doug admits. Then he spent an afternoon with the 'guru' Frank Callan – and the rest is modern snooker history.

'I learned more in that three hours than I had done in the previous 34 years', he said. 'It's amazing what Frank knows about the game'. But whilst ample praise has been heaped upon the bespectacled Lancastrian, it ought to be remembered that his star pupil was always a natural.

Born in Tir-y-Berth in the Rhymney Valley, he became Junior Valley Champion at the age of 15, and by the time he joined his dad down the mine a year later, he was one of the best players in South Wales. But career prospects in snooker during the decline of the '60s were limited, to say the least –

there being only three or four professionals in the game – and Doug did not entertain the almost unthinkable gamble of playing snooker as a trade.

But then a bet of the more familiar kind led him towards the promised land. 'I used to back horses', he explains, 'and when I won £36 – quite a bit in those days – I decided to take the missus and kids to Pontins for a week'. There, while wife Yvonne introduced young Andrew and Yvette to the delights of the holiday camp, Doug enjoyed himself on the green baize. Playing in the snooker tournament, and receiving 25 points per frame from John Spencer, the holidaying Welshman became the first amateur to win a £1,000 first prize!

WORLD AMATEUR CROWN

Two years later, after winning the Welsh title for the second time and collecting the world amateur crown in Johannesburg, Mountjoy turned pro. He said: 'I was given an ultimatum by my firm. It was either them or snooker, so I packed up work . . . and as soon as I turned pro doors seemed to open for me, I was one of the lucky ones'.

> 'I just didn't feel I had anything to offer the game', he says, 'and was having a terrible time. But once I'd started to understand Frank Callan's methods, I lost my fear. Very quickly, I realized what could be done and though I was yet to do it on the table, deep down, I began to feel superior.'

Luck was certainly on his side when a late invitation to the '77 Benson and Hedges Masters at the Drury Lane Theatre launched his career in the best possible manner. A semi-final win over Alex Higgins was followed by a 7–6 victory over compatriot, Ray Reardon. And appearances in the quarter-finals of the World Championship and the final of the Super Crystalate UK Open of that year, consolidated a marvellous start to the paid ranks.

The UK title fell to him the following year, along with the Benson and Hedges Irish Masters and – as a member of the Welsh squad – the World Team trophy. Now an established star, Mountjoy played the burgeoning circuit to the full, but could not quite capture the supreme honour – the World Championship. Steve Davis saw to that, and if his 18–12 defeat in the 1981 final may have been the overture to Davis' career, it was something of a watershed for the Welshman.

WORLD RANKINGS FROM 1983–4

SEASON	WORLD RANKING
1983–4	12
1984–5	15
1985–6	15
1986–7	14
1987–8	14
1988–9	24

'My game started slipping after that', he says sorrowfully. He had brushed off the potentially devastating effects of Bell's Palsy to notch a magnificent 145 break against Ray Reardon in the '81 semi-final at Sheffield, but his confidence began to go and two more Welsh professional titles were his only successes in the mid-'80s.

It was after a 13–1 pasting by Neal Foulds in the 1988 World Championship, that the Mountjoy finally approached Callan. 'All I had wanted was to play like I used to do, but I never dreamed of titles – certainly not two in a row!' said Doug.

But with the Mercantile Credit Classic to add to his epic UK win over Stephen Hendry, that's what the much-rejuvenated Welshman achieved either side of Christmas, 1988. 'I don't believe in fairy-tales either', he smiled. But from the way he's playing, there are signs that he is getting quite used to the reality.

FACT·FILE

NAME: DOUGLAS JAMES MOUNTJOY

DATE OF BIRTH: JUNE 8, 1942

BIRTHPLACE: TIR-Y-BERTH

TURNED PROFESSIONAL: 1976

FIRST MAJOR WIN: BENSON AND HEDGES MASTERS v RAY REARDON, 1977 (7–6)

BIGGEST PAY DAY: £88,000 FOR WINNING THE TENNENTS UK OPEN, 1988 (INCLUDING A HIGHEST-BREAK PRIZE OF £8,000)

JOHN PARROTT

Liverpool has a fine tradition of providing top class sportsmen, but one area where they seemed to be lacking was snooker. However, that situation was rectified when John Parrott emerged on the scene in the early 1980s as one of the young pretenders to Steve Davis' crown. Brought up by his father, Alan, after his parents split up, John's home was just off Penny Lane, the Liverpool street immortalised by the Beatles. And it was in the local Garston League that John was given the chance to prove himself as a great competitive player. At 16 he was regularly knocking in century breaks. But if it hadn't been for a rainy day in Liverpool, John might never have taken up snooker in the first place.

Good bowls players, John Parrott and his dad were scheduled to play together one day during the school holidays, but rain curtailed the match. So, looking for alternative entertainment, they ventured into the Dudley Institute snooker club and John took to the game like the proverbial duck to water – which was quite appropriate considering the weather outside at the time!

Parrott left the New Heys Comprehensive School with six O-levels. However, ambitions of further education were to go by the board as he had set his heart on playing professional snooker. Thus, under the guidance of manager Phil Miller, John set off on the road that has today made him one of the country's most accomplished and popular players.

Winner of Junior Pot Black in 1982 and 1983, John certainly displayed confidence in front of the television cameras, and that experience held him in good stead for the future. Yet apart from gaining international honours, Parrott left the amateur game without any national titles behind him. But that meant nothing, as his current professional record shows.

He turned professional in 1983 and in his third tournament, the Lada Classic at the Spectrum Arena, Warrington, he caused sensation after sensation. Following his elimination of Doug Mountjoy by 5–4 in the qualifying competition, he beat Alex Higgins quite emphatically 5–2 on his 'senior' television début. In the next round he knocked out one of the golden boys at the time, Tony Knowles, even more decisively, 5–1. That led him into a semi-final appearance against Steve Davis.

Undoubtedly the large crowd was partisan. After all, Warrington is only a stone's throw from Liverpool. Parrott won the first frame and kept edging in front by one until Davis made it 4–3. John showed great composure to come back to 4–4, before letting the occasion get the better of him and allowing Davis to run out the 5–4 winner.

After winning Junior Pot Black in 1982 and 1983, it was apparent that John had the right television face – a very important asset in this age of mass media coverage!

GIANT LEAP

In the next tournament, the Embassy World Championship, Parrott again beat Tony Knowles in the opening round. But then he lost a close encounter with Dennis Taylor, going down 13–11. As a result of these early successes, the young Liverpudlian jumped from nowhere to 20th in the rankings in his first year. And that giant leap was one of the many he has since taken as he has constantly moved towards the No. 1 spot.

He followed up a great début season by reaching the quarter-final of the World Championship in 1985, but lost another great battle. This time it was the former champion Ray Reardon who outlasted him, finally going through 13–12.

In 1986, still waiting to reach his first major final, John was soundly beaten 9–3 by Neal Foulds in the semi-final of the Tennents UK Open. But that first final was not too far away. In the top 16 for the first time in 1987/1988, Parrott justified his position by reaching the final of the Mercantile Credit Classic at Blackpool, and yet again he was engaged in a great match with Davis.

WORLD RANKINGS FROM 1983–4

SEASON	WORLD RANKING
1983–4	–
1984–5	20
1985–6	18
1986–7	17
1987–8	13
1988–9	7

It was their third meeting in a ranking tournament and only one frame had separated both players in the other meetings – each to Davis' advantage. At the end of an intense final at Blackpool it was Davis who was victorious again, but once more it was a close affair, 13–11. Davis built up what seemed like an unassailable lead at 9–4 and then 10–6, but Parrott came back to win five frames in succession to lead 11–10.

Unfortunately, Parrott missed a vital red when 31–16 up in the 22nd frame. This let Davis in, and he went on to win the three frames necessary to take the title and deprive John of his first ranking tournament success.

Today, John Parrott still has Phil Miller as his personal manager, but he is now part of the Ian Doyle stable that also controls Stephen Hendry and Mike Hallett. It is certainly one of the strongest teams in the professional game. All three are clean-cut and represent just the image that snooker wants.

FACT·FILE

NAME: JOHN STEPHEN PARROTT

DATE OF BIRTH: MAY 11, 1964

BIRTHPLACE: LIVERPOOL

TURNED PROFESSIONAL: 1983

FIRST MAJOR WIN: ICI EUROPEAN OPEN v TERRY GRIFFITHS, 1989 (9–5)

BIGGEST PAY DAY: £50,000 AS RUNNER-UP IN THE EVEREST WORLD MATCHPLAY CHAMPIONSHIP, 1988 (INCLUDING A HIGHEST-BREAK PRIZE OF £10,000)

RAY REARDON

Just as Steve Davis has dominated snooker in the 1980s, so Ray Reardon held the sport in an iron grip throughout the previous decade. Six World Championships – four in succession – put the stamp of greatness on this laugh-a-minute Welshman, who together with John Spencer and Alex Higgins formed a colourful trio that led snooker into the television age. Yet Ray has always insisted, almost certainly because of his experiences as a young man working down the mines, that: 'Snooker's just a game. It isn't a matter of life or death'.

It is no coincidence that Ray Reardon was the role model for a young Steve Davis, and it is a measure of the respect he has for him that the Romford superstar took a leaf out of the great man's book during his win in the 1988 Everest World Matchplay event. 'I'd been beaten in successive tournaments and I was lacking consistency', admitted Davis. 'I thought to myself, Reardon wouldn't be too pleased with the way I am playing at the moment and that helped get me back on course.'

Steve Davis is neither the first nor the last great player to compliment Reardon, who won the Welsh Amateur Championship in 1950 and slowly but surely forged himself into a modern-day legend. But not before learning the harsh facts of life – and nearly death – down a coalmine.

At 14, Ray followed in his father's footsteps by becoming a miner, and over the years was content to learn his snooker trade among the amateurs. In 1957 however, he was involved in a mining accident and trapped for three hours under tons of rubble. This episode persuaded him that he should leave the pits. Instead he joined his family in Stoke and enrolled in the police force.

After dropping out of the amateur game for several seasons, Reardon returned in great triumph to win the 1964 English Amateur Championship from John Spencer, who was destined to become his main rival in the years that followed.

MANNA FROM HEAVEN

Snooker was at its lowest ebb when Reardon eventually turned pro in 1967, with just a handful of professionals operating what was effectively a closed-shop. There were no tournaments as we know them today and precious little prize money and exhibition work. But Reardon was a fighter and when, in 1970, Pontin's offered him a summer season of exhibition matches at holiday camps, it was manna from heaven for a struggling pro.

After his victory in the 1971 World Championship, an invincible aura began to develop about his game. In his prime it was said, quite justly, that the very fear of facing Reardon across the green baize was worth two blacks a frame to him – and how he took advantage of that!

Pontin's faith in Ray was rewarded the following year when, with renewed confidence, he won the World Championship – a prelude to the series of great battles he had with John Spencer and Alex Higgins throughout the Seventies, from which he emerged for the most part on top.

Thanks to the colour that Spencer, Higgins and Reardon brought to the game, the snooker revival began in earnest. Reardon won the first edition of Pot Black, the one-frame weekly series. Then, when the World Championship became an Embassy-sponsored event, with a new home at Sheffield's Crucible, Reardon recaptured his glory days by winning the last of his six titles. That was in 1978, though by the turn of the decade he appeared to be in decline.

But snooker's first modern superstar was not about to go quietly, and in 1982 three months of hard work in his local billiard hall paid off handsomely when he again reached the World Championship final, only to lose a classic encounter 18–15 to Higgins. Yet Ray still wasn't finished, because later that year he lifted the Professional Players' Tournament first prize and added the Yamaha Organs International the following season – beating Jimmy White in both finals.

That really should have been it, but Reardon still had a few more tricks to perform. Without doubt the greatest safety player of all, he forced his way into the 1985 World Championship semi-finals after tying John Parrott up in knots. And in 1988, after one of the most dismal periods of his glittering career, when eye trouble plagued him constantly, he inflicted a 5–0 whitewash on world champion Davis, in the British Open at Derby.

Reardon, president of the WPSPA, still seems destined to cause the odd upset here and there. Indeed, in January 1989 he shocked the life out of young Stephen Hendry by taking him all the way in a nine-frame thriller. The young Scot won the final frame, but his admiration for the Welshman knew no bounds. How many other superstars will be singing Reardon's praises in the years to come?

WORLD RANKINGS FROM 1983–4

SEASON	WORLD RANKING
1983–4	2
1984–5	5
1985–6	6
1986–7	15
1987–8	38
1988–9	40

FACT·FILE

NAME: RAYMOND REARDON

DATE OF BIRTH: OCTOBER 8, 1932

BIRTHPLACE: TREDEGAR, GWENT

TURNED PROFESSIONAL: 1967

FIRST MAJOR WIN: WORLD CHAMPIONSHIP v JOHN PULMAN, 1970 (39–34)

BIGGEST PAY DAY: £20,000 FOR REACHING THE SEMI-FINALS OF THE EMBASSY WORLD CHAMPIONSHIP, 1985

JOHN SPENCER

It was slightly warped, shaped like the back leg of a dog and there was a nail holding the butt end together. Yet, with this unlikely cue, John Spencer made an indelible impression on the world of snooker, winning no less than three World Championships from 1969 to 1977. Today, he is better known as a BBC TV commentator, yet it should not be forgotten that, together with Ray Reardon and Alex Higgins, he pioneered the modern game through the '70s as snooker swept into the champagne era.

After National Service, followed by a ten-year break from the game, John Spencer was persuaded to resume his amateur career in 1964. He proceeded to reach the final of the English Amateur Championship two years running, carrying off the title in 1966 and being hailed a hero in his native Lancashire.

Spencer finished runner-up in the World Amateur Championship of that year, and after another brief lay-off was accepted into the professional ranks, managing to persuade a sympathetic bank manager that he had a great chance of winning the 1969 world title at his first attempt, if he could just raise the £100 entry fee! Fortune smiled on him as he beat reigning champion John Pulman, followed by Rex Williams and then Gary Owen in a one-sided final, to lift the £1,300 prize.

Having lost his title to Reardon and then regained it in 1970, Spencer looked likely to dominate the sport, especially after winning a series of other titles, including TV's Pot Black twice. But brash newcomer Higgins put the brakes on John's ambitions with his never-to-be-forgotten 1972 World Championship victory. And whilst fierce rivalry from Higgins and Reardon never allowed John to become complacent, his stock sank a little lower when in the 1973 World Championship semi-final he let slip a 19–12 lead over the Welshman and went down 23–22.

BROKEN CUE

As if that wasn't enough, his troubles were compounded a year later when his beloved cue was broken in four places. It had been lying beside him in the passenger seat when he was involved in a bad car crash. The cue was expertly repaired but, although Spencer won his next event, it was never the same again. Then he struck on the brilliant idea

What set Spencer apart from his rivals was his unique Rolls Royce style, which enabled him to screw balls to prodigous lengths, whilst retaining immaculate control over the cue ball. Unlike the power shots of Jimmy White or Alex Higgins, it involved minimum output for maximum result and, combined with exceptional long potting, often gave him the openings from which to sew up frames.

of using a Canadian two-piece instrument – which has since revolutionised the manufacture of cues. Spencer reasoned, sensibly, that it would be much easier to transport a cue around in a half-size case!

The feeling in the game at the time was that nothing could beat a one-piece cue for accuracy. But Spencer was to prove the knockers wrong in 1977 when, in the first Embassy World Championship played at Sheffield's Crucible Theatre, he went all the way to clinch his third title.

The revival fizzled out when unknown South African Perrie Mans beat him in the opening round of his 1978 title defence. But he pushed his name to the fore again the following year at Slough, Buckinghamshire, when he became the first player to record a maximum 147 in tournament play. But even then he had helpings of bad luck. The pockets on the table at the Fulcrum Centre were later adjudged to

WORLD RANKINGS FROM 1983–4

SEASON	WORLD RANKING
1983–4	16
1984–5	13
1985–6	20
1986–7	34
1987–8	28
1988–9	27

be oversized, so his achievement was never officially acknowledged. To make matters worse, the Thames Television camera crew, who had covered the last three days, were on a meal-break at the time. To cap it all, Spencer and his opponent Cliff Thorburn arrived late, so spectators who saw the cameras idle believed the match had been put back and wandered off. As a result only a handful of people witnessed John knock in his historic maximum!

Imagine Spencer's chagrin when three years later, in the second round of the Lada Classic, at the Oldham Civic Centre, he sat and watched opponent Steve Davis create history by making the first official competitive 147 on television.

But drama of a different kind lay ahead for the circuit's great practical joker when he discovered, during the 1984/85 season, that he had a rare eye disease which induced double vision. Not surprisingly, his form disappeared completely and for the first time he lost his top 16 ranking. Although John's health did recover, thanks to special drugs which controlled the eye disorder, and despite reaching a ranking quarter-final in 1988, the glory days have surely gone.

FACT·FILE

NAME: JOHN SPENCER

DATE OF BIRTH: SEPTEMBER 18, 1935

BIRTHPLACE: SALFORD, MANCHESTER

TURNED PROFESSIONAL: 1967

FIRST MAJOR WIN: WORLD CHAMPIONSHIP v GARY OWEN, 1969 (46–27)

BIGGEST PAY DAY: £9,000 FOR REACHING THE QUARTER-FINALS OF THE DULUX BRITISH OPEN, 1987

KIRK STEVENS

White suits, white shoes and long hair – these were the trademarks of Kirk Stevens, who brought an air of flamboyancy into the world of professional snooker in the 1980s. His youthful verve was imitated by many players up and down the country, and he became a favourite with one of the biggest sections of the viewing public, the British housewife! But, despite some spectacular performances and a rapid rise into the top echelons of the game, Kirk was overtaken by public controversy and problems in his personal life – setbacks he has yet to recover from.

Born in Toronto in 1958, Kirk Stevens started hustling his way around the local pool and billiard halls when he was just 15, using the Golden Cue club as his home base. He had a difficult childhood. His parents had split up and, when he was 18, Kirk's mother was killed in an arson attack on her Toronto home. That experience left him badly scarred, but he found that it also left him motivated to succeed at something which might allow him to escape.

Kirk turned professional in 1978, made his British début in the 1979 World Championship and qualified for the Crucible where he met the seasoned campaigner Fred Davis. The all-white suit of the 20-year-old seemed more appropriate for a Broadway musical than the sober atmosphere of a snooker arena. But, despite Stevens' new approach to the game, it was the old hand Fred who won 13–8.

A year later it was the same suit, but a different

story. On the opening day of the tournament, Stevens came within a whisker of collecting £5,000 for setting a new championship record break. He was on 136 and had only the black left for a 143. It was a fine cut, and one that he would expect to make in practice. But in the tense atmosphere of the Crucible it was a different matter, and Stevens missed the pot.

CLASH WITH HIGGINS

Nevertheless, Kirk went on to beat ex-champion John Spencer, and then Eddie Charlton, before becoming the youngest ever semi-finalist. His opponent in that game was Alex Higgins. What a match these two extrovert characters provided – the Irishman eventually pulling away to win 16–13. Nevertheless, Stevens had arrived.

Kirk had some consolation for the defeat by White in the 1984 Benson and Hedges Masters, because he compiled a maximum 147 break in the ninth frame. 'I couldn't believe how I felt. I was just enthralled in it, lost in it', was how he described the achievement. His elation was such that he said he would never have swapped that moment for anything – not even a place in the final!

He broke into the top 16 after that success, and in 1984 reached No. 4 in the rankings – despite never having won or even reached the final of a ranking tournament. Stevens was always a hard man to beat, but he could never quite make the breakthrough. Semi-final defeats in the 1981 Yamaha International Masters by David Taylor, the 1982 Jameson International by Tony Knowles, the 1983 Lada Cars Classic by fellow Canadian, Bill Werbeniuk, and the 1984 Benson and Hedges Masters and Embassy World Championship by Jimmy White, all frustrated Stevens.

The clash with White at the Crucible in 1984 is widely regarded as one of the game's great matches. White built up a 5–3 lead after the first session but Stevens led 8–7 overnight. Stevens went 12–10 in front with one session left, but then White won five on the trot to go 15–12 up. However,

WORLD RANKINGS FROM 1983–4

SEASON	WORLD RANKING
1983–4	7
1984–5	4
1985–6	5
1986–7	9
1987–8	21
1988–9	37

Stevens pulled back to 15–14 before the Londoner finally went through 16–14.

In the following season, Steve Davis beat Stevens 9–2 in the semi-final of the Coral UK Championship. But three months later Kirk had his revenge with a 9–7 win over Davis in the semi-final of the Dulux British Open, thereby reaching his first ranking final. His opponent was Silvino Francisco. Francisco however won 12–9, and it was that game which heralded the start of Kirk's decline.

Francisco made allegations in the tabloid press about Steven's drug taking. These allegations sparked a public scandal – he later admitted that he had a cocaine problem and was intent on sorting it out. But, despite a lot of sympathy, the damage had been done.

The drop from No. 5 in the rankings to a position outside the top 32 took just three seasons, and since 1985 Stevens has achieved no better than the last eight in a ranking event. But it must not be forgotten that Kirk brought a fresh approach to the game of snooker. There have been many imitators but none have captured the imagination like the young Canadian did in the early 1980s.

FACT·FILE

NAME: KIRK STEVENS

DATE OF BIRTH: AUGUST 17, 1958

BIRTHPLACE: TORONTO, CANADA

TURNED PROFESSIONAL: 1978

FIRST MAJOR WIN: CANADIAN PROFESSIONAL CHAMPIONSHIP v FRANK JONIK, 1983 (9–8)

BIGGEST PAY DAY: £30,000 AS RUNNER-UP IN THE DULUX BRITISH OPEN, 1985

DENNIS TAYLOR

Dennis Taylor was just another snooker player until 12.23am on April 29, 1985 – the moment that changed his life. Up until then Taylor had always been regarded as a tough competitor, but no-one could have foreseen the events of that never-to-be-forgotten night when he became Embassy world champion after defeating Steve Davis in one of the most dramatic matches ever played. A record 18.5 million television viewers stayed up to see Dennis kiss the trophy few believed would ever be his.

It was not until the 1985/86 season, his 14th as a professional, that Dennis Taylor proved himself as a winner. And how he did so. It took a traumatic family bereavement to give this transformation impetus. The death of his beloved mother in Coalisland, County Tyrone, caused Taylor to withdraw from the quarter-finals of the Jameson International and return to Ireland. 'All of a sudden, snooker didn't mean that much to me', recalled the Ulsterman, who had to be persuaded by his family to compete in the next tournament on the circuit, the Rothmans Grand Prix.

Taylor had never won a major title. But, carried along on an emotional wave, he fought his way through to beat Cliff Thorburn 10–2 in the final and pocket the £45,000 first prize. 'To be honest, I can't remember too much about it. But I did feel a determination I had never experienced before. I had to win for my mum', he said later. In fact, if his family had not insisted, Dennis would never have taken part – the event being barely three weeks after his mother's funeral.

As so often happens after a first major victory, Taylor's form deteriorated for a while. But shortly before the World Championship his game improved, and he beat Alex Higgins 10–5 to regain his Irish Professional title.

Sustaining the momentum, Taylor had emphatic victories against Silvino Francisco, Eddie Charlton, Cliff Thorburn and Tony Knowles on his way through to the final at Sheffield's Crucible Theatre. But there seemed no way back when he lost the first eight frames to defending champion Steve Davis. Yet remarkably, Dennis won the second session 7–1 and went to bed on the Saturday night only 9–7 down. 'It's amazing the psychology of this game. I was thinking I had won the opening day, even though I was still behind', he said.

Taylor puts a lot of his success down to the upside-down, window-sized spectacles that have given him better vision on the table. 'I said after I lost 13–11 to Steve Davis in the 1983 World Championship that the best was still to come. It's all down to the glasses', he declares.

Mentally, Taylor knew that he could cope with anything after that. He levelled the match at 15–15, before falling behind again at 17–15 with three frames to play. He again drew level at 17–17, then potted the final ball of the final frame to provide an unforgettable climax to one of the greatest matches ever seen.

HERO'S WELCOME

As world champion, Taylor received a hero's welcome from the people of his home-town, Coalisland, and another rapturous reception when he returned to his adopted town of Blackburn. He was now financially secure for life and signed a five-year contract with Matchroom supremo Barry Hearn to look after his business interests.

After climbing to No. 3 in the rankings after his World Championship triumph, Taylor has slipped down the list in recent seasons. But he has enjoyed considerable success in non-ranking tournaments. He won the Benson and Hedges Masters in 1987, and earned £170,000 in prize money in the space of ten weeks at the start of the 1987/88 season – winning tournaments in Japan, Canada, Ireland and England. He also finished runner-up to Stephen Hendry in the Rothmans Grand Prix in 1987, and was a member of the Irish team that completed a hat-trick of wins in snooker's World Team Cup during the same year.

Throughout his career Dennis Taylor has remained very much a family man who does not like spend too much time away from wife Patricia and their three children, Denise, Damian and Brendan. Though, like many of his fellow professionals, Dennis devotes many spare hours to raising money for charity. Indeed it is easy to see why this jovial Irishman has always been one of the most popular players on the circuit. 'Dennis Taylor is snooker's Mr Entertainment', says manager Barry Hearn. 'Dennis is the court jester. He has entertained snooker fans all over the world.' His quick wit and impish sense of humour make him an ideal man for exhibitions. But don't let the jokes fool you, because on the match table he continues to be one of the fiercest competitors in the game.

WORLD RANKINGS FROM 1983–4

SEASON	WORLD RANKING
1983–4	13
1984–5	11
1985–6	4
1986–7	3
1987–8	8
1988–9	10

FACT·FILE

NAME: DENNIS JAMES TAYLOR

DATE OF BIRTH: JANUARY 19, 1949

BIRTHPLACE: COALISLAND, COUNTY TYRONE

TURNED PROFESSIONAL: 1971

FIRST MAJOR WIN: IRISH CHAMPIONSHIP v ALEX HIGGINS 1982 (16–13)

BIGGEST PAY DAY: £60,000 FOR WINNING THE EMBASSY WORLD CHAMPIONSHIP, 1985

CLIFF THORBURN

Abandoned as a baby by his mother, and brought up by his father and grandmother in Victoria, British Columbia, Cliff Thorburn has learned life the hard way – both on and off the table. He developed his talent for snooker in the late '60s and early '70s, playing for keeps – the title of his biography – in the pool halls of Canada and the United States. He went on the road, living the life made familiar by films like *The Hustler* and *The Colour of Money*, where you won or you didn't eat. It was a tough life, but it didn't stop him winning the World Championship and becoming the most successful non-British player in snooker history.

'I was broke sometimes, hungry and cold, but I was doing what I wanted to do', recalled Thorburn of those early days on the road. There he spent hour after hour perfecting his technique so that it would remain rock-solid under pressure. At the time he had little idea that there was a snooker World Championship, and no idea of how to enter or become a tournament professional. But in 1970 he saw Fred Davis and Rex Williams play in his home town, Toronto, and found there was another side to the game.

The following year he played John Spencer in Canada, learned more about the World Championship and, as a result, made his first trip to Britain in 1973, losing 16–15 to Rex Williams in the second round of the tournament after first defeating Dennis Taylor.

In the years that followed, Thorburn – commuting across the Atlantic – earned a reputation as one of the toughest competitors in the game. And nothing has changed. Nicknamed 'The Grinder' for his uncompromising style of play, Cliff does not have the natural flair of a Jimmy White or an Alex Higgins. But as White once said: 'Anyone who calls Cliff boring doesn't know anything about the game'.

Thorburn reached the first of his three World Championship finals in 1977, losing 25-21 to John Spencer. But three years later he became the first overseas player to win the world title, beating Alex Higgins 18–16 in the final.

MOVE TO BRITAIN

It was then that Cliff decided to make Britain his permanent base. But the move backfired and after two disappointing seasons he decided to return to Toronto. Immediately, his game began to improve and he won the Benson and Hedges Masters at Wembley in 1983 – the first of three Masters titles.

It was during the 1983 World Championship that Thorburn made history by compiling the first ever 147 maximum break in the tournament. Those 36 shots were worth a £13,000 jackpot – yet many people only remember that the break began with a fluke!

When he returned to Britain the following time, his determination, concentration and ability to perform under pressure took him to a series of memorable victories in the 1983 World Championship. His 13–12 second-round win over Terry Griffiths provided the Championship's latest ever finish – 3.51am – to its longest ever session – 6 hours and 25 minutes.

He was two frames down with three to play in the following two rounds but came through on both occasions, beating fellow Canadian Kirk Stevens 13–12 in the quarter-finals and Tony Knowles 16–15 in the semis. But those three exhausting matches had taken their toll. When he faced Steve Davis in the final, Cliff, drained of stamina and emotion, had nothing left to give, and he lost 18–6.

Thorburn had climbed to No.2 in the world rankings by the end of the 1984/85 season, but the man otherwise known as 'The Methodical Mountie' has never quite been able to reach the peak. He gradually slipped from 2nd to 4th, then from 5th to 6th as a result of failing a random drugs test during the MIM Britannia British Open in 1988. For this he was subsequently fined £10,000, banned from two world ranking tournaments, and had two points deducted from his total in the ranking list, thereby dropping him another place.

It was a testing time for Thorburn and his family. But, typically, Thorburn gritted his teeth and took the flak to reach the semi-finals of the '88 World Championship. But that's not surprising, because Cliff, who by then had joined Barry Hearn's Matchroom team, has always been able to cope with the mental pressures of playing professional sport – he is also a very good golfer.

'This last year has been more than a little tough on me', he admitted during the 1989 Mercantile Credit Classic at Blackpool. But when the going gets tough the tough get going, and while Thorburn may never realise his ambition of becoming world number one, 'The Grinder' has not been blunted yet.

WORLD RANKINGS FROM 1983–4

SEASON	WORLD RANKING
1983–4	3
1984–5	3
1985–6	2
1986–7	2
1987–8	4
1988–9	6

FACT·FILE

NAME: CLIFFORD CHARLES DEVLIN THORBURN

DATE OF BIRTH: JANUARY 16, 1948

BIRTHPLACE: VICTORIA, CANADA

TURNED PROFESSIONAL: 1973

FIRST MAJOR WIN: EMBASSY WORLD CHAMPIONSHIP
v ALEX HIGGINS, 1980 (18–16)

BIGGEST PAY DAY: £45,000 FOR WINNING
THE BENSON AND HEDGES MASTERS, 1986

WILLIE THORNE

Elegant as he struts around the table, effortless as he pots the balls, Willie Thorne remains an enigma. Acknowledged by his fellow professionals and the public alike as one of the most fluent break-builders in the game – he's nicknamed 'Mr Maximum' – Willie knocks in 147 breaks on the practice table with almost nonchalant ease, and has now scored more than 100 maximums. But the man with the most famous 'crown' in snooker has difficulty reproducing practice form on the match table, and his record is hardly a true reflection of his undoubted ability.

Willie Thorne had to wait until his ninth year as a professional to win his first major title – the 1985 Mercantile Credit Classic. He defeated his friend and doubles partner, Canadian Cliff Thorburn, 13–8 in the final to claim the £40,000 first prize, having first edged out Steve Davis 9–8 in the semi-final. That long-awaited victory should have been the launching pad for bigger and better things. Yet, although 1985 proved Thorne's most successful year to date, it ended in heartbreak.

He finished runner-up to Thorburn in the Langs Scottish Masters, then reached the final of the Coral UK Open at Preston, beating Paddy Browne, John Virgo, Cliff Thorburn, Terry Griffiths and Dennis Taylor along the way. Willie produced a brilliant exhibition of potting as he built a handsome lead against Steve Davis in the final. It seemed that at long last he was going to turn his talent into trophies. However, a careless miscue on the blue cost him a 14–8 lead and shattered his brittle confidence.

Davis went on to win eight of the last nine frames to pull off an unlikely 16–14 victory and cap what his manager, Barry Hearn, later described as: 'Steve's greatest performance, without any shadow of a doubt'. A bemused Thorne, who had once again managed to snatch defeat from the jaws of victory, could only reflect: 'I outplayed him and lost'.

THE MATCHROOM TROPHY

Willie reached two more ranking finals in the 1986/87 season, but lost them both. Davis beat him again in the Dulux British Open, this time by a 12–7 margin, and he went down 9–5 to Jimmy White in the Benson and Hedges Irish Masters. He did, however, manage to win the Camus Hong Kong Masters and the Matchroom Trophy – the latter coming after Willie, who signed a five-year deal with Barry Hearn's Matchroom organisation in February 1986, beat Davis 10–9 in the final. It was a rare victory against Davis, but one that the world's top player avenged in the finals of the 1986 BCE Canadian Masters (9–3) and again in the 1987 Benson and Hedges Irish Masters (9–1).

Thorne had more success overseas in 1987, beating Jimmy White 5–2 to win the Kent Cup International Masters in Peking. But the 1987/88 domestic season proved disappointing as he slipped two places down the world rankings to No. 13. His best performance came in the Tennents UK Open, at Preston, where he lost 9–2 to Davis in the semi-final.

It was also at Preston that Thorne finally made a maximum break in a major championship. It came during his fourth-round match against Tommy Murphy in the pre-televised stage. Thorne became only the fourth player to compile a 147 under tournament conditions, but the absence of the BBC television cameras denied him a £90,000 jackpot! Indeed, Lady Luck has not always smiled on Thorne. He broke his ankle in a go-karting accident just before the 1982/83 season and ended up in hospital with food poisoning just before the 1983 World Championship!

Willie Thorne has made over 100 maximum 147 breaks in his career. But he has only made one maximum in competition play – in the Tennents UK Open in 1987 against Tommy Murphy.

Willie Thorne's greatest sporting pal is none other than English international striker Gary Lineker. Wherever Gary and Willie are playing in the world they phone each other up to find out the result.

But win or lose, 'the Great W.T.' has always had a loyal band of followers, and none more loyal than his 'biggest fan', Racing Raymond Winterton. This colourful troupe of supporters match Thorne's flamboyant character. And like them, he is a sports enthusiast with a keen interest in horse racing.

Willie Thorne has certainly come a long way since winning the British Junior Championship in 1973, and he is one of the most popular figures on the circuit. He once admitted: 'I'm an easy player to beat. I can't practise hours a day on safety, hours with the rest, hours with the spider. It drives me crazy. But I suppose I'm going to have to do all those things . . . one day'. Luckily for his fellow professionals that day has still to arrive.

WORLD RANKINGS FROM 1983–4

SEASON	WORLD RANKING
1983–4	18
1984–5	12
1985–6	11
1986–7	7
1987–8	11
1988–9	13

FACT·FILE

NAME: WILLIAM JOSEPH THORNE

DATE OF BIRTH: MARCH 4, 1954

BIRTHPLACE: LEICESTER

TURNED PROFESSIONAL: 1975

FIRST MAJOR WIN: MERCANTILE CREDIT CLASSIC v CLIFF THORBURN, 1985 (13–8)

BIGGEST PAY DAY: £50,000 FOR WINNING THE MATCHROOM TROPHY, 1987

JOHN VIRGO

John Virgo carries a dour look into the snooker arena. But away from the serious business of competitive play, Virgo is one of the game's great entertainers, best known for hilarious impersonations of his fellow professionals. But that is only a small side of John Virgo, professional snooker player. Nowadays, in his capacity as the chairman of the World Professional Billiards and Snooker Association, he devotes much time to the commercial sponsorship negotiations and administrative problems of the ever-expanding professional tour, as well as providing expert commentary for TV.

Born in Salford in 1946, John Virgo learned his 'trade' in the 1970s when many top players were emerging in the Manchester area – Alex Higgins, Dennis Taylor, Jim Meadowcroft, David Taylor and many more who never gained the acclaim of their more illustrious colleagues.

Virgo won the National Under-16 Snooker Championship in 1962 and three years later was the Under-19 champion. They were the first signs that a great player was emerging. When he turned professional in 1976 the game was truly starting to take off in popularity. Pot Black had certainly helped its cause and Virgo was quick to appreciate that turning professional would ensure he was in on the 'ground floor'. However, life was certainly not easy in those early days because many other players had the same ambitions.

John made his mark on the professional game in the 1977 World Championship – the first to be held at the Crucible Theatre in Sheffield. After coming through two qualifying matches he was pitched against John Spencer, another Mancunian. At the time Spencer was the best player in the world. But Virgo gave him a tough match before Spencer went on to win 13 – 9, and eventually take the title. Virgo twice led by three frames but unfortunately, at 8 – 8, he seemed to lose his confidence. However, John followed that World Championship performance by reaching the semi-final of the inaugural UK Championship at Blackpool's Tower Ballroom, losing to the eventual winner, Patsy Fagan, 9 – 8.

TOUGH TO BEAT

By now, Virgo was gaining a reputation for being a tough player to beat and in 1979 he reached the World Championship semi-final before going down to Dennis Taylor, who led at the end of each of the five sessions. In the 28th frame John came close to the first ever 147 in the championship, after potting 12 reds and 11 blacks. But he failed on the twelfth black. 'If I'd got that he could have had the Championship', Virgo commented afterwards.

John is still much sought after for exhibition matches, as much for his impersonations as for his snooker. He got the idea of mimicking his fellow professionals from the great Irish player Jackie Rea, who used to perform a similar routine in the 1950s and 1960s.

Remarkably, up to and including 1988, John has only once been beyond the first round at the Crucible. However, before 1979 was out he had his first major title tucked under his belt. Great wins over Tony Meo, Steve Davis and Dennis Taylor put him into the final of the Coral UK Championship at Preston, where he beat the reigning world champion Terry Griffiths 14 – 13 in a great match. However, a spell in the wilderness followed, and it was not until the 1982 Jameson International that Virgo reached a major semi-final again. But this time his efforts were thwarted by fellow-Mancunian David Taylor, who beat him 9 – 5.

Regularly in the top 16, Virgo's poor results saw him drop out of that élite club in 1984. He was still playing well, but when it came to the ranking tournaments he wasn't picking up the points. He did

WORLD RANKINGS FROM 1983 – 4

SEASON	WORLD RANKING
1983–4	14
1984–5	18
1985–6	19
1986–7	19
1987–8	19
1988–9	15

reach the final of the Winfield Australian Masters in 1984, and then won the inaugural Professional Snooker League – but not only did the latter not carry any ranking points, it didn't carry any prize money either!

The slide down the rankings was held up in 1986 at the Dulux British Open, thanks largely to John's first ranking semi-final appearance since 1982. He lost 9 – 4 to Willie Thorne in a game which John described as containing: 'Some of the best snooker I have seen for a long time'. And in the same event a year later Virgo enjoyed one of the best wins of his career when he beat Steve Davis 5 – 4. It was the first time Davis had failed to reach the televised stage of a professional tournament!

Virgo returned to the top 16 at the start of the 1988/89 season, despite the pressures of being chairman of the WPSBA – a role which he assumed in 1987 after Rex Williams' resignation. So, hopefully there is much more to come from this entertaining player who, away from the world of snooker, enjoys relaxing at home in Surrey with wife Avril and the new love of his life – baby Brook – who arrived on the scene in 1987.

FACT·FILE

NAME: JOHN TREVOR VIRGO

DATE OF BIRTH: APRIL 3, 1946

BIRTHPLACE: SALFORD, MANCHESTER

TURNED PROFESSIONAL: 1976

FIRST MAJOR WIN: CORAL UK CHAMPIONSHIP v TERRY GRIFFITHS, 1979 (14–13)

BIGGEST PAY DAY: £12,000 FOR REACHING THE QUARTER-FINALS OF THE TENNENTS UK OPEN, 1988

BILL WERBENIUK

In 1984 Canada had three players ranked in the top 16 – Cliff Thorburn, Kirk Stevens and Bill Werbeniuk. Sadly, only Thorburn has retained his position, while the other two have fallen. And how sad a sight it has been to see 'Big' Bill slip out of the game. Werbeniuk always enjoyed his snooker and was one of the great characters in the game over the last decade – his bulky frame, hovering around the 20-stone mark and fuelled by vast quantities of lager, was as familiar a sight on television as Dennis Taylor's spectacles or Kirk Stevens' white suits.

Born in Winnipeg in 1947, Bill Werbeniuk later moved to Vancouver and started playing snooker at the age of nine. He won the Canadian Amateur title in 1973 and that same year turned professional. The following year he brought his talent to British shores for the World Championship, but between then and 1978 British fans saw very little of him. It was only after reaching the quarter-finals of the World Championship in 1978 that Bill decided to stay in Britain and take part in other tournaments.

He made his base at the North Midland Snooker Centre in Worksop, and reached his second consecutive World Championship quarter-final in 1979 – this time it was John Virgo who brought an abrupt halt to his progress. However, Bill gained some consolation by equalling Rex Williams' championship record break of 142 in the 18th frame. Had it been just one point higher Bill would have collected a bonus cheque of £5,000. Later that year Bill went on to reach his first major semi-final – losing 9–3 to Terry Griffiths in the Coral UK Championship.

He appeared in his first major final in 1980, as a member of the Canadian team that played and lost to Wales in the World Team Cup. But what an embarrassing tournament it was for him! In an early match against England's David Taylor, Bill's rather tight trousers split around the posterior – and what's more, the television cameras caught all the action. The Canadian team captain Cliff Thorburn was heard to quip: 'This is a needle match and I was hoping Bill was going to sew it up for us'!

WORLD CHAMPION

Embarrassment and disappointment over with, Bill eventually became a world champion in 1982 when Canada beat England to win the World Team Cup,

Bill Werbeniuk used to drink up to 30 pints of lager a day to combat a hereditary nervous disease.

Bill Werbeniuk once split his trousers on TV during a 1980 World Team Cup match against England's David Taylor.

Werbeniuk himself losing only one frame. But it was not until 1983 that the friendly Canadian reached his first major individual final. After beating Alex Higgins, Doug Mountjoy and Kirk Stevens in the Lada Classic, Bill came up against Steve Davis in the final at Warrington's Spectrum Arena. Davis was playing some of the best snooker of his career at the time and Werbeniuk did well to contain him and keep the result as close as 9–5.

At the start of the 1983/84 season Werbeniuk reached his highest ever ranking – eighth. And in the 'close season' he reached the final of the Winfield Australian Masters, only to lose to Thorburn 7–3 in the final.

Thus, Bill went into the 1984/85 season full of confidence, but it all turned sour on him. He never got beyond the second round of any tournament and he slipped six places down the rankings. A season later and he was out of the top 16.

Since then, apart from a losing quarter-final appearance in the 1986 Dulux British Open, the

WORLD RANKINGS FROM 1983–4

SEASON	WORLD RANKING
1983–4	8
1984–5	14
1985–6	17
1986–7	24
1987–8	33
1988–9	47

ebullient Werbeniuk has had little to cheer about, and his slide became so great that he slipped out of the top 32.

This decline is largely explained by the fact that Werbeniuk has always suffered from a tremor in his right hand – which is the last thing a snooker player wants! He found a 'cure' – drinking several pints of lager before each match. But that meant, of course, the substantial problem of drawing the line between curing the tremor and keeping one's senses!

The beta blocker drug, Inderal, has provided relief for the Canadian, but it is one of the drugs outlawed by the WPBSA. As a result Werbeniuk was fined and suspended after continuing to take the drug, and he went home to his native Vancouver over Christmas in 1988. 'It looks like the end of the road', he said before flying home. 'There is no other drug available. I could take other medication but I would need three times the dosage and it could possibly kill me.'

It is particularly sad to see Big Bill in such an unfortunate position – he has undoubtedly given the game so much over the years and has been one of its great characters.

FACT·FILE

NAME: WILLIAM WERBENIUK

DATE OF BIRTH: JANUARY 14, 1947

BIRTHPLACE: WINNIPEG, CANADA

TURNED PROFESSIONAL: 1973

FIRST MAJOR WIN: CANADIAN PROFESSIONAL CHAMPIONSHIP, 1973

BIGGEST PAY DAY: £8,250 FOR REACHING THE QUARTER-FINALS OF THE DULUX BRITISH OPEN, 1986

JIMMY WHITE

Jimmy White is, without doubt, one of the most talented players to have graced the game of professional snooker. In full flow, there is no finer sight on the snooker table than this impish left hander. He has earned the nickname 'Whirlwind' for his quickfire style of play, and it's certainly appropriate – as millions of fans will testify. He goes for shots others wouldn't attempt and, even if he misses, there is still that cheeky smile. He knows he should have won more titles. But it isn't that always the case with sporting geniuses who also enjoy life to the full?!

Jimmy White, together with lifelong pal Tony Meo, spent his formative years playing the snooker halls of his native Tooting. Formal education came a distant second best, as young White was being taught in a far different 'school'. In that hard part of London no quarter was given on the table and none was asked for. But there was something about the young White that set him apart. People knew even then that he was going to be a great player.

It was in 1979 when White first burst into the public eye at a snooker club in Helston, Cornwall, where he was opposed by Dave Martin in the final of the English Amateur Championship. More than 600 people crammed into this tiny venue to watch the emergence of a young man who was to rise to No. 2 in the professional ranks. Even Jimmy's mother could not get into the arena. She had to sit outside smoking nervously while the game unfolded. It was a tough match but White came through a winner – the youngest person ever to win the title.

More amateur success was to follow when, at 18, he travelled all the way to Hobart, Australia, for the World Amateur Championship in 1980. White topped his group, scraped home 5–4 in the quarter-final against Steve Newbury and beat Paul Mifsud of Malta 8–6 in the semi-final. In the final, Jimmy knocked in breaks of 80 and 101 destroying Australia's Ron Atkins 11–2. That was another landmark – he was the game's youngest world amateur titleholder. Indeed, his record was such that when he turned professional he was almost immediately tipped as a certainty to beat Alex Higgins' record of 22 years 11 months as the game's youngest professional champion.

THE WORLD HIS OYSTER

When Jimmy did win the Langs Scottish Masters in 1981 to become, at 19, the professional sport's youngest winner, the world seemed his oyster. But sadly that 'youngest ever pro champ' tag was to elude him. In 1982, he was edged out 16–15 by Higgins in the world semi-final, and in the following year he departed in the first round 10–8 to his great pal, Tony Meo.

> Even though Jimmy now travels the world first class, and has a lifestyle that his mates can only dream about, he remains 'one of the boys'. He once said: 'Even if there wasn't any money in this game, I would still be down the snooker hall. Snooker is my life. I still enjoy going down the club with my mates for a few games, a few drinks and a few laughs'.

In 1984, came his greatest chance. He had won the Benson and Hedges Masters with a 9–5 victory over Terry Griffiths and then reached the world final, where he came up against Steve Davis. The match was a classic, but it was Davis who was to hold the famous trophy aloft – beating White 18–16. The following year Jimmy lost in the quarter-finals to Tony Knowles. The record was not to fall his way.

In 1985/86 he won the Mercantile Credit Classic and the following year saw White win two ranking events – the Rothmans Grand Prix, where he beat surprise package Rex Williams 10–6; and the Dulux British Open, where he conquered Neal Foulds 13–9. After that, the titles seemed to dry up, though he did burst back to form in the 1988 BCE Canadian Masters where, in front of a packed house, he beat Steve Davis 9–4.

WORLD RANKINGS FROM 1983–4

SEASON	WORLD RANKING
1983–4	11
1984–5	7
1985–6	7
1986–7	5
1987–8	2
1988–9	2

There have been many classic matches in White's career and many more will follow. But nothing could match his 13–12 defeat of Stephen Hendry in the 1988 World Championship. It was a second round match and these two snooker superstars, great friends off the table, matched each other shot for shot as Jimmy finally came home 13–12. Such was the interest that traffic came to a standstill outside Sheffield's Crucible Theatre as fans departed the arena after the shoot-out.

As to the future? Well, Jimmy has a single-minded outlook on the pro-game. He says: 'I want to be world champion and world No. 1 in the same season'. Even when he lost his No. 2 slot on the provisional ranking list to Hendry, Jimmy said: 'It doesn't matter. As long as you are in the top four, then that's okay. Being No. 1 is the only thing that really matters'.

FACT·FILE

NAME: JAMES WARREN WHITE

DATE OF BIRTH: MAY 2, 1962

BIRTHPLACE: TOOTING, LONDON

TURNED PROFESSIONAL: 1980

FIRST MAJOR WIN: LANGS SUPREME SCOTTISH MASTERS v CLIFF THORBURN, 1981 (9–4)

BIGGEST PAY DAY: £60,000 FOR WINNING THE DULUX BRITISH OPEN, 1987

REX WILLIAMS

When Rex Williams entered the arena at the Hexagon Theatre for the final of the 1986 Rothmans Grand Prix, it was just another step along the road that he set out on 38 years earlier. Outstanding as a youngster, Rex won seven national junior titles, including the National Under-16 Billiards and Snooker Championships of 1948. And he was just 17 when he captured the English amateur title in 1951 – the youngest winner until Jimmy White came along 28 years later. From those first youthful victories right through to the present day, Rex Williams has dedicated his life to the playing, promotion and administration of billiards and snooker.

Rex Williams turned professional at the age of 18, unfortunately at a time when both billiards and snooker were starting their decline. Regular tournament play was limited and he had to make his living from a few exhibition matches. However, Rex foresaw a second coming of snooker, and was instrumental in reviving the defunct Professional Billiard Players' Association, which is now the World Professional Billiards and Snooker Association.

He also played a big part in rekindling interest in the World Professional Snooker Championship, which had not been played since 1952 (although a World Matchplay Championship had existed up until 1957). Thus in 1964 the World Championship was reintroduced, albeit on a challenge basis.

Nevertheless, it was that which was the start which eventually led to the birth of Pot Black, the television programme at the root of the present snooker boom.

Not content with that, Rex also revived the World Professional Billiards Championship in 1968, when he travelled to Australia to challenge the holder, Clark McConachy, who had not received a challenge since 1951. Williams wrested the title from McConachy, and successfully beat off four challenges before losing the crown to Fred Davis in 1980. The event became a knock-out tournament that year, and Rex was twice the winner of the new-style competition in 1982 and 1983, thereby confirming his expertise at the three-ball game.

CHAIRMAN OF THE WPBSA

Williams' involvement with billiards and snooker has extended beyond his playing and innovative skills. He set up his own cue-making – and later, pool and billiard table – business, which he still runs today. In addition, he was chairman of the WPBSA for 13 years, before resigning towards the end of 1987. Whilst there he helped guide snooker through its greatest period of growth.

In the World Championships of 1965, in a match against John Pulman, Rex created a championship record break of 142 – which stood until it was finally beaten by Doug Mountjoy some 16 years later, in 1981.

So much for Rex Williams the billiards player; Rex Williams the innovator, and Rex Williams the administrator. But what about Rex Williams the snooker player? Well, he's not too bad at that either. For a start, he holds a place in the record books as the second man after Joe Davis to compile an official maximum 147 break, which he did against Mannie Francisco at Cape Town in 1965.

Prior to 1986, his most impressive results in major tournaments were in reaching the semi-final of the World Championship on three occasions. The best chance he had of reaching the final itself was in 1972, when he led Alex Higgins by six frames at one stage, before losing 31 – 30.

After a relatively lean period, the 1985/86 season brought about renewed confidence for Williams, then 51 years old. He reached the fourth round of the Rothmans Grand Prix, went one better in the Coral UK Open and then reached the semi-final of the Mercantile Credit Classic, where he put up a great battle against Jimmy White. Ten ranking points that season elevated him into the top 16 and the following season he improved three places after reaching his first ever ranking tournament final, the Rothmans Grand Prix.

The man between him and glory was, once again, Jimmy White. They had met five times before and Williams' only win was back in 1981. But victories over Alex Higgins (5 – 1), Steve Davis (5 – 1) and Neal Foulds (9 – 8) had restored his confidence. Rex feared no one. After beating Davis he quipped: 'I feel 21 again', and boy, was he playing like a 21-year-old! But sadly for Williams there was no fairytale ending. Despite leading 5 – 2 at one stage he ended up on the wrong end of a 10 – 6 scoreline. However he pocketed a cheque for £33,000, by far the biggest of his long career.

Since then Rex has slipped out of the top 16, and certainly troubled times at the WPBSA have not helped matters. However, after 40 years in snooker he has shown he can come back once. There's no reason why he shouldn't do it again.

WORLD RANKINGS FROM 1983–4

SEASON	WORLD RANKING
1983–4	30
1984–5	31
1985–6	27
1986–7	16
1987–8	13
1988–9	18

FACT·FILE

NAME: DESMOND REX WILLIAMS

DATE OF BIRTH: JULY 20, 1933

BIRTHPLACE: STOURBRIDGE, WEST MIDLANDS

TURNED PROFESSIONAL: 1951

FIRST MAJOR WIN: NONE

BIGGEST PAY DAY: £33,000 AS RUNNER-UP IN THE ROTHMANS GRAND PRIX, 1986

CLIFF WILSON

Cliff Wilson confounded all the experts – both snooker and medical – when, after a series of remarkable performances, he squeezed his bulky frame on to the bottom rung of the ladder containing the world's top 16 players, at the start of the 1988/89 season. Snooker is supposed to be a young man's game these days, but while the young Turks practise feverishly and analyse their game plans with their equally ambitious managers and agents, this 55-year-old chuckling maverick from the Welsh valleys is a walking contradiction to that theory.

If medicals were introduced for snooker tournaments, Cliff Wilson cheerfully admits that he would fail. Apart from being overweight, he is horrendously short-sighted and has various other ailments, including problems with his wrists and his neck, which make a mockery of his position as a snooker professional.

But Wilson's attitude is simple: 'If the money is there, why shouldn't I have a go and win some of it'. But don't be fooled by his happy-go-lucky approach to tournaments because, on his day and particularly in shorter matches where he doesn't start to lose concentration, he is still one of the deadliest long potters in the game.

Wilson was born in Tredegar in 1934 and grew up alongside another genius of the snooker table, Ray Reardon. The two men used to compete in 'shoot-outs', played in front of sell-out crowds, and Cliff, one of the amateur game's leading personalities, revelled in the fierce rivalry of those contests.

But, when Reardon moved off to Stoke to pursue a career, first in the police force and then as a snooker professional, Wilson lost interest in the game. He found that he had problems with his eyes, he had a wife and four young boys to support and, what was more, he had a secure job in a steelworks. As a result, in 1957 Cliff gave up the game and did not pick up a cue for 15 years! But, as the professional game began to take off in the '70s his interest was rekindled and he reappeared on the amateur scene.

WORLD AMATEUR CHAMPION

The climax of his amateur career came in 1978, in Malta, where he won an all-British world final against a young Yorkshire lad called Joe Johnson. After a convincing 11–5 win Wilson returned to South Wales with the trophy and a bit of glory, but no real thoughts of turning professional. After all, he was middle-aged, his eyesight was none too good and he had a secure job as a foreman in the steel works.

Not many men can claim to have won the Welsh Amateur Championship three times, with a 21-year gap between the first and second victory. His first title came in 1956, the second in 1977, after he had returned to the game from his 15-year 'retirement'.

It was ironic that an offer to compete as a 'wild card amateur' in the 1979 Benson and Hedges Masters at Wembley probably made up Wilson's mind to chuck in his job and join the professional circuit. The professional association was not happy about having an amateur in their tournament so, after delicate negotiations, Cliff withdrew to prevent a major confrontation. A few months later, he threw in his lot as a professional and began his steady rise up the rankings, to 16th place at the end of the 1987/88 season.

Of course, one of the perks that goes with a place in the top 16, is a spot in the Benson and Hedges Masters. So, Wilson took his place by right at Wembley in January 1989, a decade after he had suffered the humiliation of being invited and then having to step down!

Cliff will have seen the funny side of that. He sees the humour in most situations. His booming laugh and wheezing cough (a good advertisement for the sponsor's product in the B & H Masters!) have livened up many hospitality rooms and post-match press conferences. In fact, the man who lists his No. 1 hobby as 'collecting betting slips' has the approach of an old-style amateur. If things go wrong, Cliff just laughs it all off, tells a few jokes, has a couple of pints, picks up his cheque, then heads off back to the Valleys.

Quite simply, Cliff Wilson enjoys his snooker. He loves pleasing the crowds with outrageous attempts at long pots and doubles, much as he did in those games in Tredegar against Ray Reardon, and it is not going to break his heart if he loses a match he should have won. Let us not forget that if Cliff had been born about 20 years later, his crash-bang style of all-out attack could easily have made him one of the real superstars of the professional game. Without a trace of envy or regret he says: 'I was the Jimmy White and Alex Higgins of snooker in the '50s. When I was a young man I was knocking in century breaks in four minutes when Jimmy White wasn't even a gleam in his father's eye'.

WORLD RANKINGS FROM 1983–4

SEASON	WORLD RANKING
1983–4	20
1984–5	23
1985–6	22
1986–7	23
1987–8	17
1988–9	16

FACT·FILE

NAME: CLIFFORD JOHN WILSON

DATE OF BIRTH: MAY 10, 1934

BIRTHPLACE: TREDEGAR, GWENT

TURNED PROFESSIONAL: 1979

FIRST MAJOR WIN: NONE

BIGGEST PAY DAY: £7,500 FOR REACHING THE QUARTER-FINALS OF THE ROTHMANS GRAND PRIX, 1985 AND THE MERCANTILE CREDIT CLASSIC, 1986

WORLD SNOOKER
EMBASSY WORLD SNOOKER

SNOOKER TODAY

SNOOKER HAS UNDOUBTEDLY BEEN THE BOOM SPORT OF THE 1980S, AND IS NOW LOOKING FORWARD TO THE CHALLENGE OF THE 1990s. IN THIS CHAPTER WE TAKE AN IN-DEPTH LOOK AT THE GLOBAL EXPANSION OF THE GAME, THE INEVITABLE PROBLEMS THAT HAVE ACCOMPANIED THIS GROWTH, AND THE SPECIAL HOLD THAT SNOOKER STILL ENJOYS OVER THE BRITISH SPORTING PUBLIC.

The Crucible Theatre, Sheffield – snooker's most famous venue and home to the Embassy World Championship. The arena has hosted some of snooker's greatest matches.

SNOOKER TODAY

Professional snooker has been the sporting success of the 1980s. A game that was once the oft-quoted sign of a misspent youth has developed into a multi-million pound international industry. It is a phenomenon that almost defies belief – after all, why should two players knocking coloured balls around a green table produce an almost hypnotic hold on a British public. What's more their appetite for the spectacle shows no sign of waning!

Yet despite its massive popular appeal (or perhaps because of it!) snooker is a favourite target for certain critics in some of our newspapers and magazines. As soon as each new snooker season commences, the doubters are in full flow. 'Why is there so much snooker?' they cry in unison. Of course, the simple fact is that a majority of the viewing public demands hour after hour of snooker, and, in a democratic society, the majority usually gets what it wants.

THE TELEVISION AUDIENCE

In the dark days of the 1950s and 1960s snooker had looked to be on the brink of oblivion (for an account of the history of the game, see pages 10–61). But then along came colour television and a host of remarkable players – Ray Reardon, six times world champion, Steve Davis, the game's Mr. Cool, and, of course, Alex 'Hurricane' Higgins, to name but a few. An irresistible combination, they pushed the game to the forefront of British sporting life.

Some of British television's highest viewing figures attest to that success. 18.5 million viewers tuned in to BBC2 at 12.23am to watch Dennis Taylor pot the final black against Steve Davis and win the 1985 Embassy World Championship. 15.2 million ITV fans saw Davis beat Jimmy White in the 1987 Mercantile Credit Classic final. And 13.5 million switched on their sets to witness the final stages of Doug Mountjoy's epic defeat of Stephen Hendry in the 1988 Tennents UK Open.

INCREASED SPONSORSHIP

The proliferation of snooker on the television, accompanied by ever-increasing viewing figures, has inevitably attracted big money into the game

Dennis Taylor prepares to sink the final black to beat Steve Davis in the 1985 World Championships. It was 12.23am.

– notably from the tobacco giants who, banned from advertising directly on television, were quick to spot the potential in hours of high-profile sporting coverage in return for sponsorship.

That is why Embassy, Rothmans, and Benson and Hedges have been long-term supporters of the sport. Even when televison ordered them to reduce the number of signs they could have around the arena and change the cigarette-packet-colour-schemes of the décor, they didn't bat an eyelid and kept ploughing in the money. They consider their investment worthwhile, otherwise they would not have kept it going for so many years. In fact, Benson and Hedges have signed on as sponsers until 1996 – in line with the £11 million contract to continue snooker coverage on BBC. (The current ITV contract lasts until 1992.)

The new BBC contract was signed in Deauville, France during the new European Open, and the agreement is a clear indication of television's long-term commitment to the game. Nick Hunter, assistant head of BBC TV sport, flew to France to seal the deal, and he said afterwards: 'The game now has more personalities than ever before and the standard of play has gone through the roof. The FA Cup final, the Grand National and the Derby are top drawer events that are part of our sporting heritage. The World Snooker Championship is now very close to those events'.

However, Hunter, who was one of the inspirations behind the snooker boom, then touched on the squabbles that have plagued snooker. 'It saddens me that differences aired publicly in snooker couldn't have been sorted out behind closed doors. I don't subscribe totally to the view that there is no such thing as bad publicity. Even so, snooker remains one of the most popular sports on television and this new contract will allow our viewers to continue seeing the best players in the world competing in the world's top tournaments.'

THE WPBSA – AND THE FUTURE

The World Professional Billiards and Snooker Association (the WPBSA), the game's governing body, were naturally delighted with the BBC contract, because it gives them the power to negotiate with potential sponsors knowing that there is guaranteed television time. Del Simmons, the WPBSA contracts negotiator, said: 'In total this package could be worth up to £40 million. I am delighted'. Whilst John Virgo, chairman of the WPBSA, added: 'Snooker is in a very healthy position and the BBC have helped make the game what it is today. The game is spreading worldwide

WPBSA chairman John Virgo (right) signing the contract that guarantees snooker on British television until 1996. Looking on are (left) BBC's Nick Hunter, and Del Simmons of the WPSBA.

but this BBC deal has protected it where it is strongest and that is in the UK'.

What's more, the contract guarantees that the World Championship will stay at the Crucible Theatre until 1996. And, as Crucible administrator Geoffrey Rowe has said: 'Sheffield is to snooker what Wimbledon is to tennis'. So, in both the short and long term, snooker seems to have a solid base in the UK. However, what of those 'differences' that Nick Hunter of the BBC referred to?

SQUABBLES

With prize money topping £4 million in 1988–'89, it is perhaps not surprising that there have been squabbles between the WPBSA and Barry Hearn's eight-man Matchroom stable, which includes Steve Davis and world No. 2, Jimmy White. In fact, at the WPBSA Annual General Meeting in January 1989, there was an attempt by Hearn to unseat four members of the board. The move failed, though it was interesting to see the line-up at the meeting – a sprinkling of players accompanied by lawyers and accountants representing each side.

BARRY HEARN AND THE WPBSA

An accountant by trade, and a dynamic business-man, Barry Hearn was a member of the WPBSA board until he resigned in 1987 because of a clash of interests. He believes that 'managers should not be members of the WPBSA board. They should manage their own players and not make decisions for all the players'. Hence, two of the people he sought to unseat from the board were Ian Doyle, chairman of the Cuemasters outfit, and Framework chairman, Howard Kruger. The at-times uneasy relationship between Matchroom and the WPBSA has surfaced again in a difference of opinion as to what is best for the future of the game, at home and abroad. Happily, there seems to be a new mood of 'burying the hatchet'.

EXPANSION OVERSEAS

With Steve Davis, millionaire, superstar and many times world champion, now seen more times on television in one year than Her Majesty the Queen and Prime Minister Margaret Thatcher, and with television coverage of tournaments at near saturation point – some 400 hours are shown on

Ian Doyle (above) and Howard Kruger (below centre, with young stable stars David Roe, left, and Tony Drago, right) have found themselves in dispute with Barry Hearn who once tried to unseat both men from the board of the WPBSA.

Neal Foulds (above) after winning the £25,000 first prize in the 1988 Dubai Free Masters with a 5–4 win over Steve Davis, while (below) Davis shakes hands with local player Attiq Qubesi before the start of a first round match in the tournament.

British screens each year – the game has been asking itself: 'Where do we go from here?'

Well, to start with there has been a big push into new markets overseas. At the beginning of the 1988–'89 season the WPBSA announced an extension to the six ranking tournaments that are held throughout the British season. For the 1988–'89 season the additional tournaments played were the BCE Canadian Masters in Toronto and the ICI European Open in Deauville, France, whilst four extra ranking events were scheduled for the 1989–'90 season across the world – in Thailand, Hong Kong, Dubai and Europe.

However, there are those who think that the push to spread the ranking tournament abroad is taking place too quickly. The Matchroom squad's leading player, and world No. 1, Steve Davis is on record as saying: 'Canada was the wrong place for a ranking tournament. France was the wrong place (Steve said nobody would turn up at Deauville – and he was proved right). So is Dubai? I should know, I have been there'.

THE WPBSA AND IMG

On the other hand, the WPBSA, who are linked with Mark McCormack's International Management Group, are convinced that they are right – that

the world is more than ready for major international snooker tournaments rather than the eight-man specialist events that have been the mainstay of overseas matches up to now, and that snooker should, and indeed must be allowed to blossom and grow in places like Thailand and Hong Kong as quickly as possible.

Of course, it is not without significance that it was Barry Hearn who pioneered the sport's push for worldwide recognition in the early days. His growing Matchroom squad put on tournaments in Hong Kong, Thailand, China and Japan. Even Brazil, which is, it should be said, hardly the most likely snooker outpost, was paid a visit by world champion Steve Davis. So, it is hardly surprising that there has been a clash of opinion over the best way to develop the game abroad!

INCREASED MEMBERSHIP

In 1989, with expansion in mind, the WPBSA proposed increasing its membership of playing professionals from 128 to 160. However, this was turned down by the voting members of the WPBSA

Malta's Tony Drago in a happy mood after receiving the Overseas Player of the Year trophy at the WPBSA's awards dinner in London in 1988.

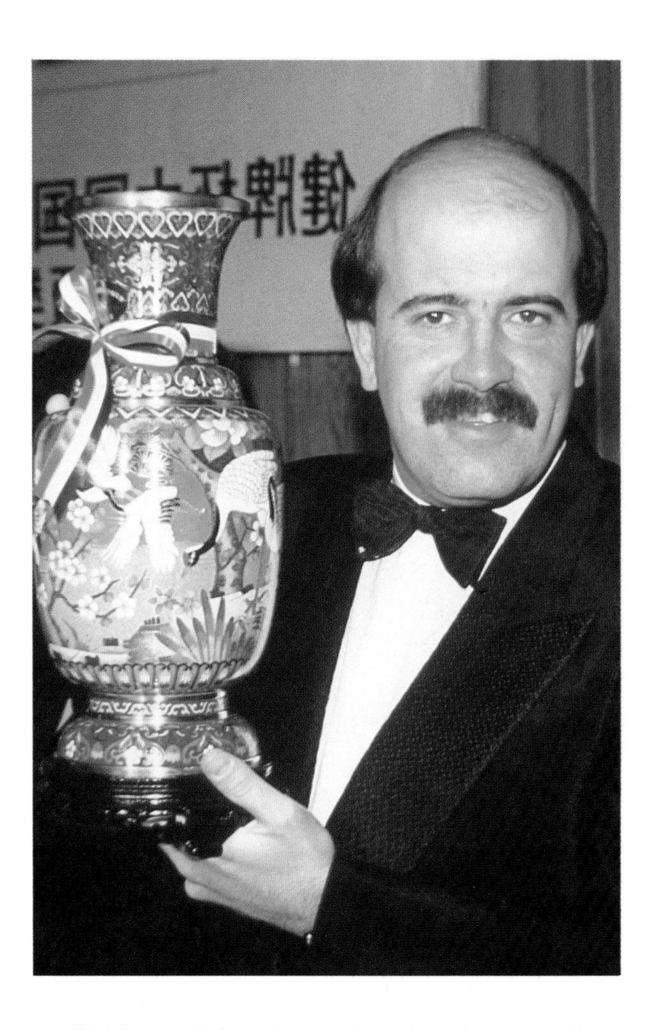

Willie Thorne (above) won the 1987 Kent Cup China International Masters in Peking defeating Jimmy White in the final, while Steve Davis (right) celebrates after his win over John Parrott in the final of the 1988 Everest World Matchplay in Brentwood.

– that is, those players who have been in the top 32 of the ranking list for the previous two years. It was not that they felt the WPBSA should stay a closed shop. Rather, that they just did not feel the proposed method for increasing the membership was right.

However, if snooker is to succeed overseas then, in the long term, it *must* increase its international membership. There must be more overseas professionals. Wherever snooker is played from now on, the marketing of the game will be so much easier if there are already professional players in the countries which are to stage tournaments.

At present, virtually all of the new professionals who progress through the Pro Ticket and play-off system are from the UK – though one notable exception in 1989 was James Wattana, the World Amateur Champion from Thailand. Wattana is one of the most talented young players ever to come through the amateur ranks. And he has already built up a very strong reputation as a naturally gifted player who can progress to the very top of the

EVEREST
WORLD MATCHPLAY

professional tree. But even so, Wattana, born in Bangkok, learnt his snooker in the UK – based in Bradford and playing on the British amateur circuit while waiting to join the élite group of 128 playing professionals.

It is clear that there must be more Wattanas if the game is to achieve its goal of making snooker as popular abroad as it is in this country.

DOMESTIC DEVELOPMENTS

Whilst the WPBSA control and run most of the major tournaments, there are exceptions, such as the Everest World Matchplay Championship and the Matchroom League – both conceived, run and promoted by Barry Hearn. The Matchplay offered the first-ever £100,000 first prize and featured the top 12 players in the world based on one season's rankings – as opposed to the normal two years for other tournaments. 'This gave us the best players on current form', said Hearn. (The second ton-up first prize was soon to follow – Steve Davis, 1989 winner of the Embassy World Championship picking up a cool £105,000.)

The Matchroom League, on the other hand, has to some extent replaced the old exhibition circuit in the snooker clubs up and down the country. In the 1970s, most professionals would supplement their income by visiting clubs for exhibition work. That meant matches against local amateurs, trick shots and an evening of quickfire jokes that was guaranteed to delight the local supporters. But with the ever-increasing number of tournaments most professionals have little or no time to entertain club audiences (though some players, like Cliff Wilson and Ray Reardon continue to do so).

In the 1980s, players like Davis and White are much more likely to parade their talents for multinational companies staging a celebrity evening for their employees and clients. That means a £5,000 per night appearance fee for someone like Davis – and that is a price totally out of the reach of the small club owner.

Hence the Matchroom League has been vital in keeping a 'live' link with the ordinary snooker fan. The majority of tournaments take place at the same venue year after year which means that, unless people are willing to travel large distances, the only snooker that most people will see will be on their television screens. However, by including more than thirty venues in the UK each year, League snooker has taken the game back to its roots and proved to be an outstanding success with 'live' audiences – which is just what snooker needs.

NOVELTY TOURNAMENTS

So, what do the 1990s hold for snooker? Television is guaranteed, exposure through other media is certain, the players at the top will stay as big-name personalities, prize money and sponsors will continue to increase – and no doubt there will be more disputes between interested parties over the best way of going about things.

Perhaps the one real fear for the future is that the tournaments are all too much the same – that, apart from the World Championship, they are all much of a muchness. That is why the Fersina Windows World Cup is so important. It is a team tournament that has often been criticised for being a 'novelty event'. The format of three players per country playing two frame matches was, in some circles, considered not to be 'proper snooker'. That might be so, but the crowds loved the format – and the paying punters are the ones that really matter!

Cliff Thorburn (right) becomes the eighth player to join the Matchroom team. Barry Hearn (left) and Steve Davis welcome Thorburn aboard.

To illustrate the point that so called 'novelty events' can provide genuine excitement as well as world-class snooker, take the World Cup final in Bournemouth in 1989, when England retained their title with one of the greatest finishes ever in a major tournament. England's Steve Davis and New Zealand's Dene O'Kane came to the table for the last frame decider with the scores level at 8 – 8. The frame lasted 73 minutes and Davis finally won on a re-spotted black – the first time that a final had been decided on a re-spot. This was yet another case of a snooker match gripping the nation.

THE WAY AHEAD

But does snooker need more events like this? Cricket, once a boom sport after the Second World War, went into decline when spectators got fed up with watching county matches that lasted for three days. The modern style of living demanded a result on the same day. Thus one-day cricket was born and, it could be argued, saved the sport from extinction.

At the moment, the viewers and spectators are quite happy with the snooker tournaments on offer. But you only have to listen to some of the comments in the bars and clubs to realise that the game must look at different formats to maintain the public's interest in the future.

However, those days are still to come and, despite the behind-the-scenes wranglings, snooker is in a very healthy state. As we have seen, there is money in the game, guaranteed television and not too many controversies, The cynics who wrote off snooker as a 'five-year wonder' have been proved completely wrong. The world is waiting – and now it is up to snooker to see whether it can get it right in the push for overseas acceptance.

THE AMATEUR GAME

WITHOUT A STRONG AMATEUR GAME TO NURTURE THE STARS OF TOMORROW, PROFESSIONAL SNOOKER WOULD FALL INTO INEXORABLE DECLINE. BUT HOW DO YOU MOVE UP FROM THE AMATEUR RANKS TO THE PROFESSIONAL CIRCUIT? TO SHOW HOW IT CAN BE DONE, WE LOOK AT THE FICTIONAL PROGRESS OF A YOUNG SNOOKER STAR AS HE AIMS TO EMULATE HIS HERO, WORLD CHAMPION, STEVE DAVIS.

The early days. John Parrott (left) pictured as an amateur before he stepped so successfully into the pro ranks. Now Parrott has risen to No. 2 in the world.

THE AMATEUR GAME

Amateur snooker, like any other amateur sport, existed for a long time before players were able to pack up their jobs and start to make a living from their chosen hobby. Indeed, whilst professonal snooker players have existed for many years, it is only during the boom of the last ten years that they have emerged as sporting 'moneybags'. Players of yesteryear, like Joe Davis, were nationally known figures but relative paupers compared to the millionaires of today.

Nowadays, snooker's top professionals can command large sums of money, and not just for winning matches. A substantial part of their income is derived from endorsing products and making public appearances. That is the glamour side of the sport, but even to start achieving this sort of status, a player needs to serve his apprenticeship in the amateur ranks.

Of course, the word 'amateur' is a rather loose description, because all players are entitled to win prize money and there are many, many competitions in the UK and throughout the world where large cash pots are available for the participants. Quite simply, everyone who picks up a cue is a player. The professionals are those who have been admitted to the World Professional Billiards and Snooker Association. And that's where the real money lies – the WPBSA tournament circuit is currently worth more than £4 million a year!

TURNING PROFESSIONAL

How do you become a professional? How do you make that transition from non-professional tournaments to professional status and, who knows, an appearance on snooker's greatest stage – at the Crucible Theatre, Sheffield, the home of the Embassy World Professional Championships?

In years gone by, players could apply to join the WPBSA by virtue of being the national amateur champion of their own country, being a regular international player or by maintaining an outstanding amateur career. However, those rules of selection have now changed and, perhaps, the easiest way to see how you can make it to the professional ranks is to follow the blossoming career of Micky Black, a purely fictional character who comes to believe that he can one day take over as world No. 1 from Steve Davis.

A picture from the family album with a young amateur, Stephen Hendry and father, Gordon.

AN EARLY START

Our Micky begins playing at the age of eight when proud mum and dad give him a small snooker table for his birthday. Micky loves playing the game and the family takes to eating in the kitchen as the snooker table seems to have permanent residence on the dining-room table! By the age of ten, Micky is already developing an eye for the game and tells his dad, Bill, that he wants to be a professional snooker player when he grows up. The days when everybody wanted to play football for England have long since passed!

Bill enjoys a pint or two of beer and is a keen player at his local working men's club. He even manages to get through one or two rounds of the Christmas Handicap. But he knows nothing about the structure of the game – how it is run in the United Kingdom as an amateur sport. The one thing Bill does know is that, on the night he enjoys his regular snooker foursome with his workmates, there is a League match taking place on another table which all the members refer to as 'The Match Table'. Bill, whose best break is a modest 16, has never dared test his meagre talents on this 'holy of holies'. But he promises Micky, who by now is beating dad regularly on the table back home that he will make some inquiries. Micky's best break on the small table now stands at 38!

THE BILLIARDS AND SNOOKER FOUNDATION

Luckily, the club captain is able to introduce Bill to a visiting captain who also happens to be secretary of the local League. He tells Bill to write to the Billiards and Snooker Control Council in Leeds, as they organise all the national competitions in England and also run some United Kingdom and British Isles tournaments. Off goes the letter and back comes a reply from David Ford, the Secretary and Chief Executive of the B&SCC, advising Bill to take Micky along to seek the help of his nearest qualified snooker coach. Included in the reply is a list of the qualified coaches in the area and an explanation of the work carried out by the Billiards and Snooker Foundation.

The Foundation is jointly sponsored by the B&SCC and the Billiards and Snooker Trade Association. The B&STA is an association of most of the major manufacturers of equipment. Collectively, these two bodies finance the work of the Foundation, whose prime object is to teach the basics of snooker and billiards to those under the age of 18.

THE LOCAL COACH

Micky reads the literature and is surprised that the Foundation introduces 3,500 new young players to the game each year. He is quickly in contact with the local coach to explain his needs. Luckily, he finds that the coach lives fairly close to his home. (This is often the case, the Foundation having a fairly widespread network of personnel.) Of course, young players would have to travel a bit further in order to get formal coaching if they live in outlying villages.

Micky is one of the lucky ones because the coach has a vacancy the following Saturday morning. He explains to Micky that he must be at the local Snooker Centre at 10am sharp. Micky passes the phone over to his dad who discusses the very modest charges and prepares to take his offspring to his first coaching lesson. Bill is secretly pleased that he will avoid the Saturday morning crush down at the local supermarket!

Micky is really excited and is up at 7 o'clock on the Saturday morning. It is usually nearer 10 o'clock when Micky crawls out of bed after watching television in his bedroom. But not today! Down at the club, the coach explains what they will be doing over the next six weeks. The first priority is to give Micky and five other pupils the basis of a first-class technique that will stand them in good stead whatever level they achieve in their playing careers.

Bill soon discovers that snooker clubs today are, in many cases, up-market establishments with restaurants and bars attached. Meanwhile, Micky works hard, gets on with the tasks outlined by his coach and persuades his dad to let him actually join the club so that he has the chance to practise between lessons.

LOCAL COMPETITIONS

It doesn't take long for the coach to recognize that Micky has ability and suggest that he enters some local competitions when he has finished his training course. Now we will see what Micky is made of! He is a sensible lad, and soon realises that it was not as easy as it looked when he watched Steve Davis score three century breaks in a row. But he is on his way, and over the next three years, as long as his schoolwork maintains a high standard, Micky is allowed to enter as many competitions as he wishes. He wins a few at local level and then starts causing a few surprises in the rest of the county. The county selectors have started to take notice!

THE ENGLISH CHAMPIONSHIP

After some successes in the junior tournaments, Micky is advised to enter senior tournaments as well and, in particular, the English Championship. Micky fills in the form and, much to his delight, manages to beat a couple of senior players in the early rounds before eventually losing! But it has been a good run and good experience even if the senior players weren't too pleased at being beaten by a 13-year-old kid! Meanwhile, Micky is still playing at the same local club and the manager, hoping that he has a potential champion on his hands, starts giving Micky free practice time on the table.

LEAVING SCHOOL

By now Micky, coming up to school-leaving age, is a regular member of the county side and last year reached the last 16 of the English Championship. Bill and Mary are still supporting their son all the way. But what is young Micky going to do for a living? He has worked hard at school but managed just a couple of exam passes. When asked by the Careers Officer, Micky says: 'I want to be a full-time snooker player'.

While Micky and his mum and dad are talking over the future, the owner of the club has decided that Micky could become a potential champion. Out of the blue the owner invites Micky and Bill along for a chat and offers the young man a sponsorship contract. This means that Micky can enter the major tournaments, receive a small wage and, of course, practise whenever he likes. In return Micky will work at the Snooker Centre, where he will carry out such duties as booking and maintaining the tables and serving in the cafeteria.

The decision is made. Micky will leave school and attempt to become a full-time professional by accepting the job offered at the Snooker Centre. And luckily for Micky everything goes well. He works hard, continues winning a few tournaments and the club owner now decides that, at 17, the time is right for Micky to concentrate on gaining a place in the professional ranks.

JOINING THE PROFESSIONAL RANKS

There are three ways of helping to gain admission to the WPBSA: 1. By winning the English Championship. 2. By becoming the International Billiards and Snooker Federation World Champion. 3. By coming through the Pro-Ticket Series.

If Micky was to win the English Amateur he would probably be invited to represent England in the IBSF World Snooker Championship. The IBSF was set up in 1973. They are the world governing body for snooker and more than 40 countries are involved in the Federation. They organise the World Championship for non-professional players every year, and have held the tournament in exotic places such as Australia, India, New Zealand and Canada. This time the event is to be held in Singapore.

Micky also enters the three Pro-Ticket tournaments which currently carry ranking points for admittance to the professional ranks. The eight qualifiers, plus the English champion and the IBF champion, then take part in play-offs against the lower ranked professionals.

In admitting new players to the professional ranks, the winners of the IBSF World Championship and the English Championship go through to the play-offs. In theory, it is possible for a player to ignore the Pro-Ticket tournaments. But this is far too big a risk to take. The English Championship is open to *all* players, so Micky will be facing the cream of talent from all over the United Kingdom.

THE QUALIFYING TOURNAMENTS

Micky has a busy year, but is beaten in the quarter-finals of the English Championship. Even so, he finds that he does not have time to lick his wounds and must now concentrate all his thoughts on the important Pro-Tickets. He packs his suitcase and together with mum and dad travels around the country to play at the holiday centres owned by Warner's and Pontin's.

To the delight of his family and friends, Micky wins the first two Pro-Ticket tournaments, collects £6000 and gains maximum points. But he is still not home and dry as there is still one Pro-Ticket to go. In this, Micky battles through to the final and comes face to face with the winner of the English Championship, who is off to Singapore the following week for the IBSF Championship. Having got this far, Micky knows he has earned sufficient ranking points to qualify for the play-offs for professional status, but pride is at stake.

Unfortunately he is beaten in a memorable match and his opponent jets off to fight for the world title.

One for the future? Lee Walker from South Wales receives a prize from six-times world champion Ray Reardon during one of Ray's highly-successful coaching sessions at Brean Sands Holiday Camp.

adidas

UP AGAINST THE PROFESSIONALS

The real crunch comes during the following year as the professionals finish the qualifying rounds for the Embassy World Championship. The bottom ten know that they have to take on the English amateur champion, the IBSF world champion and the eight Pro-Ticket qualifiers – one of whom is Micky.

It's the biggest day of his life as he travels to Preston and fortunately, after a hard-fought battle, Micky comes through to enter the professional ranks, ready to join Steve Davis and company on the long and hard road to glory and riches. All that dedication and hard work have paid off. Together with proper coaching, financial backing and the support of his parents, Micky has made it on to the first rung of the professional ladder.

THE OVERSEAS CHALLENGE

At the moment, players from the United Kingdom make up the vast majority of the new professionals, though that is now gradually changing. James Wattana of Thailand, who won the IBSF World Championship in 1988 and thereby qualified for the professional ranks for the 1989–'90 season, proved that the overseas challenge is going to get stronger and stronger as the years go by. Snooker is now truly international, with the European and Asian Federations slowly but surely producing players of world class.

There is no doubt that professional and amateur snooker has been the boom sport of the 1980s, and its popularity shows no sign of waning, with more and more youngsters turning to the game and more and more competitions being held all over the United Kingdom. So, whilst Steve Davis might be the richest and best-known player in the world, it is youngsters like our fictional Micky Black who will ensure the future of the game.

USEFUL ADDRESS

Any enquiries concerning coaching, tournaments and the rules of the game can be addressed to: The Billiards and Snooker Control Council (The B&SCC, est. 1885), at Coronet House, Queen Street, Leeds, LS1 2TN. Telephone: 0532 440586.

James Wattana, here with manager Roger Haycock, is one of the most promising new professionals.

RULES OF THE GAME OF SNOOKER

AUTHORISED BY

THE BILLIARDS AND SNOOKER CONTROL COUNCIL

•

THE BILLIARDS ASSOCIATION

ESTABLISHED 1885

•

THE BILLIARDS CONTROL CLUB

ESTABLISHED 1908

•

AMALGAMATED 1919

•

CHAIRMAN

STAN BROOKE

SECRETARY AND CHIEF EXECUTIVE

DAVID FORD

SECTION 1 • EQUIPMENT

1 • TABLE (METRIC)
2 • BALLS
3 • CUE
4 • ANCILLARY

SECTION 2 • DEFINITIONS

1 • FRAME
2 • GAME
3 • MATCH
4 • BALLS
5 • STRIKER
6 • STROKE
7 • IN-HAND
8 • IN PLAY
9 • ON
10 • NOMINATED
11 • POT
12 • BREAK
13 • FORCED OFF
14 • FOUL
15 • SNOOKERED
16 • ANGLED
17 • OCCUPIED
18 • PUSH-STROKE
19 • JUMP SHOT
20 • MISS

SECTION 3 • THE GAME

1 • DESCRIPTION
2 • POSITION OF BALLS
3 • MODE OF PLAY
4 • PLAY FROM IN-HAND
5 • SIMULTANEOUS HIT
6 • SPOTTING COLOURS
7 • TOUCHING BALLS
8 • EDGE OF POCKET
9 • FREE BALL
10 • FOUL
11 • PENALTIES
12 • MOVEMENT OF BALL
13 • STALEMATE
14 • FOUR HANDED

SECTION 4 • THE PLAYERS

1 • TIME WASTING
2 • UNFAIR CONDUCT
3 • PENALTY
4 • NON-STRIKER
5 • ABSENCE

SECTION 5 • THE OFFICIALS

1 • REFEREE
2 • MARKER

SECTION 1 • EQUIPMENT

1 • THE STANDARD TABLE • METRIC

DIMENSIONS
(a) the playing area within the cushion faces shall measure 3500mm × 1750mm with a tolerance on both dimensions of ±3mm.

HEIGHT
(b) the height of the table from the floor to the top of the cushion rail shall be from 850mm to 875mm.

POCKET OPENINGS
(c) (i) there shall be pockets at the corners (two at the Spot end known as the top pockets and two at the Baulk end known as the bottom pockets) and at the middle of the longer sides.
(ii) the pocket openings shall conform to the templates authorised by the Billiards and Snooker Control Council.

BAULK-LINE AND BAULK
(d) a straight line drawn 700mm (1/5th the length of the playing area) from the face of the bottom cushion and parallel to it is called the Baulk-line and the intervening space termed the Baulk.

THE 'D'
(e) the 'D' is a semi-circle described in Baulk with its centre at the middle of the Baulk-line and with a radius of 292mm (1/6th the width of the Playing area).

SPOTS
(f) four spots marked on the centre longitudinal line of the table.
(i) the Spot: 320mm (1/11th the length of the playing area) from the point perpendicular below the face of the top cushion.
(ii) the Centre Spot: Midway between the centre pockets and equidistant from the faces of the top and bottom cushions.
(iii) the Pyramid Spot: Midway between the centre spot and the face of the top cushion.
(iv) the Middle of the Baulk-line.

2 • BALLS

(a) the balls shall have a diameter of 52.5mm with a tolerance of +0.05mm – 0.08mm.
(b) they shall be of equal weight within a tolerance of
(i) 3 gms per Snooker set, and
(ii) 0.5 gms per Billiard set.

NOTE
A ball or a set of balls may be changed with the consent of the players or on a decision of the referee.

3 • CUE

The cue shall be not less than 910mm in length and shall show no substantial departure from the traditional and generally accepted shape and form.

4 • ANCILLARY

'Rests' may be used to provide a bridge for the cue.

NOTE
It is the players' responsibility to both place the rest on and remove it from the table.

SECTION 2 • DEFINITIONS

1 • FRAME

A frame is completed when
(a) conceded, or
(b) the black is finally potted or fouled.

2 • GAME

A game is an agreed number of frames.

3 • MATCH

A match is an agreed number of games.

4 • BALLS

(a) the white ball is the cue-ball.
(b) the 15 reds, and
(c) the 6 colours, are object balls.

5 • STRIKER

The person about to play or in play is the striker and remains so until completion of the stroke or break (Sec. 2 Rules 6 & 12).

6 • STROKE

(a) a stroke is made when the striker strikes the cue-ball with the tip of the cue.
(b) for the stroke to be a 'Fair Stroke' the following conditions must be met:
 (i) At the moment of striking, all balls must be at rest, and where necessary, colours correctly spotted.
 (ii) The cue ball must be struck and not pushed.
 (iii) The cue ball must not be struck more than once in the same stroke.
 (iv) At the moment of striking, at least one of the striker's feet must be touching the floor.
 (v) The striker must not touch any ball other than the cue ball as in section (a) above.
 (iv) A ball or balls must not be 'forced off the table'.
(c) a stroke is not completed until all balls have come to rest and the referee has decided the striker has left the table.

7 • IN-HAND

(a) the cue-ball is in-hand when it has entered a pocket or has been forced off the table.
(b) it remains in-hand until played fairly from in-hand or a foul is committed whilst the ball is on the table.

8 • BALL IN PLAY

(a) the cue-ball is in play when not in-hand.
(b) object balls are in play when spotted and remain so until pocketed or forced off the table.

NOTE
Using the cue to position the cue-ball:
If the referee considers the player is not attempting to play a stroke, even though the tip of the cue touches the cue-ball, the ball is not in play.

9 • BALL ON

Any ball which may be lawfully hit by the first impact of the cue-ball is said to be *on*.

10 • NOMINATED BALL

A nominated ball is the object ball which the striker declares, or indicates to the satisfaction of the referee, he undertakes to hit with the first impact of the cue-ball.

NOTE
If requested by the referee the striker must declare which ball he is on.

11 • POT

(a) a pot is when an object ball, after contact with another ball, and without any contravention of these rules, enters a pocket.
(b) if a colour, it shall be spotted before the next stroke is made, until finally potted under Sec. 3 Rule 3.
(c) if a stroke is made, with a ball or balls incorrectly spotted, and a foul is not awarded, the ball or balls
 (i) if on the table will be considered to be correctly spotted.
 (ii) if not on the table will be spotted when the foul is awarded.

NOTE
(i) It is the strikers' responsibility to ensure that all balls are correctly spotted before striking.
(ii) Subject to Sec. 3 Rules 8 & 12, reds are never replaced on the table despite the fact that a player may benefit from a foul.

12 • BREAK

(a) if a ball is potted, the same player plays the next stroke.
(b) a break is a number of pots in succession made in any one turn.

13 • FORCED OFF THE TABLE

(a) a ball is forced off the table if it comes to rest other than on the bed of the table or in a pocket.
(b) if a colour it shall be spotted as per Sec. 3 Rule 6 before the next stroke is made.

14 • FOUL

A foul is any act in contravention of these rules.

15 • SNOOKERED

(a) the cue ball is snookered when a direct stroke in a straight line to any part of every ball *on* is obstructed by a ball or balls not *on*.

NOTE
If there is any one ball that is not so obstructed, the cue-ball is not snookered.

(b) if in-hand, the cue-ball is snookered only if obstructed from all positions on or within the lines of the 'D'.
(c) if the cue-ball is obstructed by more than one ball, the one nearest to the cue-ball is the effective snookering ball.

16 • ANGLED

(a) the cue-ball is angled when a direct stroke in a straight line to any part of every ball *on* is obstructed by a corner of the cushion.

NOTE
If there is any one ball that is not so obstructed, the cue-ball is not angled.

If angled after a foul,
(b) the referee will state angled ball, and
(c) it may be played from in-hand at the strikers' discretion.

17 • OCCUPIED

A spot is said to be occupied if a ball cannot be placed on it without it touching another ball.

18 • PUSH STROKE

A push stroke is a foul and is made when the tip of the cue remains in contact with the cue-ball,
(a) when the cue-ball makes contact with the object ball, or
(b) after the cue-ball has commenced its forward motion.

PROVIDED that where the cue-ball and an object ball are almost touching, it shall be deemed a fair stroke if the cue-ball hits the finest possible edge of the object ball.

19 • JUMP SHOT

A jump shot is when the cue-ball jumps over any ball except when it first strikes the object ball and then jumps over another ball.

NOTE
If the cue-ball finishes on the far side of the object ball, even though touching it in the process, it is considered to have jumped over.

NOTE
After striking the ball *on* fairly if the cue-ball should then jump over the object ball after hitting a cushion, it shall be deemed to be a fair stroke.

20 • MISS

A miss is when the referee considers the striker has not endeavoured to hit the ball *on*.

SECTION 3 • THE GAME

1 • DESCRIPTION

The game of Snooker is played on an English Billiard Table and may be played by two or more persons, either as sides or independently.

Points are awarded for scoring strokes and forfeits from an opponent's fouls.

The winner is the player or side making the highest score or to whom the game is awarded under Sec. 4 Rule 2.

Each player uses the same WHITE cue-ball and there are twenty-one object balls – fifteen reds each valued 1 and six colours: yellow valued 2, green 3, brown 4, blue 5, pink 6 and black 7.

Scoring strokes are made by potting reds and colours alternately until all reds are off the table and then the colours in the ascending order of their value i.e. – yellow through to black.

2 • POSITION OF BALLS

At the commencement of each frame the object balls are positioned as follows:
BLACK on the SPOT; PINK on the PYRAMID SPOT; BLUE on the CENTRE SPOT; BROWN on the MIDDLE of the BAULK-line; GREEN on the LEFT-HAND and YELLOW on the RIGHT-HAND corner of the 'D'.

The reds in the form of a triangle, the ball at the apex standing as near to the pink ball as possible, without touching it, the base being parallel with and nearest to the top cushion.

NOTE
The positions for the object balls are commonly referred to by the colour, e.g. black spot, pink spot, etc.

3 • MODE OF PLAY

(a) the players shall determine the order of play which (subject to Sec. 3 Rule 10) must remain unaltered throughout the *frame*.

NOTE
The player to strike first at each frame shall alternate during a game.

(b) the first player shall play from *in-hand* and the frame starts with the first stroke.
(c) the cue ball
  (i) must first hit a ball *on,* and
  (ii) must not enter a pocket.
(d) a ball not *on* must not enter a pocket.
(e) (i) for the first stroke of each turn, until all are off the table, red is the ball *on*.
  (ii) the value of each red, or ball nominated as red, potted in the same stroke is scored.
(f) if a red is potted, the next ball *on* is a colour, which if potted is scored. The colour is then re-spotted.
(g) until all reds are off the table the break is continued by potting reds and colours alternately.
(h) if the striker fails to score the next player plays from where the cue-ball comes to rest.
(j) the colours then become *on* in the ascending order of their value (Sec. 3 Rule 1) and when potted remain off the table (except as provided for in the next paragraph).
(k) when only the Black is left the first score or foul ends the frame, unless the scores are then equal, in which case:
  (i) the Black is spotted.
  (ii) the players draw lots for choice of playing.
  (iii) the next player plays from *in hand*.
  (iv) the next score or foul ends the game.

NOTE
Aggregate Scores:
In games or matches where aggregate scores are relevant it is only when the scores are equal as a result of the last frame that the above applies.

(l) the striker shall to the best of his ability endeavour to hit the ball *on*. If the referee considers the rule infringed he shall call foul and miss.

NOTE
The ball *on* impossible to be hit:
In this situation it has to be considered that the striker is attempting to hit the ball *on*.

4 • TO PLAY FROM IN-HAND

To play from in-hand the cue-ball must be struck from a position on or within the lines of the 'D'.

NOTE
The referee will answer if asked if the ball is properly placed.

5 • HITTING TWO BALLS SIMULTANEOUSLY

Two balls, other than two reds or a *free ball* and the ball *on,* must not be hit simultaneously by the cue-ball.

6 • SPOTTING COLOURS

(a) if a colour has to be spotted, and its own spot is *occupied,* it shall be placed on the highest-value spot available.
(b) if there is more than one colour, and their own spots are *occupied,* the highest value ball takes precedence.
(c) if all spots are *occupied,* the colour shall be placed as near as possible to its own spot between that spot and the nearest part of the top cushion.
(d) if, in the case of the Black and the Pink, the space between its own spot and the nearest part of the top cushion is *occupied,* the colour shall be placed as near as possible to its own spot on the centre line of the table below that spot.

7 • TOUCHING BALL

(a) if the cue-ball is touching another ball which is, or can be, *on,* the referee shall state TOUCHING BALL.
(b) the striker must play away from it or it is a *push stroke*.
(c) no penalty is incurred for thus playing away if:
  (i) the ball is not *on*.
  (ii) the ball is *on* and the striker *nominates* such ball, or
  (iii) the ball is *on* and the striker *nominates,* and first hits, another ball.

NOTE
Movement of touching ball:
If the referee considers that a touching ball has moved through an agency other than the player, it is not a foul.

8 • BALL ON EDGE OF POCKET

(a) if a ball falls into a pocket without being hit by another ball it shall be replaced.
(b) if it would have been hit by any ball involved in a stroke, all balls will be replaced and the stroke replayed.
(c) if the ball balances momentarily on the edge and falls in, it must not be replaced.

9 • FREE BALL

(a) after a foul, if the cue-ball is *snookered,* the referee shall state FREE BALL.
(b) if the non-offending player takes the next stroke he may nominate any ball as *on.*
(c) for this stroke, such ball shall (subject to para (e)(i)) be regarded as, and acquire the value of, the ball *on.*
(d) it is a foul, should the cue-ball
  (i) fail to first hit, or
  (ii) except when only Pink and Black remain on the table, be *snookered* by, the *free ball.*
(e) if the *free ball* is potted it
  (i) is spotted, and
  (ii) the value of the ball *on* is scored.
(f) if the ball *on* is potted it is scored.
(g) if both the *free ball* and the ball *on* are potted only the value of the ball *on* is scored (subject to Sec. 3 Rule 3(e)(ii)).

10 • FOULS

(a) if a foul is committed:
  (i) the referee shall immediately state FOUL and on completion of the stroke announce the penalty.
  (ii) unless awarded by the referee or claimed by the non-striker, before the next stroke is made, it is condoned.
  (iii) any ball improperly spotted shall remain where positioned, except that if off the table it shall be correctly spotted.
  (iv) all points scored before the foul is awarded or claimed are allowed.
  (v) the next stroke is made from where the cue-ball comes to rest.
(b) should more than one foul be committed in the same stroke the highest-value penalty shall be incurred.
(c) the player who committed the foul:
  (i) incurs the penalty prescribed (which is added to the opponent's score), and
  (ii) has to play again if requested by the next player. Once such a request has been made it cannot be withdrawn.
  (iii) If a breach of Section 3.3(l) occurs, the offending player has to play again from the original position, if requested by the next player.

11 • PENALTIES

The following are fouls and incur a penalty of four points or the higher one prescribed.
(a) value of the ball *on*:
  by striking
  (i) when the balls are not at rest (Sec. 2 Rule 6).
  (ii) the cue ball more than once (2 – 6).
  (iii) with both feet off the floor (2 – 6).
  (iv) out of turn (3 – 3).
  (v) improperly from *in-hand* (3 – 4).
  by causing
  (vi) the cue-ball to miss all object balls (3 – 3).
  (vii) the cue-ball to enter a pocket (3 – 3).
  (viii) a *snooker* with *free ball* (3 – 9).
  (ix) a *jump shot* (2 – 19).
(b) value of the ball *on* or ball concerned: by causing
  (i) a ball not *on* to enter a pocket (3 – 3).
  (ii) the cue-ball to first hit a ball not *on* (3 – 3).
  (iii) a *push stroke* (2 – 18).
  (iv) by striking with a ball incorrectly spotted (2 – 11).
  (v) by touching a ball with other than the tip of the cue (2 – 6).
  (vi) by forcing a ball off the table (2 – 13).
(c) value of the ball *on* or higher value of the two balls by causing the cue-ball to hit simultaneously two balls other than two reds or a *free ball* and the ball *on* (3 – 5).
(d) a penalty of seven points is incurred if: the striker
  (i) after potting a red commits a foul before *nominating* a colour,
  (ii) uses a ball off the table for any purpose,
  (iii) plays at reds in successive strokes, or
  (iv) uses as the cue-ball any ball other than white.

12 • BALL MOVED BY OTHER THAN STRIKER

If a ball, stationary or moving, is disturbed other than by the striker it shall be re-positioned by the referee.

NOTE

This covers the case in which another agency causes the striker to touch a ball. No player shall be responsible for any disturbance of the balls by the referee.

13 • STALEMATE

If the referee considers a position of stalemate is being approached, he should warn the players that if the situation is not altered in a short period of time he will declare the frame null and void. The frame shall be re-started with the same order of play.

14 • FOUR-HANDED SNOOKER

(a) in a four-handed game each side shall open alternate frames, the order of play shall be determined at the commencement of each frame, and must be maintained throughout that frame.
(b) players may change order of play at the beginning of each frame.
(c) if a foul is committed and a request made to play again, the player who committed the foul plays again, and the original order of play is maintained.
(d) when a frame ends in a tie Snooker Rule 3k applies. The pair who play the first stroke have the choice of which player plays that stroke. The order of play must then be maintained as in the frame.
(e) partners may confer during a game but not whilst one is the striker and at the table or after the first stroke of his break.

SECTION 4 • THE PLAYERS

1 • TIME WASTING

If the referee considers that a player is taking an abnormal amount of time over a stroke, he should be warned that he is liable to be disqualified.

2 • UNFAIR CONDUCT

For refusing to continue a frame or for conduct which, in the opinion of the referee is wilfully or persistently unfair a player shall lose the game. He is liable to be disqualified from competitions held under the control of The Billiards and Snooker Council and its Affiliated Associations.

3 • PENALTY

If a game is awarded to a player under this section the offender shall:

(i) lose the game, and
(ii) forfeit all points scored, and the non-offender shall receive the value of the balls still on the table (each red counting eight points).

NOTE

Provided that where aggregate points scores apply, the offender shall also forfeit 147 points for each unplayed frame, to the number required to complete the game.

4 • NON-STRIKER

The non-striker shall, when the striker is playing, avoid standing or moving in the line of sight; he should sit or stand at a fair distance from the table.

5 • ABSENCE

In the case of his absence from the room he may appoint a substitute to watch his interests, and claim a foul if necessary.

SECTION 5 • THE OFFICIALS

1 • THE REFEREE

(a) the referee shall
  (i) be the sole judge of fair and unfair play, and responsible for the proper conduct of the game under these Rules.
  (ii) intervene if he sees any contravention.
  (iii) if a player is colour blind, tell him the colour of a ball if requested.
  (iv)clean a ball on a player's request.
(b) he shall not
  (i) answer any question not authorised in the Rules.
  (ii) give any indication that a player is about to make a foul stroke.
  (iii) give any advice or opinion on points affecting play.
(c) if he has failed to notice any incident he may take the evidence of the spectators best placed for observation to assist his decision.

NOTE

The referee will not answer a question regarding the difference in scores.

2 • THE MARKER

The marker shall keep the score on the marking board and assist the referee in carrying out his duties.

NOTE

If requested by the striker, the referee or marker may move and hold in position any light shade which interferes with the action of the striker.

RESULTS

Snooker has, of course, its personalities and its heroes in as great a number as in any other sport, but the snooker fan loves to consider at the same time the facts and figures of the game. The following is a look at the major results which have been recorded in the modern era of professional snooker – an easy-to-follow guide to who has won what and when.

FOSTER'S CHAMPIONS

YEAR	CHAMPION		RUNNER-UP	RESULT
1984	J. WHITE (Eng)	bt	A. KNOWLES (Eng)	9–7
1985	J. WHITE (Eng)	bt	A. HIGGINS (NI)	8–3
1986	DENNIS TAYLOR (NI)	bt	J. WHITE (Eng)	8–3
1987	DENNIS TAYLOR (NI)	bt	J. JOHNSON (Eng)	8–5
1988	M. HALLETT (Eng)	bt	S. HENDRY (Scot)	8–5

Previous sponsors: 1984, 1985, 1986 Carlsberg; 1987 Carling.

TENNENTS UK OPEN

YEAR	CHAMPION		RUNNER-UP	RESULT
1977	P. FAGAN (Rep Ire)	bt	D. MOUNTJOY (Wales)	12–9
1978	D. MOUNTJOY (Wales)	bt	DAVID TAYLOR (Eng)	15–9
1979	J. VIRGO (Eng)	bt	T. GRIFFITHS (Wales)	14–13
1980	S. DAVIS (Eng)	bt	A. HIGGINS (NI)	16–6
1981	S. DAVIS (Eng)	bt	T. GRIFFITHS (Wales)	16–3
1982	T. GRIFFITHS (Wales)	bt	A. HIGGINS (NI)	16–15
1983	A. HIGGINS (NI)	bt	S. DAVIS (Eng)	16–15
1984	S. DAVIS (Eng)	bt	A. HIGGINS (NI)	16–8
1985	S. DAVIS (Eng)	bt	W. THORNE (Eng)	16–14
1986	S. DAVIS (Eng)	bt	N. FOULDS (Eng)	16–7
1987	S. DAVIS (Eng)	bt	J. WHITE (Eng)	16–14
1988	D. MOUNTJOY (Wales)	bt	S. HENDRY (Scot)	16–12

Previous sponsors: 1977 Super Crystalate; 1978, 1979, 1980, 1981, 1982, 1983, 1984, 1985 Coral.

FIDELITY UNIT TRUSTS INTERNATIONAL

YEAR	CHAMPION		RUNNER-UP	RESULT
1981	S. DAVIS (Eng)	bt	DENNIS TAYLOR (NI)	9–0
1982	A. KNOWLES (Eng)	bt	DAVID TAYLOR (Eng)	9–6
1983	S. DAVIS (Eng)	bt	C. THORBURN (Can)	9–4
1984	S. DAVIS (Eng)	bt	A. KNOWLES (Eng)	9–2
1985	C. THORBURN (Can)	bt	J. WHITE (Eng)	12–10

Steve Davis on his way to a 16–14 final win over Jimmy White in the 1987 Tennents UK Championship.

YEAR	CHAMPION		RUNNER-UP	RESULT
1986	N. FOULDS (Eng)	bt	C. THORBURN (Can)	12–9
1987	S. DAVIS (Eng)	bt	C. THORBURN (Can)	12–5
1988	S. DAVIS (Eng)	bt	J. WHITE (Eng)	12–6

Previous sponsors: 1981, 1982, 1983 Jameson; 1985 Goya; 1986 BCE.

ROTHMANS GRAND PRIX

YEAR	CHAMPION		RUNNER-UP	RESULT
1982	R. REARDON (Wales)	bt	J. WHITE (Eng)	10–5
1983	A. KNOWLES (Eng)	bt	J. JOHNSON (Eng)	9–8
1984	DENNIS TAYLOR (NI)	bt	C. THORBURN (Can)	10–2
1985	S. DAVIS (Eng)	bt	DENNIS TAYLOR (NI)	10–9
1986	J. WHITE (Eng)	bt	R. WILLIAMS (Eng)	10–6
1987	S. HENDRY (Scot)	bt	DENNIS TAYLOR (NI)	10–7
1988	S. DAVIS (Eng)	bt	A. HIGGINS (NI)	10–6

Previous sponsors: 1982, 1983, 1984, 1985, 1986 Professional Players Tournament.

EVEREST WORLD MATCHPLAY

YEAR	CHAMPION		RUNNER-UP	RESULT
1988	S. DAVIS (Eng)	bt	J. PARROTT (Eng)	9–5

MERCANTILE CREDIT CLASSIC

YEAR	CHAMPION		RUNNER-UP	RESULT
1980	J. SPENCER (Eng)	bt	A. HIGGINS (NI)	4–3
1981	S. DAVIS (Eng)	bt	DENNIS TAYLOR (NI)	4–1
1982	T. GRIFFITHS (Wales)	bt	S. DAVIS (Eng)	9–8
1983	S. DAVIS (Eng)	bt	W. WERBENIUK (Can)	9–5
1984	S. DAVIS (Eng)	bt	A. MEO (Eng)	9–8
1985	W. THORNE (Eng)	bt	C. THORBURN (Can)	13–8
1986	J. WHITE (Eng)	bt	C. THORBURN (Can)	13–12
1987	S. DAVIS (Eng)	bt	J. WHITE (Eng)	13–12
1988	S. DAVIS (Eng)	bt	J. PARROTT (Eng)	13–11
1989	D. MOUNTJOY (Wales)	bt	W. JONES (Wales)	13–11

Previous sponsors: 1980, 1981 Wilsons Classic; 1982, 1983, 1984 Lada.

ICI EUROPEAN OPEN

YEAR	CHAMPION		RUNNER-UP	RESULT
1989	J. PARROTT (Eng)	bt	T. GRIFFITHS (Wales)	9–8

BENSON AND HEDGES MASTERS

YEAR	CHAMPION		RUNNER-UP	RESULT
1975	J. SPENCER (Eng)	bt	R. REARDON (Wales)	9–8
1976	R. REARDON (Wales)	bt	G. MILES (Eng)	7–3
1977	D. MOUNTJOY (Wales)	bt	R. REARDON (Wales)	7–6
1978	A. HIGGINS (NI)	bt	C. THORBURN (Can)	7–5
1979	P. MANS (SA)	bt	A. HIGGINS (NI)	8–4
1980	T. GRIFFITHS (Wales)	bt	A. HIGGINS (NI)	9–5
1981	A. HIGGINS (NI)	bt	T. GRIFFITHS (Wales)	9–6
1982	S. DAVIS (Eng)	bt	T. GRIFFITHS (Wales)	9–5
1983	C. THORBURN (Can)	bt	R. REARDON (Wales)	9–7
1984	J. WHITE (Eng)	bt	T. GRIFFITHS (Wales)	9–5

Doug Mountjoy, the winner, and runner-up Wayne Jones after the 1988 Mercantile Credit Classic.

YEAR	CHAMPION		RUNNER-UP	RESULT
1985	C. THORBURN (Can)	bt	D. MOUNTJOY (Wales)	9–6
1986	C. THORBURN (Can)	bt	J. WHITE (Eng)	9–5
1987	DENNIS TAYLOR (NI)	bt	A. HIGGINS (NI)	9–8
1988	S. DAVIS (Eng)	bt	M. HALLETT (Eng)	9–0
1989	S. HENDRY (Scot)	bt	J. PARROTT (Eng)	9–6

ANGLIAN WINDOWS BRITISH OPEN

YEAR	CHAMPION		RUNNER-UP	RESULT
1980	A. HIGGINS (NI)	bt	R. REARDON (Wales)	5–1
1981	S. DAVIS (Eng)	bt	DAVID TAYLOR (Eng)	9–6
1982	S. DAVIS (Eng)	bt	T. GRIFFITHS (Wales)	9–7
1983	R. REARDON (Wales)	bt	J. WHITE (Eng)	9–6
1984	Three-man play-off D. MARTIN (Eng)	bt	J. DUNNING (Eng)	3–2
	S. DAVIS (Eng)	bt	J. DUNNING (Eng)	4–1
	S. DAVIS (Eng) Winner: S. DAVIS (Eng)	bt	D. MARTIN (Eng)	3–0
1985	S. FRANCISCO (SA)	bt	K. STEVENS (Can)	12–9
1986	S. DAVIS (Eng)	bt	W. THORNE (Eng)	12–7
1987	J. WHITE (Eng)	bt	N. FOULDS (Eng)	13–9
1988	S. HENDRY (Scot)	bt	M. HALLETT (Eng)	13–2
1989	A. MEO (Eng)	bt	D. REYNOLDS (Eng)	13–6

Previous sponsors: 1980 British Gold Cup; 1981, 1982, 1983, 1984 Yamaha; 1985, 1986, 1987 Dulux; 1988 MIM Britannia Unit Trusts.

BENSON AND HEDGES IRISH MASTERS

YEAR	CHAMPION		RUNNER-UP	RESULT
1978	J. SPENCER (Eng)	bt	D. MOUNTJOY (Wales)	5–3
1979	D. MOUNTJOY (Wales)	bt	R. REARDON (Wales)	6–5
1980	T. GRIFFITHS (Wales)	bt	D. MOUNTJOY (Wales)	9–8
1981	T. GRIFFITHS (Wales)	bt	R. REARDON (Wales)	9–7
1982	T. GRIFFITHS (Wales)	bt	S. DAVIS (Eng)	9–5
1983	S. DAVIS (Eng)	bt	R. REARDON (Wales)	9–2
1984	S. DAVIS (Eng)	bt	T. GRIFFITHS (Wales)	9–1
1985	J. WHITE (Eng)	bt	A. HIGGINS (NI)	9–5
1986	J. WHITE (Eng)	bt	W. THORNE (Eng)	9–5
1987	S. DAVIS (Eng)	bt	W. THORNE (Eng)	9–1
1988	S. DAVIS (Eng)	bt	N. FOULDS (Eng)	9–4
1989	A. HIGGINS (NI)	bt	S. HENDRY (Scot)	9–8

EMBASSY WORLD CHAMPIONSHIP

YEAR	CHAMPION		RUNNER-UP	RESULT
1927	J. DAVIS (Eng)	bt	T. DENNIS (Eng)	20–11
1928	J. DAVIS (Eng)	bt	F. LAWRENCE (Eng)	16–13
1929	J. DAVIS (Eng)	bt	T. DENNIS (Eng)	19–14
1930	J. DAVIS (Eng)	bt	T. DENNIS (Eng)	25–12
1931	J. DAVIS (Eng)	bt	T. DENNIS (Eng)	25–21
1932	J. DAVIS (Eng)	bt	C. McCONACHY (NZ)	30–19
1933	J. DAVIS (Eng)	bt	W. SMITH (Eng)	25–18
1934	J. DAVIS (Eng)	bt	T. NEWMAN (Eng)	25–23
1935	J. DAVIS (Eng)	bt	W. SMITH (Eng)	25–20
1936	J. DAVIS (Eng)	bt	H. LINDRUM (Aust)	34–27
1937	J. DAVIS (Eng)	bt	J. LINDRUM (Aust)	32–29
1938	J. DAVIS (Eng)	bt	S. SMITH (Eng)	37–24
1939	J. DAVIS (Eng)	bt	S. SMITH (Eng)	43–30
1940	J. DAVIS (Eng)	bt	F. DAVIS (Eng)	37–36
1941–45	No tournament held			
1946	J. DAVIS (Eng)	bt	H. LINDRUM (Aust)	78–67
1947	W. DONALDSON (Scot)	bt	F. DAVIS (Eng)	82–63
1948	F. DAVIS (Eng)	bt	W. DONALDSON (Scot)	84–61
1949	F. DAVIS (Eng)	bt	W. DONALDSON (Scot)	80–65
1950	W. DONALDSON (Scot)	bt	F. DAVIS (Eng)	51–46
1951	F. DAVIS (Eng)	bt	W. DONALDSON (Scot)	58–39
1952	H. LINDRUM (Aust)	bt	C. McCONACHY (NZ)	94–49
	F. DAVIS (Eng)	bt	W. DONALDSON (Scot)	38–35
1953	F. DAVIS (Eng)	bt	W. DONALDSON (Scot)	37–34
1954	F. DAVIS (Eng)	bt	W. DONALDSON (Scot)	39–21
1955	F. DAVIS (Eng)	bt	J. PULMAN (Eng)	37–34
1956	F. DAVIS (Eng)	bt	J. PULMAN (Eng)	38–35
1957	J. PULMAN (Eng)	bt	J. REA (NI)	39–34
1958–1963	No tournament held			
1964	J. PULMAN (Eng)	bt	F. DAVIS (Eng)	19–16
	J. PULMAN (Eng)	bt	R. WILLIAMS (Eng)	40–33
1965	J. PULMAN (Eng)	bt	F. DAVIS (Eng)	37–36
	J. PULMAN (Eng)	bt	R. WILLIAMS (Eng)	25–22
	J. PULMAN (Eng)	bt	F. van RENSBURG (SA)	39–12
1966	J. PULMAN (Eng)	bt	F. DAVIS (Eng)	5–2
1967	No tournament held			
1968	J. PULMAN (Eng)	bt	E. CHARLTON (Aust)	39–34
1969	J. SPENCER (Eng)	bt	G. OWEN (Wales)	37–24
1970	R. REARDON (Wales)	bt	J. PULMAN (Eng)	37–33
1971	J. SPENCER (Eng)	bt	W. SIMPSON (Aust)	37–29
1972	A. HIGGINS (NI)	bt	J. SPENCER (Eng)	37–32
1973	R. REARDON (Wales)	bt	E. CHARLTON (Aust)	38–32
1974	R. REARDON (Wales)	bt	G. MILES (Eng)	22–12
1975	R. REARDON (Wales)	bt	E. CHARLTON (Aust)	31–30
1976	R. REARDON (Wales)	bt	A. HIGGINS (NI)	27–16
1977	J. SPENCER (Eng)	bt	C. THORBURN (Can)	25–12
1978	R. REARDON (Wales)	bt	P. MANS (SA)	25–18

Tony Meo on his way to victory in the final of the 1989 Anglian Windows British Open.

YEAR	CHAMPION		RUNNER-UP	RESULT
1979	T. GRIFFITHS (Wales)	bt	DENNIS TAYLOR (NI)	24–16
1980	C. THORBURN (Can)	bt	A. HIGGINS (NI)	18–16
1981	S. DAVIS (Eng)	bt	D. MOUNTJOY (Wales)	18–12
1982	A. HIGGINS (NI)	bt	R. REARDON (Wales)	18–15
1983	S. DAVIS (Eng)	bt	C. THORBURN (Can)	18–6
1984	S. DAVIS (Eng)	bt	J. WHITE (Eng)	18–16
1985	DENNIS TAYLOR (NI)	bt	S. DAVIS (Eng)	18–17
1986	J. JOHNSON (Eng)	bt	S. DAVIS (Eng)	18–12
1987	S. DAVIS (Eng)	bt	J. JOHNSON (Eng)	18–14
1988	S. DAVIS (Eng)	bt	T. GRIFFITHS (Wales)	18–11
1989	S. DAVIES (Eng)	bt	J. PARROTT (Eng)	18–3

Previous sponsors: 1969, 1970 Players No. 6; 1973, 1974 Park Drive; 1975 no sponsor.

LANGS SUPREME SCOTTISH MASTERS

1981	J. WHITE (Eng)	bt	C. THORBURN (Can)	9–4
1982	S. DAVIS (Eng)	bt	A. HIGGINS (NI)	9–4
1983	S. DAVIS (Eng)	bt	A. KNOWLES (Eng)	9–6
1984	S. DAVIS (Eng)	bt	J. WHITE (Eng)	9–4
1985	C. THORBURN (Can)	bt	W. THORNE (Eng)	9–7
1986	C. THORBURN (Can)	bt	A. HIGGINS (NI)	9–8
1987	J. JOHNSON (Eng)	bt	T. GRIFFITHS (Wales)	9–7

FOSTER'S WORLD DOUBLES

1982	S. DAVIS (Eng) A. MEO (Eng)	bt	T. GRIFFITHS (Wales) D. MOUNTJOY (Wales)	13–2
1983	S. DAVIS (Eng) A. MEO (Eng)	bt	A. KNOWLES (Eng)) J. WHITE (Eng)	10–2
1984	A. HIGGINS (NI) J. WHITE (Eng)	bt	C. THORBURN (Can) W. THORNE (Eng)	10–2
1985	S. DAVIS (Eng) A. MEO (Eng)	bt	A. JONES (Eng) R. REARDON (Wales)	12–5
1986	S. DAVIS (Eng) A. MEO (Eng)	bt	S. HENDRY (Scot) M. HALLETT (Eng)	12–3
1987	M. HALLETT (Eng) S. HENDRY (Scot)	bt	C. THORBURN (Can) DENNIS TAYLOR (NI)	12–8

Previous sponsor: 1982, 1983, 1984, 1985, 1986 Hofmeister.

WINFIELD MASTERS

1983	C. THORBURN (Can)	bt	W. WERBENUIK (Can)	7–3
1984	A KNOWLES (Eng)	bt	J. VIRGO (Eng)	7–3
1985	A MEO (Eng)	bt	J. CAMPBELL (Aust)	7–2
1986	S. DAVIS (Eng)	bt	DENNIS TAYLOR (NI)	3–2
1987	S. HENDRY (Scot)	bt	M. HALLETT (Eng)	371–226 (5-frame agg.)

A pair of world champions. (Inset) Joe Johnson, 1985 winner, and Alex Higgins, 1982.

WORLD RANKINGS

WHERE THEY STAND AT THE START OF THE 1989–90 SEASON

A player's ranking for the season is evaluated on points gained in the preceding two seasons. The player keeps the same ranking for the entire season.

Points are awarded in all ranking tournaments (with the exception of the World Championship) on the following basis: Winner, 6pts; Runner-up, 5pts; Losing semi-finalist, 4pts; Losing quarter-finalist, 3pts; Fifth round loser, 2pts; Fourth round loser, 1pt; Third round loser, 1 merit pt; Second round loser, 1 'A' pt; First round loser, frames won in match.

In the World Championship, the points are: Winner, 10pts; Runner-up, 8pts; Losing semi-finalist, 6pts; Losing quarter-finalist, 4pts; Second round loser, 2pts; First round loser, 1 ranking pt unless member of top 16 who collect 2 merit pts; Fifth preliminary round loser, 2 merit pts; Fourth preliminary round loser, 1 merit pt; Third preliminary round loser, 1 'A' pt; Second preliminary round loser, frames won in match.

If players are level on ranking points, then the player who has picked up most ranking points in the immediate previous season is awarded the higher placing.

If they are still level, the merit points come into operation. Players having the same number of merit points would be placed according to the merit points gained in the immediate previous season. Further equality would bring 'A' points and frames won into the allocation of places.

			Ranking Points	Merit Points	A Points	Frames
1	(1)	S. Davis (Eng)	64	2	–	–
2	(7)	J. Parrott (Eng)	48	1	–	–
3	(4)	S. Hendry (Scot)	46	1	–	–
4	(2)	J. White (Eng)	43	1	–	–
5	(5)	T. Griffiths (Wales)	39	2	–	–
6	(9)	M. Hallett (Eng)	33	4	–	–
7	(6)	C. Thorburn (Can)	33	2	–	–
8	(10)	Dennis Taylor (NI)	29	1	–	–
9	(13)	W. Thorne (Eng)	28	1	–	–
10	(24)	D. Mountjoy (Wales)	25	4	–	–
11	(11)	J. Johnson (Eng)	24	3	–	–
12	(8)	A. Knowles (Eng)	24	4	–	–
13	(15)	J. Virgo (Eng)	22	1	–	–
14	(31)	A. Meo (Eng)	20	7	–	–
15	(22)	D. Reynolds (Eng)	19	6	–	–
16	(32)	S. James (Eng)	17	4	1	–
17	(41)	M. Clark (Eng)	16	6	–	8
18	(16)	C. Wilson (Wales)	16	3	–	–
19	(25)	S. Newbury (Wales)	15	7	–	–
20	(3)	N. Foulds (Eng)	15	6	–	–
21	(26)	B. West (Eng)	14	7	–	–
22	(19)	E. Charlton (Aust)	14	7	–	–
23	(12)	S. Francisco (SA)	14	6	–	–
24	(17)	A. Higgins (NI)	13	7	–	–
25	(14)	P. Francisco (SA)	13	8	–	–
26	(39)	D. Roe (Eng)	12	4	2	–
27	(21)	E. Hughes (Rep Ire)	11	7	–	–
28	(23)	D. O'Kane (NZ)	11	3	3	–
29	(29)	R. Chaperon (Can)	11	6	–	–
30	(20)	T. Drago (Malta)	11	8	–	–
31	(34)	W. Jones (Wales)	10	7	2	–
32	(18)	R. Williams (Eng)	10	11	–	–

Dean Reynolds, up 7 places to number 15.

			Ranking Points	Merit Points	A Points	Frames
33	(28)	David Taylor (Eng)	9	10	–	–
34	(30)	S. Longworth (Eng)	9	7	–	–
35	(102)	A. Robidoux (Can)	8	5	1	–
36	(43)	D. Fowler (Eng)	8	8	1	–
37	(38)	J. Wych (Can)	8	6	3	–
38	(27)	J. Spencer (Eng)	8	9	–	–
39	(45)	Gary Wilkinson (Eng)	8	5	2	9
40	(35)	J. O'Boye (Eng)	8	6	3	–
41	(51)	A. Chappel (Wales)	7	6	3	–
42	(33)	J. Campbell (Aust)	7	6	3	–
43	(50)	S. Duggan (Eng)	6	5	5	–
44	(54)	P. Browne (Rep Ire)	6	3	7	–
45	(48)	M. Macleod (Scot)	6	9	1	–
46	(56)	N. Gilbert (Eng)	6	8	2	5
47	(52)	M. Bennett (Wales)	5	6	5	–
48	(67)	C. Roscoe (Wales)	4	3	4	4
49	(55)	R. Edmonds (Eng)	4	5	6	–
50	(37)	K. Stevens (Can)	4	8	1	–
51	(46)	G. Cripsey (Eng)	4	8	4	–
52	(–)	M. Johnston-Allen (Eng)	3	2	4	–
53	(–)	D. Morgan (Wales)	3	–	4	3
54	(40)	R. Reardon (Wales)	3	9	2	–
55	(44)	W. King (Aust)	3	6	6	–
56	(36)	D. Martin (Eng)	3	12	2	–
57	(42)	T. Murphy (NI)	3	9	3	–
58	(64)	J. McLaughlin (NI)	2	7	6	–
59	(–)	I. Graham (Eng)	2	3	2	10
60	(73)	J. Chambers (Eng)	2	3	6	7
61	(60)	R. Bales (Eng)	2	–	12	–
62	(49)	A. Jones (Eng)	2	10	4	–
63	(57)	D. Gilbert (Eng)	2	7	7	–
64	(58)	M. Fisher (Eng)	2	2	9	5
65	(62)	L. Dodd (Eng)	1	12	2	–
66	(81)	John Rea (Scot)	1	8	3	12
67	(61)	J. Wright (Eng)	1	7	7	–
68	(63)	M. Gauvreau (Can)	1	3	10	–
69	(–)	C. Edwards (Eng)	1	2	3	5
70	(119)	R. Marshall (Eng)	1	1	5	18
71	(–)	A. Wilson (Eng)	1	1	4	11
72	(–)	N. Terry (Eng)	1	1	4	4
73	(90)	G. Scott (Eng)	1	1	6	14
74	(116)	A. Harris (Eng)	1	–	8	22
75	(53)	K. Owers (Eng)	1	7	6	–
76	(72)	M. Smith (Eng)	1	6	4	7

Steve James, up to 16 places to number 16.

			Ranking Points	Merit Points	A Points	Frames
77	(66)	R. Foldvari (Aust)	1	6	6	8
78	(65)	G. Miles (Eng)	1	5	6	10
79	(70)	B. Rowswell (Eng)	1	4	7	6
80	(68)	P. Medati (Eng)	1	3	7	15
81	(59)	P. Houlihan (Eng)	1	3	10	–
82	(69)	P. Gibson (Eng)	1	2	3	4
83	(71)	V. Harris (Eng)	1	–	7	14
84	(74)	J. Donnelly (Scot)	1	–	4	30
85	(84)	B. Oliver (Eng)	–	6	6	11
86	(82)	M. Morra (Can)	–	6	3	16
87	(75)	M. Bradley (Eng)	–	5	7	11
88	(86)	J. Bear (Can)	–	5	3	27
89	(83)	F. Davis (Eng)	–	5	5	13
90	(–)	M. Price (Eng)	–	3	3	4
91	(85)	Glen Wilkinson (Aust)	–	3	5	7
92	(89)	I Williamson (Eng)	–	3	7	15
93	(77)	B. Harris (Eng)	–	3	6	11
94	(85)	E. Sinclair (Scot)	–	3	5	34
95	(92)	J. Dunning (Eng)	–	3	5	28
96	(93)	E. Lawlor (Eng)	–	3	5	16

David Roe, up 13 places to number 26.

			Ranking Points	Merit Points	A Points	Frames
97	(76)	M. Wildman (Eng)	–	3	6	13
98	(–)	S. Campbell (Eng)	–	2	3	16
99	(–)	M. Rowing (Eng)	–	2	2	5
100	(101)	T. Whitthread (Eng)	–	2	6	14
101	(80)	A. Kearney (Rep Ire)	–	2	6	18
102	(100)	M. Darrington (Eng)	–	2	4	27
103	(87)	J. van Rensburg (SA)	–	2	4	25
104	(118)	J. Smith (Eng)	–	1	8	19
105	(113)	F. Ellis (SA)	–	1	6	13
106	(114)	J. Fitzmaurice (Eng)	–	1	5	14
107	(117)	S. Meakin (Eng)	–	1	4	21
108	(111)	D. Hughes (Eng)	–	1	4	17
109	(115)	D. Sheehan (Rep Ire)	–	1	3	39
110	(108)	M. Watterson (Eng)	–	1	2	25
111	(124)	P. Thornley (Can)	–	1	1	7
112	(88)	M. Gibson (Scot)	–	1	9	14
113	(79)	R. Grace (SA)	–	1	7	19
114	(98)	P. Watchorn (Rep Ire)	–	1	6	21
115	(94)	J. Meadowcroft (Eng)	–	1	6	16
116	(91)	G. Rigitano (Can)	–	1	5	25
117	(99)	Jack Rea (NI)	–	1	2	23
118	(78)	G. Foulds (Eng)	–	–	9	17
119	(110)	B. Kelly (Rep Ire) (NT)	–	–	6	14
120	(104)	G. Jenkins (Aust) (NT)	–	–	4	23
121	(96)	I. Black (Scot) (NT)	–	–	4	15
122	(97)	B. Mikkelsen (Can) (NT)	–	–	3	18
123	(103)	P. Fagan (Rep Ire) (NT)	–	–	3	21
124	(105)	P. Burke (Rep Ire) (NT)	–	–	2	22
125	(112)	D. Chalmers (Eng) (NT)	–	–	2	29
126	(107)	I. Anderson (Aust) (NT)	–	–	2	11
127	(106)	F. Jonik (Can) (NT)	–	–	2	8
128	(121)	D. Mienie (SA) (NT)	–	–	1	19
129	(109)	J. Rempe (USA) (NT)	–	–	1	16
130	(–)	J. Grech (Malta) (NT)	–	–	1	–
131	(123)	D. Heaton (Eng) (NT)	–	–	1	15
132	(120)	C. Everton (Wales) (NT)	–	–	1	10
133	(125)	D. Greaves (Eng) (NT)	–	–	–	12
134	(129)	B. Bennett (Eng) (NT)	–	–	–	9
135	(127)	M. Parkin (Eng) (NT)	–	–	–	6
136	(122)	J. Hargreaves (Eng) (NT)	–	–	–	4
137	(128)	B. Demarco (Scot) (NT)	–	–	–	2
138	(131)	E. McLaughlin (Scot) (NT)	–	–	–	1
139	(130)	J. Caggianello (Can) (NT)	–	–	–	–
140	(126)	M. Hines (SA) (NT)	–	–	–	–
141	(136)	L. Condo (Aust) (NT)	–	–	–	–
142	(137)	M. Francisco (SA) (NT)	–	–	–	–
143	(135)	J. Giannaros (Aust) (NT)	–	–	–	–
144	(132)	S. Mizerak (USA) (NT)	–	–	–	–
145	(134)	P. Morgan (Aust) (NT)	–	–	–	–
146	(138)	W. Sanderson (Can) (NT)	–	–	–	–
147	(133)	G. Watson (Can) (NT)	–	–	–	–
148	(–)	S. Frangie (Aust) (NT)	–	–	–	–
149	(–)	W. Postanik (Aust) (NT)	–	–	–	–

(1988/89 positions in brackets)

(NT) – Non-Tournament Status

THE NEW PROFESSIONALS

N. Bond (Eng)	B. Gollan (Can)
I. Brumby (Eng)	B. Morgan (Eng)
A. Cairns (Eng)	S. Murphy (Rep Ire)
D. Campbell (Scot)	B. Pinches (Eng)
N. Dyson (Eng)	J. Wattana (Thai)

INDEX

Entries in italics refer to captions

H

I

J

K

L

M

N

O

P

R

SNOOKER ACKNOWLEDGEMENTS

Front and back cover, 1, 2/3, 4/5, 6 David Muscroft; 8/9, 10 RoLee Ltd; 12/13 Bridgeman Art Library; 14 RoLee Ltd; 15 David Muscroft; 16/17 Bridgeman Art Library; 18, 19, 20, 21, 22, 23, 24/25, RoLee Ltd; 27 The Illustrated London News Picture Library; 29 David Muscroft; 30, 31 RoLee Ltd; 32 David Muscroft; 33 Hulton Deutsch Collection; 34 RoLee Ltd; 35, 37 David Muscroft; 38 Hulton Deutsch Collection; 40 RoLee Ltd; 41, 42 David Muscroft; 43 RoLee Ltd; 45, 46/47 David Muscroft; 52, 53 RoLee Ltd; 54 David Muscroft; 55 RoLee Ltd; 57 David Muscroft; 58 Syndication International; 59, 60/61, 62/63 Sporting Pictures (UK) Ltd; 64, 65 David Muscroft; 66, 67, 68 Sporting Pictures (UK) Ltd; 70, 71 David Muscroft; 72 S. Kendall/ Sportsphoto; 74, 76 David Muscroft; 77 Sporting Pictures (UK) Ltd; 78, 79 Eric Whitehead; 80, 82 David Muscroft; 84, 85 Eric Whitehead; 86, 87 Coloursport; 88 Eric Whitehead; 90 David Muscroft; 92 Gallagher Ltd; 94, 95 Coloursport; 96 Private Collection; 97 Eric Whitehead; 98 Private Collection; 100 Fersina Windows; 102/103, 104, 106, 108, 110, 112, 114, 116, 118, 120, 122, 124, 126, 128, 130, 132, 134, 136, 138, 140, 142, 144, 146, 148, 150, 152, 154, 156/157, 158 David Muscroft; 159 Private Collection; 160 top David Muscroft; 160 bottom, 161, 162 left, 162 right, 163, 164/165 Private Collection; 166/167, 168 David Muscroft; 171 B&SCC; 172 Private Collection; 180, 181, 183, David Muscroft; 184 Coloursport; 185, 186, 187, 188 David Muscroft.